The Renewed Pastor

Essays on the pastoral ministry in honour of Philip Hacking

The Renewed Pastor

Essays on the pastoral ministry in honour of Philip Hacking

EDITED BY MELVIN TINKER

MENTOR

Copyright © Melvin Tinker 2011

ISBN 978-1-84550-805-0

Published in 2011
by
Christian Focus Publications,
Geanies House, Fearn, Ross-shire,
IV20 1TW, Scotland.

www.christianfocus.com

Cover design by Daniel van Straaten

Printed by
Bell and Bain

MIX
Paper from
responsible sources

FSC
www.fsc.org
FSC® C007785

CONTENTS

CONTRIBUTORS

Hugh Palmer is Rector of All Souls Church, Langham Place, London. He was formerly Philip Hacking's curate at Christ Church, Fulwood in Sheffield and his successor.

Melvin Tinker is Vicar of St John's, Newland, in Hull. He is Director of Yorkshire Training and has written extensively on a wide range of theological matters, and is the author of several books, including *Evangelical Concerns* (Christian Focus).

Peter Lewis is the Senior Pastor of Cornerstone Evangelical Church, Nottingham. He is a well-known conference speaker and the author of several books, including *The Glory of Christ* and *The Message of the Living God* (IVP).

Tim Chester and Steve Timmis are Senior Pastors in Crowded House, Sheffield, a church planting initiative, and directors of the Porterbrook Network. They are the authors of *Total Church* (IVP).

Dr Peter Adam is the Principal of Ridley Theological College, Melbourne. He is the author of several books and articles, including *Speaking God's Words, A Practical Theology of Preaching* (IVP).

Paul Williams is the Vicar of Christ Church, Fulwood, and was formerly on the staff at All Souls, Langham Place, London, with special responsibility for evangelism.

Professor Don Carson is Research Professor of New Testament, Trinity Evangelical Divinity School, Illinois. He is the author and editor of many major theological books, and is a popular and respected Bible teacher of international repute.

Professor J.I. Packer was Sangwoo Youtong Chee Professor of Theology at Regent College, Vancouver, until his retirement. He is a prolific writer and frequent lecturer, but he is perhaps best known for his book, *Knowing God.*

Bishop Frank Retief was until his retirement the Presiding Bishop of the Church of England in South Africa (CESA) and founder and Senior Pastor of St James, Kenilworth in Cape Town.

David Holloway is the Vicar of Jesmond Parish Church, Newcastle-upon-Tyne. He is the author of several books, including *Ready, Steady, Grow* (Monarch) and *Church and State in the New Millennium: Issues of Belief and Morality for the 21st Century* (Hodder).

John Risbridger is Senior Minister at Above Bar Church, Southampton, and former Head of Student Ministries at the UCCF.

John Stevens is the Director of the Fellowship of Independent Evangelical Churches and founder Pastor of City Evangelical Church, Birmingham.

Professor Gerald Lewis Bray is an Evangelical theologian, prolific writer and research professor for Samford University, U.S.A. He previously taught at Beeson Divinity School, where he continues to teach specialised courses. He is the general editor of *Churchman* and the author of several major works in theology. His more popular writings include *The Doctrine of God* and *Creeds, Councils and Christ* (IVP).

FOREWORD

I was a new Christian when I first heard Philip Hacking. We were visiting relatives in Sheffield, and went to Christ Church, Fulwood. Philip was speaking that morning on Acts 9 and I can still remember his two points: 'The Damascus Road Experience' (Paul's conversion) and 'The Damascus Home Experience' (Paul's commissioning). Both 'Road' and 'Home' were long-drawn-out words in that inimitable Lancashire accent of his! It was a message that was simple, clear and, as time has proved, memorable. Twenty-five years later, our paths having crossed on several occasions in the meanwhile, I would find myself back at Fulwood as his curate and then successor!

I have had the privilege of serving under three remarkable rectors and vicars, all very different from each other. Gordon Bridger and Dick Lucas both taught me more lessons than I can remember, but Philip was also a striking model to learn from.

God seemed to give him a remarkable energy, which was still evident even in the last years of his time as Vicar of Fulwood. Lancastrian by birth and a Yorkshireman for the last thirty years of his ministry and then into his active retirement, Philip was a northerner through and through, and

I suspect at times underestimated as such by some south-
erners, who didn't always appreciate the scope of the ministry he had developed.

Famous for his love for sport, Philip knew his Wisden
nearly as well as his Bible and was full of cricketing trivia,
never mind the latest Test score! If that didn't feature in
a sermon then almost certainly the current fortunes of Sheffield Wednesday would! Under his very real human touches
there was never a doubt though that the Bible was at the
centre of his preaching as well as his ministry. Indeed, he
was far from a pragmatist, engaging both with biblical exposition and theological debate.

An ordained Anglican clergyman all his working life,
Philip had the Church of England in his bloodstream in
a way that few of us in succeeding generations have. Yet
there was nothing narrow about his loyalties and affections
and, both within Sheffield and further afield, he had a far
wider ministry than merely to Anglican circles From the remarkable Mission England meetings with Billy Graham in
Sheffield in 1985, which he chaired and championed, to the
local ministers' fraternal drawn from all kinds of denominations which ran for many years under his leadership, via his
chairmanship of the Keswick Convention and then Word
Alive, not to mention his tireless preaching at many chapels
as well as churches, Philip had a place in the heart of gospel-
loving people across the range of church backgrounds.

Like most people who have been in ministry for many
years, there was a pattern to his ministry. Indeed, there was
a pattern to nearly all his life; his secretary told me not just
where and when he and Margaret would have their holi-
days, but also which Little Chef restaurant they would stop
at on the way! He was a man of his generation, of course, and
parish ministry focused for him around the Sunday when he
would almost invariably be in the pulpit and the mid-week
Bible study and prayer meeting, which he led, teaching faithfully through the Bible week after week. I never knew when

he fitted in his preparation, for he was also a prodigious visitor around the parish. In fact, he had a healthy scepticism for those who so emphasised their Bible teaching preparation that they seemed to neglect the people in their charge.

Philip was a pastor as well as a Bible teacher. His visits may have been quick ones but they were tirelessly carried out and many was the person I would discover in later years who would tell me that 'Philip was here the day our child was born' or 'relative died'. At the back of it all he was a man of prayer and prayer for the congregation. The totally credible rumour was that Philip would regularly work his way through the electoral roll as his prayer list. Certainly he would stand with me at the vestry window watching people come to church on Sunday and not only be able to tell me their names but give a potted history of them as well. This was with a congregation of nearly a thousand people!

I remember my first bishop, Maurice Wood, giving me a rule of thumb for ministry 'Keep close to God. Keep close to the Bible. Keep close to the people.' Philip would echo that.

Of course there was an innovative side to Philip too. It would certainly be foolish to imagine him stuck in the past. He was not the most high-tech of ministers (he famously confessed to having left his Bible at a conference centre before asking his secretary if they could fax it back to him! He only learnt to email in his retirement.) All the same, it was his vision that dragged the Keswick Convention away from an increasingly sepia-tinted appearance and boldly struck out to build the current Convention Centre there. Similarly and with great foresight he pushed through the building of the Church Centre extension at Fulwood which became a seven-day-a-week resource for so many ministries. His energy helped persuade Billy Graham to come back to England a year after his Mission England tour of 1984 and this time include Sheffield in his itinerary. His breadth meant that a solidly middle-class parish like Fulwood would be linked in a real partnership with parishes both in a former mining village parish and a Barnsley housing estate.

There was something infectious about Philip's enthusiasm in the pulpit and out of it and a guileless integrity to his life and ministry. Above all, he was a gospel person. It is this which explains him more than anything else and that loyalty transcended all others. He liked to mention how it took him onto the pitch at Bramall Lane, footballing home of Wednesday's arch-rivals Sheffield United, for those Billy Graham meetings. Far more seriously, it took him to the chairmanship of Reform and the awkwardness for him of involvement in church politics, as well as putting him at odds with many in the Church of England hierarchy, not to mention old friends who did not see the dangers to the gospel cause as acutely as he did. After his retirement he returned to live in the parish at Fulwood and along with Margaret they not only proved wonderfully loyal supporters even when changes affected the ministry patterns he left behind, but he willingly and faithfully continued to visit whoever he was asked to see and so kept the gospel in front of people in their homes, as well as helping from the pulpit.

The day before I wrote this, I was back in Fulwood and heard Philip preach at a funeral. The passion was still there, the ability to speak into the occasion, the insightful engaging with the passage (he was never just a 'blessed thought' preacher) and the courage to bring the evangelistic challenge and not let the opportunity slide by, even though the vast majority were committed Christians. There were so many reasons to thank God for the good news of Jesus, but I left thinking: 'If I live to eighty, pray God the gospel is still gripping my mind and heart and tongue as powerfully!'

Here then is a book which I believe touches on so many issues that have been close to Philip's heart throughout his ministry, and which need to be close to the hearts of any pastor today.

Hugh Palmer
August 2011

I

The Pastor Renewed

MELVIN TINKER

Philip Hacking was ordained as a minister in the Church of England the year I was born. There are many things which mark Philip's remarkable ministry under God, not least his consistency. He began his service of Christ as a committed Evangelical and continued unashamedly along that path without wavering. As someone dedicated to preaching 'the whole counsel of God' Philip exemplified a ministry which had breadth (taking him on missions and preaching engagements around the world) and depth (he was a 'parish man' to the core). Few will have captured the essence of what Richard Baxter called 'The Reformed Pastor' as well as Philip. This chapter explores what this looks like in principle and practice.

The modern pastor is expected to be a preacher, counsellor, administrator, PR guru, fund raiser and hand-holder. Depending upon the size of the church he serves, he may have to be an expert on youth, something of an accountant, janitor, evangelist, small groups expert, an excellent chair of committees, a team player and a transparent leader. Of course his home life must be exemplary and he should never appear tired or discouraged, since he must always be spiritual, prayerful, warm-hearted, and passionate but unflappable. He should spend no fewer than 40 hours a week in sermon preparation, no fewer than 30 hours in counselling, at least 20 hours in regular visititation of his flock, and another 15 hours in door-to-door evangelism, and at least 20 hours on administration, another 10 on hospital calling, leaving about 50 hours for miscellaneous matters (especially being available if anyone wants to see him day or night). And then a neighbour will ask his wife: 'Excuse me, I don't mean to be rude, but I'd really like to know: What does your husband do the rest of his time, apart from you know, his work on Sundays?'[1]

This is a rather playful, tongue-in-cheek description of the expectations that are often placed upon the modern pastor by others (and sometimes himself). Although this is exaggerated, it is purposively so in order to make an important point, namely, pastors *do* come up against expectations which on the face of it appear good but which in fact are not the best because they do not accord with priorities in ministry which are in line with the Bible. Adopting a more serious tone, John Piper pinpoints the direct danger he sees as threatening today's pastoral ministry which chimes in with the caricature sketched by Carson and Woodbridge above: 'We pastors are being killed by the professionalising of the pastoral ministry. The mentality of the professional is not the mentality of the prophet. It is not the mentality of the slave of Christ. Professionalism has nothing to do with the essence and heart of the Christian ministry. The more professional we long to be, the more spiritual death we will leave in our wake.'[2] What does Piper see as the alternative to this creeping professionalism?

---

1 D.A. Carson and John D Woodbridge, *Letters Along the Way*, (Crossway, 1993), p. 127.

2 John Piper, *Brothers We Are Not Professionals* (Christian Focus Publications 2004) p. 1.

'Oh for radically Bible-saturated, God-centred, Christ-exalting, self-sacrificing, mission-mobilising, soul-saving, culture-confronting pastors!'[3] A similar longing for God to raise up such pastors lay on the heart of the seventeenth-century Puritan minister, Richard Baxter of Kidderminster. This led him to write his classic work, *The Reformed Pastor*, which is an extended treatment of Paul's farewell address to the Ephesian elders in Acts 20. Today the term 'Reformed' is associated with a certain theological tradition, namely, Calvinism. Perhaps a more accurate rendering of what Baxter had in mind would be 'Renewed', a pastor whose life and ministry has been rekindled and shaped by the Scriptures, involving a wholehearted dependence upon the Holy Spirit.

In order for the main features of the 'Renewed Pastor' to be portrayed using broad brush strokes, we shall follow Baxter's example (and indeed the Church of England's Ordinal), by focusing upon the apostle Paul's teaching in Acts 20:17-35 and his farewell address to the Ephesian elders:

From Miletus, Paul sent to Ephesus for the elders of the church. When they arrived, he said to them: 'You know how I lived the whole time I was with you, from the first day I came into the province of Asia. I served the Lord with great humility and with tears, although I was severely tested by the plots of the Jews. You know that I have not hesitated to preach anything that would be helpful to you but have taught you publicly and from house to house. I have declared to both Jews and Greeks that they must turn to God in repentance and have faith in our Lord Jesus.

---

3   John Piper, *Brothers We Are Not Professionals* (Christian Focus Publications 2004), p. xii.

'And now, compelled by the Spirit, I am going to Jerusalem, not knowing what will happen to me there. I only know that in every city the Holy Spirit warns me that prison and hardships are facing me. However, I consider my life worth nothing to me, if only I may finish the race and complete the task the Lord Jesus has given me - the task of testifying to the gospel of God's grace.

'Now I know that none of you among whom I have gone about preaching the kingdom will ever see me again. Therefore, I declare to you today that I am innocent of the blood of all men. For I have not hesitated to proclaim to you the whole will of God. Keep watch over yourselves and all the flock of which the Holy Spirit has made you overseers. Be shepherds of the church of God, which he bought with his own blood. I know that after I leave, savage wolves will come in among you and will not spare the flock. Even from your own number men will arise and distort the truth in order to draw away disciples after them. So be on your guard! Remember that for three years I never stopped warning each of you night and day with tears.

'Now I commit you to God and to the word of his grace, which can build you up and give you an inheritance among all those who are sanctified. I have not coveted anyone's silver or gold or clothing. You yourselves know that these hands of mine have supplied my own needs and the needs of my companions. In everything I did, I showed you that by this kind of hard work we must help the weak, remembering the words the Lord Jesus himself said: "It is more blessed to give than to receive."'

THE MODEL OF A RENEWED PASTOR

A role model for the way a church is to be cared for is provided by the apostle Paul himself. The simple fact that in the midst of a busy schedule Paul took time out to meet with these church leaders at all is in itself a testimony to Paul's dedicated pastoral care. As we read in verse 16, Paul was in a desperate hurry to get to Jerusalem by Pentecost. Therefore, time was of a premium. But like any good leader of God's people, Paul is never too busy to make time to meet people's real needs. While, for whatever reason, he couldn't go directly to the church in Ephesus itself, nonetheless the apostle does act strategically by calling together those who on a day-to-day basis have responsibility for oversight within the church.

As J.B. Lightfoot conclusively showed in his celebrated essay, The Christian Ministry,[4] in the New Testament, bishops and presbyters (or priests) are the same. The elders of verse 17 (presbyteroi) are called to exercise the function of bishops (episkopountes) in verse 28a, which involves 'shepherding' or 'pastoring the flock' (poimaino) in verse 28b. Commenting on these verses, John Stott observes "'Pastors' is the generic term which describes their role. In our day, in which there is much confusion about the nature and purpose of the pastoral ministry, and much questioning whether clergy are primarily social workers, psychotherapists, educators, facilitators or administrators, it is important to rehabilitate the noble word "pastors", who are shepherds of Christ's sheep, called to tend, feed and protect them.'[5] This book in general, and the present chapter in particular, is a modest attempt to take the rehabilitation forward.

The question arises: How are the elders (presbyters) to be guardians (bishops) who pastor Christ's flock? Paul provides the example.

---

4   J.B. Lightfoot The Christian Ministry, (Morehouse Publishing, 1984).
5   John R.W. Stott , The Message of Acts, (IVP, 1990), p. 323.

It is significant that in the first instance Paul draws attention to his own conduct, verses 18-19: 'You know how I lived
the whole time I was with you from the first day I came in
to the province of Asia.' Paul is claiming that the elders are
aware that he was totally consistent from the beginning of his
ministry to the end, such that how he lived matched what he
taught. This means that Paul was not a 'desk' pastor, locked
away from view. Often the modern pastor faces a temptation
to move in one of two opposite directions. The first is to be
the distant leader, maybe spending most of his time in administration and programme planning or in the study reading
and preparing for that great sermon which never comes. As
we shall see later, thorough sermon preparation is crucial, as
is prayerful planning, but not at the expense of 'walking the
factory floor' in order to get close to the people we are meant
to be serving. After all, it is to real people we are preaching,
not our absent peers, and if we are to be effective pastors we
need to know the people to whom we are speaking which
makes our preaching all the more authentic.

The other extreme is to try to be friends with everyone
by just being one of the 'regular guys', forgetting that God
has set us apart to lead under God's Word – which means
that life 'at the top' is often lonely. Both extremes are to be
avoided, one resulting in an out-of-touch professionalism,
the other a wavering man-pleasing. The Christian leader is
a *servant* leader to be sure, but a *leader* nonetheless; after all,
someone has to make decisions, offer guidance, teach and at
times rebuke. If that is what God has set us apart to do then
we can't offload that to others (hence Paul's injunction to
Titus, 'these, then, are the things you should teach. Encourage and rebuke with all authority. Do not let anyone despise
you.' Titus 2:15)

One of the most successful (and colourful) generals of
the Second World War was George S. Patton Jnr. He once
wrote: 'Trying to lead men from behind makes you a driver

and not a leader. It is easier to lead as it is easier to pull a log chain. You cannot push a log chain and you cannot push troops. ..... A leader has to be ahead of his men. You've got to know what is going on all the time. You cannot swim without being in the water.'[6] Sadly, some Christian ministers don't like to get into the water by being amongst the people in their care.

The role of 'modelling' the Christian faith, so that people see that there is integrity to the life of the pastor, is especially important in a post-modern context which has produced a generation which is suspicious of all claims to 'truth' (metanarratives), but which is nonetheless open to the impact of individual lives (personal narratives). As the apologist Ravi Zacharias has remarked, 'Whereas thirty years ago the non-Christian was concerned with the integrity of the message, now there is a greater concern for the integrity of the messenger.' This principle was central to one of the most significant pastor-apologists of the twentieth century, Dr Francis Schaeffer, which may account for why he was singularly used by God to reach those the church was finding it difficult to reach. He wrote, 'People are looking at us to see, when we say that we have the truth, whether it is possible for this truth not only to take men's souls to heaven but to give meaning to life in the present time, moment by moment.'[7] For Schaeffer, a changed life which was lived before 'the watching world' was the 'ultimate apologetic'.

The importance of integrity was also a key feature which characterised a 'Renewed Pastor' for Richard Baxter and so he urged the need to be careful about the way a pastor lived:

'Take heed to yourselves, lest you exemplify contradictory doc-

trine. Beware, lest you lay such stumbling blocks before the blind

---

6   Alan Axelrod, *Patton On Leadership*, (Prentice Hall, 1999), p. 27.

7   Francis Schaeffer, *The Church at the End of the 20th Century*, (Hodder and Stoughton, 1975), p. 88.

that you occasion their ruin. Beware lest you undo with your lives, what you say with your tongues. Beware, lest you become the greatest hindrances to the success of your own labours..... If our actions become a lie to our tongues, then what we may build up in an hour or two of discourse can be demolished with our hands in a week...Thus one proud, surly, lordly word, or one needless contention, or one covetous action may cut the throat of many a sermon.'[8]

The extent to which the apostle Paul was willing to imitate Christ and so be able to call people to imitate him (1 Cor. 11:1) is brought out by what he says in verses 33-35, 'I have not coveted anyone's silver or gold or clothing. You yourselves know that these hands of mine have supplied my own needs and the needs of my companions. In everything I did, I showed you that by this kind of hard work we must help the weak, remembering the words the Lord Jesus himself said: "It is more blessed to give than to receive."' Paul refused to burden those to whom he was ministering; on the contrary, by earning money with his 'tent making' Paul was able to use that to help the poor and so put into practice the teaching of Jesus.

Another aspect of the life of a 'Renewed Pastor' being itself a means of pastoring through modelling is the emotional cost involved. We see something of this in verse 19, 'I served (literally slaved for) the Lord with great humility and with tears, although I was severely tested by the plots of the Jews.' Although Paul may well have been tempted to take short cuts in his work and get out of an uncomfortable situation made almost unbearable because of the pressures contrived by the Jews to get rid of him, nonetheless he remained. This could account for the tears of which Paul

---

8   Richard Baxter, *The Reformed Pastor*, (Pickering and Inglis, 1983), p.32.

speaks. It was simply breaking his heart that his own people had turned against him and more importantly against God's Messiah – however, he saw it as his duty and privilege to be 'serving the Lord'. Whatever the future has in store for him, for this pastor it appears to be more of the same, verse 22: 'And now, compelled by the Spirit, I am going to Jerusalem, not knowing what will happen to me there. I only know that in every city the Holy Spirit warns me that prison and hardships are facing me.'

Difficulties, setbacks, disappointments and opposition are 'givens' in pastoral ministry and will be emotionally exacting. Such things are to be expected and endured. As one begins pastoral ministry such thoughts are far from one's mind and as such is a kind provision of God. Here is part of some advice given by John Newton to a young man of considerable gifting who is considering entering the ordained ministry:

You have, doubtless, often anticipated in your own mind the nature of the service to which you are now called, and made it the subject of much consideration and prayer. But a distant view of the ministry is generally very different from what is to be found when we are actually engaged in it. The young soldier, who has never seen an enemy, may form some general notions of what is before him; but his ideas will be much more lively and diversified when he comes on the field of battle. If the Lord was to show us the whole beforehand, who that has a due sense of his own insufficiency and weakness, would venture to engage? But he first draws us by a constraining sense of his love, and by giving us an impression of the worth of souls, and leaves us to acquire a knowledge of what is difficult and disagreeable by a gradual experience. The ministry of the Gospel, like the book which the Apostle John ate, is bitter sweet; but the sweetness is tasted first, the bitterness is usually known afterwards, when we are so far engaged that there is no turning back.[9]

There was to be no turning back for the apostle Paul because he placed his trials against the greater backdrop of his high calling as he says in verse 24, 'However, I consider my life worth nothing to me, if only I may finish the race and complete the task the Lord Jesus has given me – the task of testifying to the gospel of God's grace.'

Sometimes it is only having this long-term goal in sight which enables the pastor to persevere when the going gets tough which in turn requires the exercise of patience. Baxter helpfully comments:

We must bear with many abuses and injuries from those for whom we are doing good. When we have studied their case, prayed with them, and besought and exalted them, and spent ourselves for them, then we may still need more patience with them. We can still expect that after we have looked upon them as our won children, that there may be some who will reject us with scorn, even hate and contempt.... All this has to be accepted and yet we still need unswerving and unwearied desire to do good on their behalf...Even when they scorn and reject our ministry, and tell us to mind our own business, yet we must still persevere in caring for them. For we are dealing with distracted people who

---

9   *Letters of John Newton* (Banner of Truth, 1984), p.49.

will reject their physician. Nevertheless we must persist with their cure. He is indeed an unworthy doctor who will be driven away merely by the foul language of a patient.[10]

It is important to observe that the apostle Paul not only refers to his tears, but also his 'humility'. Humility is required to enable the pastor to carry this burden of opposition, but it is also the fruit of such trying experiences and therefore something for which we are meant to be grateful to God. By way of illustration, Eric Alexander records the following incident: 'It is said that Alexander Whyte of Edinburgh had preaching for him on one occasion a young man who was getting a bit of a reputation as a preacher. He had come to Free St George's (as it then was), and he went up into the pulpit full of a sense of what they were all expecting from him, the young luminary. Something went badly wrong, and he was shattered! He made a mess of the whole thing. He forgot what he was going to say, his mind went blank, and it was a disaster. He came down the pulpit steps, a broken-hearted man, and cried to Whyte, "What went wrong, Sir?" Whyte said to him, "Well, laddie, if you had gone up the way you came down, you would have had more chance of coming down the way you went up." How truly Calvin wrote, "The first step towards serving Christ is to lose sight of ourselves." [11] Difficulty and opposition are sometimes the tools the Lord uses to cultivate the kind of humility He wants in His pastors.

THE METHODS OF THE RENEWED PASTOR
It might be helpful to think about the imagery of the shepherd for a moment in order to consider how biblical pastoral ministry is to be undertaken.

One of the primary duties of a shepherd is to feed the sheep, or, to be more precise, to lead the sheep to the place

---

10   Baxter, *The Reformed Pastor*, pp. 23-4.
11   Eric Alexander, *Our Great God and Saviour*, (Banner of Truth, 2010), p.161.

where they can graze on good pasture. It is also the duty of a shepherd to protect the sheep from harm, especially predators. It was a failure of Israel's spiritual overseers to do these things in the days of Ezekiel which brought down God's condemnation (Ezek. 34:1-19) and His promise to raise up a Shepherd, His 'servant David', to provide proper pastoral care, a promise fulfilled in the Lord Jesus Christ (Ezek. 34:20-31 c.f. John 10:1-18).

So it is with God's spiritual under-shepherds (1 Pet. 5:2-4). Their task is not to entertain the flock but to feed the sheep from the nourishing pasture of God's Word. Therefore, first and foremost pastoral ministry is a *teaching* ministry. This is brought out by the verbs used by Paul to describe what he had been doing during his three years in Ephesus: 'preach' verse 20, 'taught' verse 20, 'declared' verse 21, 'testified' verse 24, 'preaching' verse 25, 'proclaiming' verse 27, 'warning' verse 31.

This positive aspect of providing for God's sheep moves in two directions.

First, there is a move *outwards* to those who have not yet been brought into the sheep fold as we see in verse 21, 'I have declared to both Jews and Greeks that they must turn to God in repentance and have faith in the Lord Jesus Christ.' Evangelism is part of pastoral work, not a separate activity. Secondly, there is the move *inwards* to the members of the church itself, verse 27 'I did not shrink back from proclaiming to you the whole will of God'; verse 32 'I commit you to God and to the word of his grace which can build you up.' Reaching out and building up are the aims of pastoral ministry and proclaiming God's Word is the primary means, together with prayer (v. 36). 'When all has been said and done, a pastor should remember what his principal roles are: to preach and to teach and to care tenderly for the flock. If you get caught up in a CEO mentality (your essential goal is to direct a smoothly running church), and yet the Word of

God is not preached with knowledge and the Spirit's power, the ordinances are not faithfully administered, worship and prayer and evangelism are no longer central (protestations notwithstanding), and there is neither deep and growing knowledge of God nor any church discipline, then you have become a leader of a slick organisation rather than a pastor of Christ's church. Keep focused on your calling.'[12]

The model as set before us in Paul shows clearly that a pastor's teaching of the Bible must be both *intensive* and *extensive*. Paul's teaching was intensive in that it was deep and left no stone unturned. Accordingly, he taught about the nature of God's grace and kingdom (vv. 24-25) and of the vital necessity of repentance and faith (v. 21). He also did not 'shrink back' from teaching anything which would be of value (v. 20), covering the whole of God's plan of salvation (v. 27). It was extensive because he wanted to reach as many people as possible with the gospel, Jews and Gentiles, residents and visitors. The extensive nature of Paul's ministry is reflected in the thoroughness of his methods, teaching publically (synagogue and lecture hall) and privately (people's homes), by day and night (vv. 20, 31). 'He shared all possible truth with all possible people in all possible ways. He taught the whole gospel to the whole city with his whole strength.'[13]

Let us tease out some of the implications of Paul's approach.

First, in order to share 'all possible truth with all possible people' means that the pastor himself must be a competent student of the truth. He must not only master the truth of God's Word but be mastered by it. He also has to be thoroughly conversant with the context in which he is ministering – the larger Western post-modern context and the particular local context of those he engages with. The

---

12   Carson and Woodbridge, *Letters Along the Way*, p.238.

13   Stott, *The Message of Acts*, p.328.

image of the expository preacher pedantically labouring away point by point through his text, locked into the world of the sixth century B.C. with the occasional reference to sixteenth-century Geneva, may be a travesty but may contain more than an enough grain of truth to warrant the charge that the evangelical pastor is sometimes perceived to be out of touch with the world which most of our congregations inhabit. The result is not so much a 'renewed pastor' but a 'reified pastor', having an outlook set in concrete! What is more, if we do not help our people to think and act Christianly in relation to their world they will become isolated and estranged, unable to relate their faith to their situation and that is when an unhealthy pietism begins to set in. We are not to overreact to irrationality and the subjective (hallmarks of post-modernity) by becoming overly rationalistic and emotionally detached. Neither is the answer to be found in simply dipping into the modern world for a few illustrations for sermons. The key word is *engagement*, which is precisely what we see occurring in the ministry of the apostle Paul in Ephesus. It is in developing the skills required under God to enable the hearer to enter into the world of the Bible (which is really their world too) and allowing the world of the Bible to critically impact the world of our hearers. When there is this coming together of the Word and the World, a tension is created because of a clash of world views and that is when engagement takes place. We will then not have to plead for the Bible's relevance; people will see it and, indeed, *feel* it for themselves, and so God's Word will be commended to believers and unbelievers alike. This is what Dr John Stott refers to as 'double listening': listening to the Word and the World and bringing them together in critical engagement.

Practically, this implication is that the pastor must keep up his study of the Bible, not first and foremost to provide material for his sermons, but to feed his own soul. He will also keep up with his wider Christian reading. It has been

remarked that one can tell when a pastor has stopped thinking by looking at the date of the last book he bought which
is gathering dust on the shelf of his study! But he will also
keep abreast of the world's thinking and allow Scripture to
be brought to bear on it. That is, he needs to read non-Christian books and articles so keeping his finger on the secular
pulse. This will require time, energy and self-discipline.

However, he is not to become a recluse – after all, Paul
taught, 'house to house'.

Visiting is becoming a neglected aspect of modern evangelical ministry, partly because of a renewed emphasis on the
importance of preaching, with the resulting perceived need
for more time for sermon preparation. But, apart from the fact
that one-to-one ministry of the Word (which is not necessarily a formal study but wisely relating the Bible to the people
we meet) is something modelled by Jesus, it is not to be seen
as somehow detracting from preaching because it earths the
sermon in reality. As the pastor gets to know the people in his
care, then his teaching can be more pertinently and sensitively
applied. Visitation not only provides colour to what otherwise could become abstract sermons, but vitality to the minister. He himself becomes a much more fully rounded character by personal interaction, more sympathetic and caring.
People will sense this when he enters the pulpit and so will
give his words more attention, knowing he is the one who has
shown care for them by visiting them. The old rule of thumb
still has its value that, 'a pastor should not be seen out of his
study in the morning and not seen in it in the afternoon', the
former being reserved for study and the latter for visiting. In
this Philip Hacking provides an outstanding model as almost
every afternoon he would engage in consecutive visiting in his
parish of Fulwood as well as setting an outstanding example
of being a serious student of Scripture. It was not, therefore,
surprising that his preaching was characterised by warmth
and authority, passion and persuasion.

The other entailment of what Paul describes here is sheer hard work, a point taken up by Baxter: 'The work of the ministry must be done with much diligence and effort, for it is of infinite importance to others and ourselves. It is our task to save ourselves and others from temptation, to overcome the devil, to demolish his kingdom, and to set up the kingdom of God. It is our duty to help others attain eternal glory. These are vast works to be done, so how could these works be done with careless hands and minds. See then that this work is done with all your might. Study hard, for the well of spiritual knowledge is deep, and our brains are shallow.'[14]

The warning given by the veteran pastor Eric Alexander still needs to be heard and heeded by pastors today if they are to be 'renewed': 'There is an absolutely vital principle of guarding your mornings, because one of the grave dangers of ministry as I see it (and I see it in myself, in my own life) is the danger of becoming masters in the ignoble art of "pottering" or "trifling."'[15]

Such trifling is soon seen to be out of place when we bear in mind the other aspect of the work of a shepherd – protecting the sheep from wolves; after all, there are crooks as well as shepherds! In verses 25-29 Paul is looking to the future and speaks of dangers from without, verse 29 'After I leave, savage wolves will come in.' He also speaks of dangers from within, verse 30 'Even from your *own* number men will arise.' The local church is an 'endangered' species from one point of view. There is never a moment when it is not under threat. Just as it is built up by the truth of God, it is torn down by the lies and half-truths of Satan. Wolves have only one aim, to harm the sheep. They may well be sincere – wolves are consistently wolf-like, true to their natures – but they are dangerous.

Prior to the 1998 Lambeth conference, the worldwide gathering of Anglican Bishops, Bishop John Spong of

---

14   Baxter, *The Reformed Pastor*, p.14.
15   Alexander, *Our Great God and Saviour*, p.158.

Newark, New Jersey, issued twelve theses for what he called a 'new reformation'. These included the view that 'theism' as a way of defining God was dead and that the concept of Jesus as a kind of incarnation of God was 'nonsensical'. He also rejected the idea of Jesus dying for our sins, the authority of Scripture and the existence of universally binding moral principles. Not surprisingly, during the twenty-four years during which he was Bishop church membership in his diocese fell by 35 per cent, 81 per cent faster than the national rate of decline.

Perhaps what is more disturbing is the fact that from *within* this good apostolically founded church would spring up some pastors who through a distortion of the truth will draw people away after them, which means away from the teaching of the apostles. Not that they necessarily set out to do that, wanting to form another church, though some will. Often it happens through a gradual drift by not keeping a check on their own spiritual lives. That is why this prophecy is prefaced in verse 28 with a warning to the leaders to 'Keep watch over *yourselves* and the flock.' The sobering reality is that there is no reason in principle why any 'sound' evangelical minister could not one day find themselves distorting God's truth; sadly, history is littered with such tragic examples, those who have compromised and eventually abandoned the truth or wavered in terms of moral behaviour. How is this to be guarded against?

Pastors need pastoring too. It is not insignificant that eldership in the New Testament is always a plurality; pastors need to hold each other accountable. But this is also a responsibility shared by the congregation. This will involve support by their prayers, offering feedback, encouragement as well as being constructively critical. It is also why ministers need to go to conferences where they can be fed and kept on track. Many of us have all seen those old black-and-white corny werewolf films; the moon comes out and the poor fellow starts to grow excessive hair on his hands and then his face. This is followed by the enlargement of canine teeth and other wolf-like features. It is a *gradual* transformation. Such is the spiritual degeneration warned of here whereby gamekeeper turns into poacher. Here again is Richard Baxter: 'It is possible for preaching to succeed in the salvation of others without bringing holiness to our own hearts or lives. Many shall say on that day, "Lord, have we not prophesied in your name?" and they will be answered: "I never knew you; depart from me ye that work iniquity" (Matt. 7:22-3 KJV). How many have preached Christ and yet perished because they lacked a saving interest in Christ?'[16] As the Australian evangelist John Chapman has said, pastors must look out for the enticement of the big three temptations: 'Girls, gold and grog'!

By now many of us may well feel like the apostle Paul when he cried out, 'Who is sufficient for these things?' What enables the pastor to keep working hard, not giving up and staying on the straight and narrow (apart from the work of God's grace of course, v. 32)? The answer lies in having the right motivation.

THE MOTIVATION OF THE RENEWED PASTOR

To be properly motivated in pastoral ministry one must have a proper understanding of God's church. What this is, Paul reminds the Ephesian elders of in verse 28: 'Keep watch over yourselves and all the flock of which the *Holy Spirit* has made you overseers. Be shepherds of the *church of God* which he bought with *his own blood*.' No church is the 'minister's church' in terms of it being his possession. It is *God's* church. All three persons of the Trinity have invested themselves in gathering this flock together. In the great economy of salvation, it is God the Father who appoints to save us, God the Son who bleeds for us as an atoning sacrifice, and God the

---

16   Baxter, *The Reformed Pastor*, p. 34.

Holy Spirit who makes that work effective in the life of the individual in regeneration and sanctification and gives gifts to the church for the well-being of His people, including the gifts of pastor-teachers (Eph. 4:11-13).

To know that he was caring for the precious children of God was all the motivation Paul needed to have in order to keep on keeping on. So much so, that his main concern was not losing his life but ending his life well, verses 22-24: 'And now, compelled by the Spirit, I am going to Jerusalem, not knowing what will happen to me there [here is an apostle who didn't know the future – so why should we?]. I only know that in every city the Holy Spirit warns me that prison and hardships await me. *However*, I consider my life worth nothing to me, if only I may finish the race and complete the task the Lord Jesus has given me – the task of testifying to the gospel of God's grace' (emphasis mine). To start the ministry is a fairly easy thing to do; one is usually young and full of idealism. The challenge is finishing the ministry as one began it. This will only happen if we encourage each other to see the church as Christ sees it, infinitely precious, worthy of our care and utmost attention. As usual, Richard Baxter lays down the challenge clearly and forcefully:

Let us then hear the words of Christ, whenever we feel the tendency growing in us to become dull and careless. 'Did I die for them and you will not look after them? Were they worthy of my blood and yet they are not worthy of your labour? Did I come down from heaven to seek and save that which was lost, and you will not go next door or to the next street to seek after them? Compared with mine, how small is your labour and condescension? I debased myself to do this, but it is your honour to be so employed. Have I done and suffered so much for their salvation,

and was I willing to make you a co-worker with me, and yet you
refuse that little which lies within your hands?'[17]

The call is really to love Christ's flock. The pastor might
reply, 'but they are not all that lovely' – maybe, but then,
neither are we and yet Christ shed His blood for us. There
is a basic unconditional love which is required of the pastor,
a love which is not native to himself but which comes
from above. And this is a love which is to be shown to
the congregation and not hidden away. A young Scottish
minister was rebuked in the early days of his ministry when
an older member of the congregation came to see him. After
some flattering words about his first year at the church, the
older man said, 'Yes, everything in the garden's lovely – or
nearly everything. My boy, the garden is still waiting for the
blossoming of one flower without which the garden of no
minister can be perfect. I know we are not everything we
ought to be, and no doubt we need a lot of scolding; but we'd
all be a great deal better if only you would try sometimes
instead of lecturing us, to show us you love us!'[18]

It would be a pity if this chapter gave the impression that
the whole life and well-being of the church depended upon
the pastor. One of the major steps towards being renewed as
a pastor is to remember that ultimately the church is God's
church and He loves the people far more than we will ever
love them. The doctrine of the sovereignty of God worked
out in His Providence is meant to reassure us that 'our work
in the Lord is not in vain'.

After the warning of the rise of false teachers and recount-
ing his own labour, it is instructive that Paul commits the
elders and their churches to God's care in the following way:
'Now I commit you to God and to the word of his grace,

17   Baxter, *The Reformed Pastor*, p. 91.
18   Cited by Jonathan Prime in *The Practical Preacher* (Christian Focus 2002),
      W. Philip (Ed.), p. 96.

which can build you up and give you an inheritance among all those who are sanctified.' God is the ultimate Shepherd of His sheep, each one is known to Him by name, His Word sets them apart, builds them up and guarantees that the work will be finished and the eternal inheritance received. These final words by Carson and Woodbridge echo this theme and form a suitable conclusion for the encouragement of the 'Renewed Pastor':

We must learn to relax in the Lord and rest in the assurance that He is building His church. I have met many frustrated pastors who are exhausted in the Lord's service. Somehow they have converted that sense of exhaustion into a sign that they are following Christ as true disciples. At the same time they confess that they are irritable and frustrated. I do not believe that this pattern of existence is what the Lord generally intends for His servants. How encouraging on the other hand to encounter the pastor who, despite all the challenges and difficulties of the ministry, possesses a serenity of spirit. From what does this serenity spring? You know that he spends time with the Master and meditates on the Word of God. He is following the lifestyle set forth in Psalm 1. [19]

---

19   Carson and Woodbridge, *Letters Along the Way*, p.238.

2

The Pastor at Prayer

PETER LEWIS

Effective pastoral ministry can only be maintained by prayer. Philip Hacking may be known for many things, not least as a man of prayer. In this chapter, another 'long-stay' pastor, Peter Lewis, warmly engages with this important topic. The challenges as well as the privileges of prayer for the pastor are carefully laid out against the rich backdrop of the Trinitarian nature of God and His loving purposes for the world.

I find prayer easy; I find prayer hard. I pray a great deal; I don't pray nearly enough. I feel great confidence and satisfaction as I pray; I often get up apologising to the Lord for the poverty of my prayers.

All these things are true of me and always have been. I could not live without prayer; life would not be life in its abundance without prayer; a prayer-less life would be, for me, life with its colour washed out, its vibrancy lost. Yet my greatest struggle with prayer is that I find prayer a struggle; my most common guilt is that I miss my more substantial times of prayer and intercession sometimes for days and even weeks on end. And only when I regain my disciplines do I regain my equilibrium.

ONE PASTOR AT PRAYER

My prayer times usually begin with a short reading from Scripture because this sets my mind and heart in the right context and perspective: my prayers become a response to God's Word which must always be first. Then I turn to the hymn book and steadily work through its contents, reading one or two hymns and settling on those lines which most move me.

After that I begin my prayers with the Lord's Prayer in which I use each line of the prayer to stimulate other prayers: for the hallowing of God's name, the spread of the gospel, the daily needs of family and others, forgiveness sought and freshly given, protection from temptation, testing and evil, etc. Then I turn to our church list, containing all the core members of the church and pray for between twelve and twenty-five of them at a time, parents and children.

After that I turn to Operation World and pray for the country of that day (selecting only a few statistics and never trying to make up for previous omissions). This might take between half an hour and an hour. I do this no more than three days of the week, two other days being taken up with praying with others.

Without prayer I weaken. All the books I read cannot make up for prayer, all the sermons I preach cannot make up for prayer, all the conversations with my fellow human beings cannot make up for prayer to our Father in heaven; but when I pray I rise up stronger even when I think I have prayed poorly.

To say 'I want to get on with my work' and to neglect prayer is somewhere between arrogance and folly: arrogance which thinks it can do anything without God and folly as ridiculous as a car driver saying 'Never mind about stopping for petrol let's get on with the journey.'

Above all else I am mindful that my relationship with God is a *personal* one. The metaphors of Scripture include parent, husband, lover and friend. As Eugene Petersen insists:

God is not someone or something to be talked <u>about</u> ... God is not

an idea to be studied ... God is not a problem to be solved. God is

a <u>thou</u> to whom we speak, not an <u>it</u> that we talk about. Prayer is

the attention we give to the One who attends to us.[1]

Prayer has been called 'eye-contact with God'! In Scripture it is called 'seeking the Face of God'. And the important thing there is to know that in such seeking there is finding; for He is in the seeking as well as the finding: encouraging, accepting, honoured and pleased. I think it is to Bernard of Clairvaux that we owe the wonderful prayer: 'I never come to You but by You; I never go from You without You'.

PERVASIVE PRAYER
Canon Bruce Duncan, an expert on the Myers-Briggs Type Indicator, has written an unusual book, *Pray Your Way*, exploring prayer from within the personality type of the one praying. It is very liberating as well as encouraging, showing us all that we pray more than we know and urging us all to go further in the disciplines that are always necessary. For instance, he writes:

Some types, especially IN types, [introvert, intuitive] tend

to be perfectionist. INFPs and INTPs [F is for feeling, T for

thinking, P for perception; many pastor-teachers are in these

two categories] are often fascinated by the whole idea of prayer.

They collect books on the subject...but find it difficult to engage

in a disciplined structured relationship with God...T types [we

intellectual types!] can easily fail to recognise the prayer that is

already there in their intellectual activity[2]

---

1   Eugene Peterson *Run with the Horses: The Quest for Life at Its Best* (IVP, 1983), pp.266-7

2   Bruce Duncan, *Pray Your Way*, (Dartman, Longman and Todd, 1993), p. 71.

To a great extent the pastor-teacher prays by reading, the evangelist prays by witnessing, the missionary prays by journeying; those that speak of the Lord together and about His work are praying even as they talk. Yet each and all need the disciplines of both private structure and church community; the insight and stimulus of others' prayers and prayer-lives; and the balance that sees what is right for them as individuals.

C.H. Spurgeon rarely spent twenty minutes together on his knees yet scarcely a quarter of an hour passed in all his reading and writing when he did not lift up his heart in fervent prayer and praise; on the other hand, the contemporary Scottish preacher Andrew Bonar was famous for his disciplined, controlled prayer life and his Diary shows a very different approach.

Some of our heroes are legendary for their prayer lives. We all remember the instances in E.M. Bounds' little books on prayer with their stirring examples of the mighty: Luther at times was spending three hours at the start of the day in prayer; the seventeenth-century Scottish preacher, John Welch, thought the day ill-spent if he did not give five or seven hours a day to prayer; Bishop Ken was up at three to pray, Richard Alleine at four, etc., etc.. A long line of us have tried in our youth to follow such examples. And failed!

Not many of us have had the courage to say with Steve Farrar that, important and wonderful as they were and are, these are *abnormal* and not meant to be the model for most of us. They are the giants that inspire us and instruct us by their lives and teaching but we are not all meant to be what they were or do what they did; we are meant to be ourselves, inspired and stretched and humbled by such mighty figures. As Farrar puts it, 'I respectfully suggest that they are no more the norm for prayer than an Olympic medal winner in the marathon is the norm for joggers'.[3]

---

3   Steve Farrar, *Point Man: How a man can lead his family* (Multnomah, 1994), p. 142.

By the way, be sure to read his outstanding book *Finishing Strong*, a book specially written to keep ministers on the straight and narrow; all ministers should read this or resign at once! It's also hugely quotable in sermons (thought that would get you!)

THE PROBLEMS OF PRAYER

Even Andrew Bonar, famous for his constant prayer-life, said he never went to prayer without a struggle with the flesh. Why? Why is it we have so often to force ourselves to pray? Why is it that we want to be up and doing, reading books, preparing sermons, visiting, organising and a hundred and one other things? Why is it that we fall back into periods when we have failed to pray regularly, seriously, systematically and in intercession for others?

Speaking personally I find that last kind of prayer the hardest and most demanding – intercession. Doxological prayer through the day I find easy; intercessory prayer on my knees or at my desk I find hard. One of our retired missionaries who for forty years had a special ministry of intercession with her husband once said to my wife: *'Prayer is hard work!'* – and as such it should be regarded and planned and practiced. No-one gets into shape and fit by taking out a subscription to the local gymnasium – or by spending only five minutes a day in it either (Farrar calls prayer 'aerobic kneeling'!). But why is prayer harder than it need be for many of us?

First, because *prayer is, of all actions, one of pure faith.* We speak to the air, we think unuttered thoughts, we pray for people and situations far away who are entirely unaware of us. We speak of the power of prayer but that same prayer cannot turn over a page of the Bible in our hand or lift a feather off the ground, for the power of prayer lies in the goodness of God: His will, His response, His operation and co-operation. In itself it is the weakest thing; in God's response it is made the strongest. Intercessory prayer is a sustained act of faith in God.

Secondly, because *of all actions it is one which Satan is most concerned to interrupt*, to diminish in our lives, and to mock with his temptations. Always he is the enemy of faith; for without faith it is impossible to please God and he wants to stop us pleasing God. Prayerlessness makes God a stranger; it casts our identity in doubt; it diminishes us; on the other hand, when we pray we grow: we remember who we are; we stand on high places and look outward and forward to an eternal landscape. Furthermore, Satan knows what harm is done to his kingdom and hold on men and women by prayer; as Ronald Dunn puts it: 'Satan has no defence against this weapon; he does not have an anti-prayer missile.'

Thirdly, *we face such a world of need both near and far that in prayer we hardly know where to start or stop*. However it is always better to do something than to do nothing and in prayer one thing is certain: nothing is lost. If we do not value prayer as we should, God does; if we feel crushed by prayer that seems weak, confused, desperately inadequate, it is because we do not see it transformed in the hands of God as He does with it what He has planned and what only He can do. If we saw what Christ does with the crumbs of our poor prayers we would have prayed more and offered Him loaves! 'Prayer', said an old Puritan divine, 'is the muscle that moves the arms of Omnipotence'. We may feel our prayer-life is hardly muscular – but we know more about the nervous system these days and a very effective message can travel along a very slender nerve.

In a world of need and a church in that world which needs our prayers, we must set to and get on with the work. There are helps. I use Operation World, that marvellous encyclopedia of information and guidance, and periodically urge it on the church here (there is a children's version too).

Among the greatest problems I have with prayer is the problem of 'self', that malign shadow that follows all my moves including those made when the light is strongest. I enter the cathedral of my quiet times but again and again I find myself in a little side-chapel dedicated to 'me' and worshipping before an altar on which is mounted not a cross but a mirror! So prayer becomes a series of sometimes desperate attempts to drag myself back from my preoccupations with my own ambitions or disappointments, fears or resentments, pride or guilt.

As for *the problem of wandering thoughts*, they are the daily and inevitable problem of prayer. Philip Henry, the father of Matthew, in his diary lamented that if his thoughts in prayer were written down interleaved and interrupted by his distractions they would be an unreadable mess. The Puritan preacher Thomas Manton once said it was like taking a pack of spaniels out for a walk without a lead! Familiar?

Yet the most wonderful thing about prayer is that God has provided for all our inadequacies: there is grace to cover all our prayers too as well as our sins. We must never see our prayers as if they stood alone; always we are in conversation with the Three that make all the difference in the world – and in the next.

TRINITARIAN PRAYER

When I pray, I do so as a theologian and a child, a son and a sinner, an intercessor with authority and a dependant in all humility. I have great joy in Trinitarian prayer: lifted up into the company of the holy Three-in-One, facing the glory of Each and All, speaking to One and then Another of their perfections and their gracious place in the plan of redemption. I pray marvelling at my Heavenly Father who has loved and chosen me, kneeling before the Son who died for my sin and rose for my justification, and opening my deepest heart to the Holy Spirit who with amazing patience and love is making me holy too.

John Calvin wrote 'That passage of Gregory of Nazianzus vastly delights me: "*I cannot think on the one without quickly being encircled by the splendour of the three; nor can I discern the three without being straightway carried back to the one*" [Inst. Bk. 1 chap. xiii sect. 17]. Wonderful!

Prayer gives God the glory of all His perfections. Prayer gives God the credit of His existence, His nature and His character. It glorifies God in His omnipresence (God is never out of earshot from our prayers), His omniscience (God always knows what He is doing with our prayers) and His omnipotence (God can do all He intends to do with our prayers). Prayer adores Him in the beauty of holiness and celebrates His character: His authority, His wisdom and His love. It delights in Him above self; sometimes it stands with Him against self; always it calls on Him to transform self into the image He intended at the first.

The three greatest encouragements to pray are that we have:

- *a listening God*   (Matt. 6:6)
- *a praying Christ in heaven*   (Heb. 4:14-16; 7:25)
- *and a praying Spirit on earth*   (Rom. 8:26-27)

So there is this great river of prayer flowing between the Persons of the Blessed Trinity: the Father, the Son and the Holy Spirit. <u>And yours are being taken up into it</u>, joined with it, flowing with it in its mighty current. Is that not a staggering thought? Through all eternity Father, Son and Holy Spirit have had communion, fellowship, joyful interaction, and the tremendous testimony of God's love is this: that we are taken up in the divine work, we become part of the eternal conversation, our prayers are used to fulfil the sovereign plan.

When you realise this and take it deeply into your prayer life then it will have two effects:

First, you will not simply see your prayers on their own; you will not evaluate them as if they were on their own; and you will not fall victim to the temptation to abandon your prayers and prayer-life as hopelessly weak and inadequate and useless. Instead you will see the larger picture; you will see this great river of prayer within the Godhead and your own prayers and prayer-life as part of it.

And secondly, however small a part your prayers may be of the heavenly intercession of Christ or the mighty movement of the Holy Spirit in His ministry of prayer on earth, whatever drops of that great river of prayer within the Godhead your own prayers are, they are hugely significant and truly effective. Prayer cannot fail when it is according to the will of God because it is part of this bigger picture and this greater power.

Therefore, every day of your life stand aware as you pray and pray with a sense of wonder and privilege and confidence, and never give up on your prayers but instead give God the glory and the praise of all your intercessions.

Prayer combines in unique ways weakness and strength. It stops us in our tracks and tells us that we can do nothing as we ought and as we need without Him to whom we pray. And yet it also lifts up our heads and tells us that we 'can do all things through him who loved us'. Prayer is the signature of God under the story of our lives – one of two signatures, his and ours – which says '*This is our story*' and '*Nothing was done without me!*'

Our prayers not only connect us with 'infinities and immensities' but also with the lives and people around us in a host of ways: the saved and the unsaved, young and old, sick and well.

PASTORAL PRAYER

'Hello, I was praying for you this week.' The child in our church to whom I was speaking looked rather astonished at the idea (but I bet he told his mother!). The fact is I pray for all our church members and their children, and I quite often tell someone on a Sunday morning 'I was praying for you this week'. It is always a blessing and an encouragement to know someone has prayed for us.

Many years ago Dr Martyn Lloyd-Jones said to me 'My wife and I pray for you every day'. I was as astonished as the little boy and I hope he was half as encouraged as I was! Some years later, after Dr Lloyd-Jones's death, I mentioned it to his wife: 'I *still do*' she said emphatically.

In fact, all the members of Cornerstone know that I pray for them and it means a lot to them as well as to me. If you pray for someone, tell them. Another man, this time from my home village in Wales, prayed frequently for me in my early ministry. His name was Tom Gwilym and he lived a deeply godly and set-apart life in a community that did not understand him.

Whenever my wife, Valerie, and I visited him in his tiny old-fashioned cottage, he always prayed on his knees at the end of our visit and always began his prayer with 'And...' This was, I believe, because he lived a life of prayer and so it was natural to continue the conversation with his Lord in this way. The ministry denied to him was given to me – and he strengthened it with his own prayer-life.

When we pray seriously and earnestly for a person, we are being used as a means of grace and blessing to them in the will of God. As we might say to a friend 'Let's go over and visit such and such a one', so our heavenly Father says to us 'Let's go over and bless such a one'. In prayer we become partners with the activity of God; it is a huge privilege for us and a marvellous condescension on His part.

PERSISTENCE IN PRAYER

Jesus preached two parables to promote persistence in prayer – The friend at midnight and the unjust judge – and urged His followers, 'Keep on asking...seeking...knocking' and it <u>will</u> be given you, you <u>will</u> find, the door <u>will</u> be opened'.

In the parable of the unjust judge Jesus tells the story of a woman's forlorn cause; she seems to have no chance in a man's world, without a protector or advocate and with a stronger, noisier crowd shouldering its way to the front and a man in power who doesn't care. Yet, by her persistence and the judge's fear of dishonour, her cause triumphs. What chance does the kingdom of God have in a world of unjust judges, a world where the laws of the kingdom are the laughter of men, where love, humility, meekness, forgiveness seem defenceless against pride, selfishness and greed?

But into just such a world Christ Jesus has brought the beginnings of God's future kingdom; the only one that will last forever. The beginning of that kingdom was very small: Jesus once compared it to a mustard seed planted in the ground. It grew, but against the hostility and muscle of the world it seemed to have no chance. Yet it grew on and on. Jesus, in another metaphor, described His kingdom as being like yeast: growing silently in the dough of history, growing secretly, unstoppably. But not easily or evenly. There would be opposition and setbacks. It would be scorned, hated, opposed and threatened. And it always will be until He comes to judge the world in righteousness in one final act.

Meantime, there are to be two great forces of prayer in a world of injustice and suffering and rebellion against God: they are the prayers of Christ in heaven and the prayers of God's people on earth.

> So far as the Church in history and on earth is concerned therefore the great connecting link between world history and the heavenly session of Christ is to be found in prayer and intercession.[4]

As you pray do not baulk at praying for great things. Pray over the Muslim 10/40 window: 'Thy kingdom come'; pray over India: 'Thy kingdom come'; pray over the Western nations and African countries: 'Thy kingdom come'. For it is on such a wave of prayer, gathering through the centuries, that the Lord of glory will come in the hour appointed by His Father.

---

4   Thomas F. Torrance, *Space, Time and Resurrection* (T. and T. Clark, 1976) p. 138

'Then Jesus told his disciples this parable to show them that they should always pray and not give up' (Luke 18:1). But why, someone may ask, 'Why does God not answer prayer immediately? He has the power, he has the will, and he has the goodness so why do we have to work through opposition, delay and unbelief? Perhaps because he himself has to work through opposition, delay and unbelief.

Perhaps he is reminding us that we are dealing with people who need to be persuaded not puppets who simply need a different string pulled. Perhaps he is calling us to be partners with him in his wisdom, his patience, his persistence and his love. Perhaps too he is showing us that we are fighting a long battle with eternal consequences and building a kingdom which is here to last. That takes time. A cardboard kingdom could be put up in no time but an eternal kingdom takes rather longer!

God's work in people is not easily done; we are not puppets, we are moral agents. *Prayer takes time to work because God takes time to work – in all of us.* He has to work against much ignorance and many prejudices; against fears, inconsistencies and follies. God's work in people is a delicate, complex and very special one. It is remarkable that He offers to share that work with us and asks us to work with Him. This is a very great privilege; it involves much faith and prayer, much thoughtfulness and consistent living on our part. We so often do not fulfil these conditions. We wonder why the delay is so long when we are part of the problem. We sometimes complain about our spiritual experience (or lack of it) but God might more often complain about our spiritual zeal (or lack of it).

When you pray recognise that the opposition and their reluctance to face God is strong and persistent. That is why prayer must be strong and persistent. God is rejected every day so why should we complain if we are rejected every day? Yet God comes back every day with persistent mercy so why should we not come back every day with persistent prayer?

God's persistence only wins through after many rebuffs and He calls us to share in that work too. That is why the apostle Paul writes to the Romans: 'I urge you brothers [and sisters] by our Lord Jesus Christ and by the love of the Spirit to join me in my struggle by praying to God for me' (Rom. 15:30).

PRAYER AS SPIRITUAL WARFARE

'What is the nature of petitionary prayer?' asks David Wells in a major book on world mission and answers his own question: 'It is in essence rebellion – rebellion against the world in its fallenness, the absolute and undying refusal to accept as normal what is pervasively abnormal.' Later he continues: 'Petitionary prayer only flourishes where there is a two-fold belief: first, that God's name is hallowed too irregularly, His kingdom has come too little, and His will is done too infrequently; second, that God Himself can change this situation.'[5]

Prayer becomes rebellion against the rebellion of earth. It fights for God and it knows that it fights on the winning side. As Karl Barth put it in a memorable line: 'To clasp the hands in prayer is to rise up against the disorder of the world.'

John Piper uses a favourite metaphor in his book on world mission, *Let the nations be glad*: 'Life is war...prayer is primarily a wartime walkie-talkie for the mission of the church as it advances against the powers of darkness and unbelief. It is not surprising that prayer malfunctions when we try to make it a domestic walkie-talkie so that we can call headquarters for everything we need as the kingdom of Christ advances in the world. Prayer gives us the significance of front-line forces, and gives God the glory of a limitless Provider. The one who gives the power gets the glory. Thus prayer safeguards the supremacy of God in missions while linking us with endless grace for every need.'[6]

---

5   Ralph D. Winter and Steven C. Hawthorne, Editors, *Perspectives on the World Christian Movement – Reader*, 4th Ed. (William Carey Library, 2009), pp. 224-5.

6   John Piper, *Let the Nations be Glad* (IVP, 2010), p. 41

Paul reminds us that it is prayer which puts on the whole armour of God (Eph. 6:18) and is so aware of its potency even in the hands of the weakest that he asks for prayer to continue and complete his own ministry (Eph. 6:19-20) – even though he is in chains for the gospel. This is not a war without wounds and the persecuted church should never be far from our own prayers and the public prayers of our churches. We must join our voices with those of suffering Christians around the world who are surrounded by hostility and penalised by discrimination.

Our churches should also be encouraged to pray for missionaries, those who labour in the hard places of the earth. In our own church we often have more than twenty of our members serving abroad and we pray for one or another of them in every service. To have a time specifically set aside for world missions, the persecuted church, various countries in trouble, etc., keeps our people thinking globally. We can become too parochial in our concerns.

We need too, in the public prayers of our churches at different times, to pray for our own nation and for our people in their working lives and contexts. The areas of government and education, medicine and business, media and culture are also theatres of conflict where the Christian voice must be heard. Our present culture is poisoned by materialism, sexual permissiveness and cynicism; the media increasingly feed the basest instincts and the prevailing philosophy lurches between a godless scientism and a pagan mysticism. It fails a generation and undermines the future. The churches and the Christians feel helpless and weak before such forces but prayer and a truly biblical perspective will be a strong counter to that and remind us that at the end of the day it is God's kingdom which is destined to stand and grow and inherit the eternal future.

The great need of the hour is for a repeat of the work of God which arrested the nation 250 years ago in the days of Whitefield and the Wesley brothers. Then too, society was as promiscuous as it is now, and to a great extent the church was in worse state than today. Yet God did a work which began to change not only the present but the future and affected British life for generations in another century.

So we too may be a challenge to the present and a part of the future; sowing the seeds of Christian witness and praying for a new harvest in a new generation. We can do so confident that no prayer is lost, no witness that does not register in the heart of Christ, and determined that we too will always pray and never give up.

PRAYER AS VICTORY-SONG

Someone has said that the Bible begins with 'Let there be light' and ends with the Hallelujah Chorus! Certainly the gospel of the empty tomb proclaims the victory of God in Christ and our prayers must be on that basis. We live as the people of God and we must pray as the people of God. If sometimes our prayers become dull or formal or weary, how often it is because our prayers lack the elements that Paul repeatedly mentions alongside prayer and to be included in it: the elements of victory, joy and thanksgiving: *'Be joyful always; pray continually, give thanks in all circumstances for this is God's will for you in Christ Jesus'* (1 Thess. 5:16-18 cf. Phil. 4:4-7; Col. 4:2, etc.). Without this, no wonder if our prayers become weary and lifeless. We produce shopping lists – and who can sing or dance to a shopping list? A friend of mine says whenever you come to God for a new blessing be sure you bring Him a receipt for the previous one.

When we forget this we soon start to pay the price even in our prayer-lives. Our prayers become a worry list that only deepens our preoccupations with our anxieties. We dwell on our fears and forget how often we have been guarded, guided and kept. Our lives are crowded with the blessings of God; our generous and good God and Father. If we have a prayer list we ought perhaps to make a blessing list and write down or type a thousand things until our fingers ache.

APPENDIX: GOD AND ONE MAN'S PRAYERS

One of our church members is Elsie Harris. Elsie and her husband John (now in heaven with the Lord) worked for the Leprosy Mission for forty years, mostly in Nepal and Congo.

One week a while back Elsie received a letter. The letter relates to a time in their early career, about thirty-five years ago. To understand this you need to know that John and Elsie had a very profound and sustained prayer ministry of which John spoke very little, a ministry of intercession which reached into every day (and night) of their lives.

In 1969 they were living and working in the Kathmandu valley about twenty miles from Kathmandu. In those days no-one was allowed to witness to Christ to Nepalese. Expats in the hospital could have their own services but there was to be no evangelism whatsoever. It was a closed country.

During their work John and Elsie had become increasingly burdened about the nearby Lille Valley. It was then a place of such spiritual darkness and occult power that the missionaries used to say it could be felt by Christians who passed near.

One day in the leprosy hospital a mother brought a child who needed some attention though she did not have leprosy. The child was very dirty and scruffy, and as John was talking with the mother and the child he felt a tremendous conviction that this ten-year-old would be used to open up the notorious Lille valley to the gospel.

It seemed a ridiculous thing but John felt the assurance of the Holy Spirit that it would certainly come to pass, and he covenanted with God to pray every day for the child and this outcome.

He prayed for seventeen years, every day without fail, even when they left Nepal to take up leprosy work in Congo. In 1986, when visiting Nepal, they heard from a paramedic friend named James that the Lille valley had opened up to the gospel.

Soon after, he wrote with details that entire families had become Christians through the witness of one woman. John asked simply and without show 'What is the name of this woman?' His friend said 'Daya' – it was the very person John had treated so many years before!

Not long after John died, Daya wrote to Elsie to say that James, the paramedic, had told her it was John who had treated her as a girl and prayed for her through all the years. Neither she nor her mother had ever known of John's conviction but now she was writing to Elsie to say that there were now whole groups of worshippers in the Lille valley.

Later Elsie had another letter from her to say they were standing strong in the faith of Jesus Christ. There is now even a plaque to John Harris there in open celebration of the gospel of Jesus Christ.

That, it seems to me, is a modern example of what we read in the Acts of the Apostles: the power of the Spirit at work in a deeply spiritual person, God sharing His secrets with a praying man and taking him up into partnership, God doing mighty things through believing prayer. But remember, this was a case of a *given* assurance, a prophetic revelation of God's Spirit, and it was given to a man of prayer. God does not tell His secrets to those who only drop in for a chat.

3

The Pastor as Theologian

TIM CHESTER AND STEVE TIMMIS

It has long been recognised that orthopraxis arises out of orthodoxy, which means that whatever else a pastor is, he is a theologian. Philip Hacking's teaching and ministry were shaped by and reflected Reformed theology at its best. In this chapter two well known UK 'pastor-theologians', Tim Chester and Steve Timmis, tease out how theology enriches ministry and ministry is the proper setting for theology and that both are meant to serve the purpose of God's mission in the world.

There are many aspects of Philip Hacking's long and fruitful ministry that are worthy of both commendation and emulation. His commitment to his local 'parish' is definitely one of them. There were very few weeks in the year when at some point Philip would not be seen walking around the parish knocking on the doors of his parishioners. One of the main drivers of this habit was his commitment to evangelism. He loved nothing more than explaining the gospel to people for whom he had a real sense of responsibility. They may rarely set foot in their local church, but few would deny him the opportunity to set foot in their home.

But this practice was also driven by theological convictions. As his wider ministry grew, it ensured he remained earthed in the concerns of his parish and so the life issues of his parishioners. This familiarity with ordinary, local people helped shape his preaching. It was partly through these conversations that he knew how to shed the light of the gospel onto the real questions of real people.

1. THEOLOGIANS MUST BE EARTHED IN THE MISSION OF THE CHURCH

Theology is the conversation between God's Word and God's world. Theologians seek to exegete God's Word through the disciplines of biblical studies and systematic theology that we might then apply God's Word to His world. And we seek to exegete God's world through the disciplines of cultural and historical analysis, philosophical engagement and missiological reflection that we might then understand God's world in the light of His Word. The role of the theologians is to mediate this conversation between God's Word and God's world.

One of the key questions, therefore, for theologians is this: With whom are we in conversation?

The greatest danger is that we lose connection with God's Word. Then the conversation is an internal conversation within a closed world. The world speaks to the world and the voice of God is never heard. One of the key motifs of John's Gospel is that Jesus is 'from heaven'. In other words, He brings revelation and salvation from outside the human condition. This is why pastors must be theologians.

But there is a second danger and that is the danger of losing connection with God's world. That, too, creates an internal conversation, the internal conversation of academics or churchmen. Then we no longer mediate the conversation between God's Word and God's world. This is why theologians must be involved in the mission of the church and its pastoral ministry.

Reformed philosopher Paul Helm complains that too many systematic theologies are 'an intramural product, consisting of lots of conversations among exclusively Christian theologians'. He continues:

The general features or movements of current culture only merit discussion insofar as they have been taken up by or unconsciously reflected in the published work of members of the guild. As far as I can see the numerous works in systematic theology recently produced among conservative theologians (Grudem, Frame, Reymond, Kelly and now Horton) all seem to play on the same field and in more or less the same way, so that while we all may have our favourite, there is, frankly, little to choose between them, except depth of pocket or size of shelf. Is this, a kind of Theological Correctness, that contributes to the feeling of many that systematic theology is inherently dull? I hazard the hope that when the present cycle of systematic theology writing has run its course, the next cycle, while thoroughly conservative in orientation, will be wider, broader, more expansive, allowing some genuine, substantive differences of opinion and so, if nothing else, widening consumer choice. Perhaps such a change will be forced on new authors whether they like it or not. Ought not a modern systematic theology to engage with Islam? ... 'Do Christians and Muslims worship the same God? Christian providence or Muslim fate?'[1]

It was not always like this. Augustine's *City of God* was a conversation with an empire in decline. One of Thomas Aquinas' main works, *Summa Contra Gentiles*, was written as a manual in apologetics for missionaries, especially those facing the advance of Islam. John Calvin's *Institutes* was written

---

1   Paul Helm, Review Article of Michael Horton, *The Christian Faith: A Systematic Theology for Pilgrims on the Way*, reformation21.org, April 2011, www. reformation21.org/shelf-life/the-christian-faith-a-systematic-theology-for-pilgrims-on-the-way.php.

to instruct laypeople. The works of the Puritans were for the most part pastoral in intent, many starting life as sermons.

Above all the New Testament documents themselves, the source data as it were, were missional and pastoral documents. They were written by missionaries for missional situations. John's Gospel is written that people might believe (John 20:31). Paul's letters are written to new church plants as they wrestle with the challenges of growth. A century ago theologian Martin Kähler famously claimed that mission was 'the mother of theology'. Missiologist David Bosch comments: 'The New Testament writers were not scholars who had the leisure to research the evidence before they put pen to paper. Rather, they wrote in the context of an "emergency situation", of a church which, because of its missionary encounter with the world, was *forced* to theologise.'[2]

Take the epistle of Romans as an example. Romans is often regarded as the most 'theological' book in the New Testament. Certainly it is the most systematic in its presentation of truth. But the reality is that it is a missional document from start to finish.

Paul writes to express his intent to visit the church in Rome (1:8-13) and to make Rome a launch pad for a new mission to Spain (15:23-24). But a visit from Paul was not necessarily welcome news! Everywhere he went he attracted controversy. He was controversial among Christians because he said Gentile converts did not need to adopt a Jewish identity. He was even more controversial among unbelievers who persecuted him wherever he went. So Paul is writing to say, 'This is who I am. This is what I preach. This is my gospel.'

The letter begins and ends in the same way:

● an outline of Paul's 'gospel' (1:1-2; 16:25)

● which focuses on 'Jesus Christ' (1:4; 16:25)

---

2   David J. Bosch, *Transforming Mission: Paradigm Shifts in Theology of Mission* (Orbis, 1991), p. 16.

- which is attested through the prophets in the 'holy writings' or through the 'prophetic writings' (1:2; 16:26)

- which is for 'all the Gentiles' or nations (1:5; 16:26)

- calling them to 'the obedience of faith' (1:5; 16:26)

This topping and tailing of the letter with the same motifs employing the same language suggests these themes are central to all that transpires in between. The letter of Romans is a defence of Paul's mission to the nations and a defence of Paul's gospel for the nations.

The central theme is then the righteousness of God because Paul's mission to the Gentiles calls God's righteousness into question. Paul's gospel calls into question the righteousness of God because in the 'court case' between God and humanity, sinners are declared righteous through faith in Jesus Christ. God's righteousness – in the sense of God's doing right by His character – is thereby called into question. Romans is the 'demonstration' that God can be both 'just and the one who justifies the man who has faith in Jesus' (3:26). But Paul's mission also calls into question the righteousness of God because in the 'court case' between Israel and the nations, God appears now to be siding with the nations. And in the Hebrew judicial system to vindicate one party was to condemn the other. God's righteousness – in the sense of God's doing right by His Word – is thereby called into question. He appears to be forsaking His covenant promises to Israel.

In his introduction and conclusion Paul emphasises that his gospel and his mission were *promised beforehand in the prophetic writings*. In other words, Paul is claiming that mission is not just his personal version of Christianity or his specialist interest. This is the Bible story. So in Romans Paul revisits the Bible story in the light of what Jesus has done. He tells the story of creation (ch. 1), of Adam as humanity's representative (ch. 5), of humanity's Fall into sin (ch. 1), of Abraham's calling (ch. 4), of Israel's calling (chs. 2, 9–11), of the Exodus (ch. 6), of the giving of the law at Mount Sinai (ch. 7), of God leading Israel through the wilderness into a new inheritance (ch. 8). This is biblical theology in the service of mission.

Paul is showing how Jesus fulfils the Old Testament *with the result* that people from all nations can become part of God's people simply through faith in Jesus without having to become Jewish or follow the Jewish law. This message is for '*all*' nations. Paul was controversial because people thought he was inventing this new idea of Gentile mission. But in the letter of Romans is Paul saying, 'No, this was always the plan. Mission is not some trendy idea that I invented. It's the climax of the story.' This is the logic of the letter. And this is its ambition: '*It has always been my ambition to preach the gospel where Christ was not known.*' (15:20)

The point for our purposes is that the New Testament is a missional document. It means it is difficult truly to understand the gospel and epistles if you are not likewise engaged in mission. Reading the New Testament in the academy is like reading a Haynes manual in your living room. If you really want to understand a Haynes manual you need to have a car in front of you.

Tim Keller makes a similar point in relation to preaching. 'You tend to preach to the people you listen to and talk to during the week,' he says. 'If you only read books by other evangelical pastors then you'll answer them in your preaching because you tend to get out of the biblical text answers to the questions you are asking and the questions you are asking have to do with the conversation partners you have during the week – both literal and the people you're reading.' If you are engaging with secular people then you will naturally engage them from the text when you're preaching. Plus 'the Christians will hear you talking to their non-Christians friends and they'll end up bringing them.'

The most effective way to evangelise a non-Christian through your preaching is to so inhabit that person's worldview ... to be so conversant with that person's questions and issues, but as ... a confident believer, [that] you give them a glimpse of what they would look like if they were a Christian ... [Otherwise] they cannot imagine ever being anyone like you.[3]

Young pastors, Keller argues, need to spend less time preparing and spend more time with people. This is what will make them a better preacher. Pastoral counselling crystallises and personalises the application of the gospel to life.

It is a very great mistake to pit pastoral care and leadership against preaching preparation. It is only through doing people-work that you become the preacher you need to be – someone who knows sin, how the heart works, what people's struggles are and so on. Pastoral care and leadership is to some degree sermon preparation. More accurately, it is preparing the preacher, not just the sermon.[4]

Peter Collier, a long-standing member of Christ Church, Fulwood, and a personal friend of Philip, tells a story that illustrates this point well. On one occasion, a number of young trainees were in Sheffield to help take part in a parish mission. As they were standing in the coffee bar they took the opportunity to ask Philip how he structured his days. He explained his practice of study and prayer in the morning, followed by a couple of hours of parish visitation after lunch. One of the young men replied that surely the practice of

---

3   Tim Keller, *Preaching to the Heart*, audio lectures (Ockenga Institute, 2006).
4   Tim Keller, 'Ten Questions for Expositors – Keller,' unashamedworkman. wordpress.com, 4 April 2007.

visiting was outdated and wouldn't his time be better spent in sermon preparation. Philip, looking at him with a mixture of pity and despair, said, 'Do you not think I'm preparing my sermon all the time I'm visiting the people?'

It is often noted that theologians in non-confessional institutions are in danger of losing touch with the authoritative and sufficient standard of God's Word in the face of academic peer pressure. This is clearly a real danger. But we also need to recognise that theologians in confessional settings can also go astray by losing touch with God's world. They need to ensure they are rooted in the mission of the church through significant and meaningful involvement in the life of a local church.

But we also need a new breed of practitioner-theologians who are engaged in serious theology in a missional context, rather than an academic context. This will not be the calling of every pastor, but it should be the calling of some and be seen as an equally valid, and maybe more valid, way of doing theology.

2. PASTORS MUST BE EARTHED IN THE THEOLOGY OF THE CHURCH

So theologians must be earthed in the mission of the church. But there is a profound sense, too, in which all pastors must be theologians. That is, all of their practice and preaching must express deep theological convictions. Without this firm theological anchor, they will be driven by 'fads and fancies' and default to mere pragmatism.

This, though, does not mean pastors must be up to date with academic debates or experts in biblical, historical and doctrinal studies. For a pastor wanting to be effective in the local church and seeking proactively to shepherd the people in his care, such an aim is unrealistic and unhelpful. In fact, it would prove a significant distraction from the task to which the Lord has called him.

We must avoid the tyranny and seductions of academia. For some men in the pastoral ministry, the attraction of academia can be irresistible. Not only are books often more manageable than people, there is also a certain kudos that comes from being well regarded in academic circles. In an evangelical culture prone to idolising intellectual prowess, we should not underestimate the lure of the published article in a respected journal.

When then does it mean?

1. Pastors need to reflect theologically on contemporary issues

Evangelical theology proceeds on the basis that God has revealed Himself. It presents the word of truth concerning the character and purposes of God as revealed in the gospel concerning His Son and our Saviour Jesus Christ. So the only theology worthy of the name evangelical is rooted deeply in the Scriptures.

This means that theological reflection outside of the Bible is speculative and fanciful. Everything we need to know about God is to be found in His Word. The Scriptures set both the extent and the limit of our thoughts and reflections. This is one area where we are currently susceptible as evangelicals. The authority of the Bible is almost everywhere among us assumed, but our confidence in the sufficiency of Scripture is not so certain. But if the Bible is not sufficient then it is not authoritative. Without its sufficiency it becomes nothing more than a reference point: significant but not decisive. It is precisely because the Scriptures are sufficient that they function as the 'final authority in all matters of faith and conduct.'

So if we are to reflect theologically on contemporary matters, we must read the times through the lens of God's revealed truth. This is what John Stott describes as 'double listening'. Pastors need to listen both to God's Word and to their context. They need to work as hard at understanding the one as they do the other.

There is a danger inherent in pastoral ministry of being absorbed by the immediate pastoral needs of the people for whom we have responsibility. When this happens, we find ourselves sucked into a small world of personal problems and difficulties. Of course, these are often real and pressing. Being responsible for people means we have to shepherd them skilfully through issues and questions. But we must avoid the pitfall of being so distracted by these immediate needs that we no longer see the larger picture. To do so is short-sighted as it is this bigger context that shapes the questions and provides the distinctive texture of our struggles.

It was said of the men of Issachar, who stood with David in battle, that they 'understood the times' and so 'knew what Israel should do' (1 Chron. 12:32). That sort of insight will come from Spirit-directed, deep engagement in both God's Word and His world.

This commitment to cultural and biblical engagement is also important in helping pastors disciple ordinary believers living everyday lives. People need to see how we engage theologically with the world so that they can learn how to engage for themselves. We can never be satisfied with mere professions of faith. A church comprising 'mere' converts is a dereliction of our duty. It is the pastor's responsibility and privilege to 'equip the saints for works of service' (Eph. 4:12, NASB). At the heart of those 'works' is the ability to engage with their world in a way that is distinctive. It is the truth of God's Word, rightly taught and pertinently applied, that enables Christians to live well in the world. It is through living 'the good life' in the mess and complexity of contemporary living, through joys and sorrow, failure and success, that we commend the Saviour.

But so many Christians are simply unaware of how to do this. They do not know how to relate to the contemporary world in which they live. They are often confused by the philosophical complexity, bemused by the moral ambiguity and overwhelmed by the rapid rate of change. Pastors need to model real theological engagement with the world in a way that trains others to do this for themselves. Only then will we present to the world a credible and intriguing faith.

2. Pastors need to recognise the essentially simple nature of theology.

Engineers often talk about the quest for simplicity in design. They move, or at least aspire to move, from complexity to simplicity. The opposite is often true in theology and that is never more so than in our theology of pastoral care. It is self-evidently true that every human being is different. You only have to look at the human face to see infinite variation on a theme. How much more when it comes to the complexities of personalities, backgrounds, influences and gene pools?

But there is also much about the human condition that is common to every person across cultures and history. It is perhaps one of the most profound insights of theology to be able to assert that we are sinners who need a Saviour. Peel back the complexities of our circumstances and you will discover the irreducible core of a heart that was made to love God and others, but which has now turned in on itself, becoming obsessively and compulsively self-loving. All of our sin is in some way an outworking of this essential condition. Pastors need to have confidence in the gospel and its power to address issues in a way that transcends particulars.

This is not to say we can go rushing arrogantly and insensitively into every situation, imagining that we have the magic pill that will solve every ill. Such naivety is both arrogant and foolish. We must always deal with the differing issues that people face with humility and care. But we must also deal with them with a robust confidence in the gospel to speak into their lives whatever the texture and hue of their situation. Evangelical theology, we have said, is 'a word of truth about God, His character and purposes, as revealed in the gospel concerning His Son'. Such a theology is able to speak directly into people's lives with a penetrating and liberating pertinence. It is evangelical theology alone that, not only diagnoses the human condition, but also treats it. This is why pastors need to be competent and confident theologians.

3. Pastors need to guard the flock by being alert to dangerous trajectories

Our mandate is Paul's address to the Ephesian elders where in Acts 20:28-30 Paul instructs them to pay careful attention to 'the flock of which the Holy Spirit has made you overseers'. He warns them of the inevitability of 'fierce wolves' coming in among them, men who say 'twisted things, to draw away disciples after them' (ESV). The role of a pastor is to guard the flock from such men and their seductions. To do this we need to know what we are talking about. We need men who are steeped in the truth of the gospel.

But guarding the flock is more than addressing clear error. Heresy does not wear a badge any more than false teachers will come among the flock baring their teeth and with blood dripping from their mouths. It is common for predators to roll in the excreta of the animals they are hunting to disguise their smell, to enable them to get closer without being detected. This is why we speak about 'wolves in sheep's clothing'. Just because it looks like a sheep and smells like a sheep doesn't mean it is a sheep!

This, then, is why we need to be alert to where trajectories of thought will lead. Heresy rarely begins with a clear rejection of truth. It starts with a change of emphasis. We need to spot the forks in the road where a change of emphasis today will lead to a divergent path tomorrow. This is often subtle and insidious. We need to listen for what is *not* being said with as much diligence as we listen to what is being said.

For example, it is not uncommon to hear preachers talk effusively about Jesus, the Father, the kingdom of God and mission. Following Jesus is an adventure that is all about living life to the full by realising our potential. Evangelism is calling people to the good life and inviting them into the kingdom of God which, as we all know, is a party. Of course, all of these assertions are true. But they are not the whole truth. Following Jesus is also about taking up the cross, counting the cost and suffering for the Saviour. Unless all of these aspects of discipleship are understood fully and presented clearly, then the trajectory will be away from truth and into error.

Another example might be spiritual experiences. If someone has had an experience that is intense and meaningful, it is important to listen to how they speak to others about it. If the focus in their counsel of others is that experience so that they try to make it normative for others then the trajectory is away from the sufficiency of Christ and the centrality of the cross. The gospel is our reference point and we are to always shepherd people back to Christ and His finished work.

This is not straightforward. We do not want to pounce on everything people say. This is why pastors must be competent theologians who are able to lead God's people with sound judgment. Two principles will help.

First, hold shepherds to a higher standard than sheep. If you constantly correct a new Christian they may soon become discouraged. They are learning and we need to give them time to learn. But those who teach God's Word are held to a higher standard. They are more likely to teach error through a deliberate choice rather than through ignorance of the issues.

Second, preach the whole counsel of God. This principle allows us in one context to emphasise truth with full rhetorical force without constantly qualifying what we are saying. But over time we should present a full view of truth that reflects the weight of Scripture. Consider, for example, the roles of human responsibility and divine sovereignty. Our teaching must reflect the biblical emphases without diminishing the weight of either. So there will be times when we are handling a specific passage when we focus in on our responsibility to make our calling and election sure. At those times we do not need to, nor is it helpful to, qualify it constantly with 'of course, we all know that God is sovereign ...' What God's people need to hear at that point is their responsibility because that is what the text says. But at other times we will emphasise God's sovereignty, speaking words of reassurance to people, calling them to work hard at following Christ while resting in His grace.

Philip Hacking was not an academic theologian. Nor did he ever claim to be. But if theology is nothing more nor less than 'a word of truth about God, His character and purposes, as revealed in the gospel concerning His Son' then he has to be among the most gifted of his generation. Because Philip knew truth he knew when to take a stand on key issues, not only as he shepherded his people but also as he played a leading role at a national level.

4

The Pastor as Preacher

PETER ADAM

Philip Hacking is a preacher. Clear, well-earthed Bible expository preaching delivered with warmth and passion has always been the hallmark of his ministry. Not surprisingly he has inspired many would-be preachers (including the editor) to give over their lives to this noble task. In recent years there has been something of a renaissance in expository preaching in the UK with a focus on what makes a good sermon. In this chapter, Peter Adam takes a step back and asks a more fundamental question: what makes a good preacher?

This chapter is about preparing preachers, not about preparing sermons. Why? Aspiring preachers often ask 'Show me how to preach a good sermon.' Ministers sometimes ask 'How can I train someone to preach a good sermon?' There is, however a more basic question, namely, 'How should we prepare preachers?' For the sermon comes from the preacher. Preparing a preacher is more basic than preparing a sermon. It is more basic, and so more neglected: more basic, and so more important.

For words express our inner character: as Jesus Christ taught us, 'it is out of the abundance of the heart that the mouth speaks' (Luke 6:43-5, ESV). His words have particular application to preachers and teachers of God's Word, for those who teach will be judged with greater strictness (James 3:1).

So this chapter is not about how to preach or how to pre-pare a sermon. It is about how to prepare a preacher. Who we are is fundamental to what we say and do, for character is expressed in words and actions, and all we say and do is formed by our personal and Christian identity. That is why Paul wrote to the Corinthians, who were so focused on gifts, about the need for love. A gifted person who has no love is a danger to others, so a gifted and able preacher who has no love is a danger to others. For, 'Knowledge puffs up, but love builds up' (1 Cor. 8:1). And, if I am loveless, then 'I am nothing', and 'I gain nothing' (1 Cor. 13:1-3). No wonder Paul encouraged the Corinthians to 'pursue love' in order to edify others (1 Cor. 14:1, ESV).

As Paul made this point about character and gifts in general in 1 Corinthians, so he made the same point about elders in Titus 1. In his list of requirements for elders his main focus is on character: 'blameless...not arrogant or quick-tempered...not addicted to wine, or violent or greedy for gain... hospitable, a lover of goodness, prudent, upright, devout, and self-controlled... (and with) a firm grasp of the word that is trustworthy in accordance with the teaching, so that he may be able both to preach with sound doctrine and to refute those who contradict it' (from Titus 1:6-9, NRSV). Here are aspects of character and actions that are required, aspects of character and actions that disqualify, and then, finally a firm grasp of the trustworthy message, and gifts of teaching and refutation.

Similarly, when Paul commended good ministry and warned against bad ministry, he wrote not only of the con-tent of the message but also of the style of ministry. So he wrote: 'For you put up with it when someone makes slaves of you, or preys on you, or takes advantage of you, or puts on airs, or gives you a slap in the face' (2 Cor. 11:20, NRSV). And, in contrast, 'If I must boast, I will boast of the things that show my weakness' (2 Cor. 11:30).

So too James looked for lively faith to be expressed in a tamed tongue: and this will only be found in those who are 'wise and understanding' with the 'wisdom from above', that is from God (James 3:13, 17 ESV). Wise words come from wise people: a message of special importance for those who are teachers in the church (James 3:1).

These matters are of great importance and urgency today. For there are three powerful and persuasive ideas in the Christian world-view in many places that damage how we think about and evaluate ministry, whether ministry we do, or ministry we receive or support.

1. The cult of celebrity has infiltrated the church, and the world recognises celebrities by their wealth, success and popularity, not by their character. Celebrities have replaced heroes. We in the church may be less likely to be mesmerised by conspicuous wealth, but we honour those who have the trappings and resources of wealth, and we are bewitched by success and popularity.

2. We, like the world, are also bewitched by gifts. We fall into the trap of thinking that if someone is very gifted, Christian character and personal maturity must also be present. That may be the case, but sometimes great gifts replace character and maturity. Some are appointed for their great gifts and lose their way because of their weak or vicious character.

3. We also assume that there must be easy steps to achieve great aims; there must be short cuts which will enable us to achieve greatness without too much effort. We want to bypass long-term and costly learning and discipline, to win without blood, sweat and tears. Of course there are some who are so spectacularly gifted by God that they leap forward. However, in most cases God's gifts mean more demands. Like the gospel, ministry gifts are freely given, but are costly to receive.

We see clues to preparing preachers in 2 Timothy. The climax of the letter comes in chapter 4, in Paul's solemn charge to Timothy: 'In the presence of God and of Christ Jesus, who will judge the living and the dead, and in the light of his appearing and his kingdom, I solemnly urge you: preach the word' (4:1, 2).[1]

What then of Paul's instructions before and after this charge? How do they relate to it?

We can see them as Paul explains the preconditions, the pre-commitments that are necessary if Timothy is to be ready to 'proclaim the message.' Let me summarise them in fifteen instructions that Paul gave to Timothy directly, or through him to those he was to train. For the purpose of this letter is to encourage Timothy to good ministry, and especially the ministry of teaching and training teachers and preachers for their ministry. These two aims are complementary, for the teachers and preachers will learn from Paul's instructions to Timothy, as also from the instructions that Timothy is to pass on to them. So the letter is about teachers and preachers, for the benefit of Timothy and those he trains. The evidence that Paul had in mind this narrow group, rather than the church in general, is this: all the instructions to Timothy about his own ministry; the mention of the 'faithful people' in 2:2; the instructions to those who teach in 2:14ff; and the reference to the training of 'the man of God' (an Old Testament term for a prophet) in 3:17. If the church is meant to hear these instructions (as in 4:22, 'grace be with you'), that would be so they would welcome good ministry, and reject bad ministry.

All of these instructions are relevant for those 'faithful people' being trained by Timothy, and so relevant for us as we train preachers.

1. Fan into flame the gift of God.
In 1:5-7 Paul encouraged Timothy by writing of his sincere faith, and then reminded him of what he needed to do to be

---

1   I use my own translation. See also the comparable passage 1Timothy 6:2-16.

useful in ministry, that is to fan into flame the gift of God that he has received. What would be the sign that Timothy is not doing this? The sign is 'fear' (1:7), and faint heart never did good ministry. And what will be the sign that Timothy fans his gift into flame? Power, love and self-discipline (1:7).

The gift of God that Timothy received through the hands of Paul is likely to have been the Holy Spirit: the gift that he received through the hands of the elders is likely to have been the gift of teaching (1 Tim. 4:13, 14).[2] This instruction is fundamental: if Timothy is not constantly fanning into flame the Holy Spirit within him, then he will not be able to make good progress in reading the Scripture, exhorting and teaching (1 Tim. 4:13). Fear or cowardice provide no platform for ministry.

Notice too the three positive signs of the Holy Spirit: power, love and self-discipline. What a great combination! And how easily and unwisely we separate them. Power without love is abusive or manipulative; love without power is ineffective; and great power and great love without self-discipline are self-indulgent and erratic. We need preachers who constantly fan into flame the Holy Spirit within them, and so are marked by power, love and self-discipline in their sermons, as in all of their ministry.

2. Don't be ashamed: suffer for the gospel.
In 1:8 Paul challenged Timothy not to be ashamed, but to join in suffering for the gospel. He must give up embarrassment, to embrace suffering. For here, as in Romans 1, Paul assumed that a natural response to the gospel is shame, not faith, joy or proclamation! Paul reinforced his challenge by pointing to his example: 'of this gospel I was appointed a herald and an apostle and a teacher. That is why I am suffering as I am' (1:11, 12).

---

2 So Philip H Towner, *The Letters to Timothy and Titus*, NICNT (Grand Rapids/ Cambridge, Eerdmans, 2006), pp. 457-61

Some poor Indian evangelists once asked me if their suffering for the gospel meant that they were doing something wrong, when those in the West seemed to be suffering-free. I replied that the normal Christian life and normal Christian ministry both require suffering for the gospel, according to the New Testament.[3] Timothy was not to be ashamed of the gospel, nor of Paul, the gospel messenger. In this he was to follow the example of Onesiphorus, who was 'not ashamed of my chains' (1:16). Identifying with persecuted gospel messengers is even more demanding than identifying with the gospel and suffering for it, but both are required of Timothy, and of all who want to lead and preach. However, notice the two sweeteners added to this bitter pill: 'join with me' and 'by the power of God' (1:8). Sweet fellowship and great power support those who suffer for the gospel.

We may think that Paul's focus on the sufferings of the gospel teachers and preachers is overstated. Yet he himself was facing martyrdom, and when churches face persecution (which is their usual condition), leaders are often in the frontline. Perhaps we should include in our commissioning services the question: Are you willing to suffer for the gospel? Preachers should be able to give a positive reply!

3. Guard the gospel

This gospel came in the form of what Timothy heard from Paul, a 'pattern of sound teaching' (1:13). It is the 'good deposit', entrusted to Timothy, which he must 'guard', and he is to do so 'with the help of the Holy Spirit' (1:14). It is possible not to be ashamed of Christ, but to be ashamed of the gospel. Such embarrassment will disable good preaching! And Timothy was called to guard Paul's gospel, not as a mere intellectual exercise, but with faith and love, and with the Holy Spirit's help (1:13, 14). For the Spirit is 'the Spirit of truth' as he was named by

---

3   See references to suffering and persecution in this letter: 1:8-12; 2:1-13; 3:10-12; 4:6-8, 14-18.

Christ (John 16:13). Timothy needed intellectual rigour as well as personal bravery, and a deep dependence on the Holy Spirit to guard the gospel. If he does not do so, he will be a feeble preacher. And he must do so on his own, for 'everyone in the province of Asia has deserted me' (1:15).[4] Onesiphorus (present in Rome with Paul) provided not only comfort for Paul but also an encouragement to Timothy. Onesiphorus shows us what not being ashamed of the gospel looks like in practice, as will Timothy, if he guards and teaches that gospel.

4. Be strong to teach and train.
In 2:1 Paul challenged Timothy to be strong to teach. What kind of strengths are needed to teach and train?

Firstly, personal and theological faithfulness or reliability, intellectual rigour and faithfulness were necessary if Timothy was to guard and teach the gospel, the good deposit, here described as 'the things you heard me say in the presence of many witnesses' (2:2).

Secondly, insightful selection of people and also the ability to teach and train others effectively are necessary if Timothy is to teach and train 'faithful people who will also be qualified to teach others' (2:2). Timothy and the people he trained needed strengths in understanding the truth and strengths in understanding people. 'Truth-smarts' by themselves are not sufficient, nor are 'people-smarts': preachers, teachers and trainers need both. Timothy needed the ability to select and train faithful people to teach others. This is a truth-centred ministry, and also a people-centred ministry.

This was a striking moment in the history of the church of Jesus Christ. As apostles like Paul died out, the gospel of Christ must be guarded and taught in the future. Paul was achieving a very specific and demanding generational change, as the warning of 'terrible times in the last days'

---

4   Ephesus, where Timothy was working, was the capital city of the Roman province of Asia.

(3:1) made clear.[5] Paul had a proactive plan to preserve gospel ministry: he was thinking beyond Timothy's welfare, and he was helping Timothy to see his ministry in a longer timescale, with greater aims and hopes than the immediate edification of his hearers. Timothy must see his ministry as part of a long-term gospel strategy: and, more immediately, as Timothy must soon leave Ephesus to join Paul in Rome (4:9), others must be left there to continue gospel ministry.

Paul underlined the cost of teaching and training others for ministry with the call to endure hardship, as a soldier, and athlete, and hard-working farmer (2:3-7). Yet he also encouraged Timothy with the words, 'be strong *in the grace that is in Christ Jesus*' (2:1, emphasis mine). As he tried to be strong, Timothy would experience the grace of Christ Jesus: so too, when he reflected on Paul's words, the Lord would give him understanding (2:7). There is both personal responsibility and divine grace: not one or the other, but both.

Paul further reinforced the cost of ministry by reminding Timothy of the gospel of Christ, for which Paul was suffering (2:9). Why did he suffer? It was 'for the sake of the elect, so that they too may obtain the salvation that is in Christ Jesus' (2:10).

Paul then added yet more encouragement, with the trustworthy saying of 2:11-13. Those in ministry should be aware of the suffering that is theirs because of their ministry: but this is only part of the suffering required of all believers, and God in His grace will one day reward and honour those who suffer and endure now. We suffer for Christ or we deny Christ: yet Christ remains faithful to His gospel promises, even if we are faithless. Paul expects the triumph of God's grace through Christ's faithfulness.

5. Remind and warn those you train.
Timothy was to remind those he was training of the comforts and challenges of the instructions that Paul has already

---

5   See also 4:3

given, especially the trustworthy saying of 2:11-13. I take it that the unidentified 'them' of 2:14 is not the church but the 'faithful people' of 2:2. There is no indication that a wider group is addressed; 'those who listen' indicates that teachers are addressed; and 2:15 addressed Timothy, indicating that church leaders are in mind.[6] Religious words can be destructive: they may have no value, and only damage those who receive them. A good warning for all preachers and teachers!

6. *Present yourself to God.*

Preachers, church leaders, teachers and trainers are often rightly focused on those to whom they minister. This is appropriate, for our work is with people. Yet ultimately we, like Timothy, have 'an audience of one', namely God. So Timothy must present himself to God as a workman who will gain God's approval, as later Paul commissioned him 'in the presence of God and of Christ Jesus' (4:1). The most important question is what God thinks of our ministry, and Paul, in his instructions to Timothy, gives us some important insights into what God expects. Timothy is to present himself to God, and correctly handle the word of truth (2:15). This is by way of contrast with 'quarrelling about words', and 'godless chatter' 2:14, 16. He will correctly handle the word of truth if he is faithful to Paul's gospel and straightforward in his presentation of that gospel. He must teach the truth, the whole truth and nothing but the truth. The obvious contrast is with that godless chatter that comes from ungodly people; teaching that is diseased and destructive, and that wanders from the truth (2:16-18).

---

6   This view is supported by George W. Knight III, *The Pastoral Epistles: A Commentary on the Greek Text*, NIGTC (Grand Rapids/Carlisle, Eerdmans/Paternoster, 1992), p. 410, by William Hendrickson, *The Epistles to Timothy and Titus*, (London, The Banner of Truth Trust, 1959), p. 261, and by Handley C. G. Moule, *The Second Epistle to Timothy: A Devotional Commentary*, (London, The Religious Tract Society, 1906), p. 87

7. Trust God even when disaster hits God's people.

God's church is to be the 'church of the living God, the pillar and foundation of the truth' (1 Tim. 3:15). As in Numbers 16, when some rebelled against Moses and so against God, so in Ephesus, some have deserted Paul's teaching, and so have deserted God. Yet, 'the Lord knows those who are his' (2:19, see Num. 16:5). And the Lord Jesus is still present in His church, to preserve and to judge. So the presence of the Lord (reminiscent of Rev. 2, 3) leads to comfort, yet is also a warning to turn away from wickedness. Timothy, like all preachers and teachers, needed to be comforted with the conviction that God in Christ is present in his church, and is able to save and to judge.

8. Be made clean, holy, useful to the Master, and prepared to do any good work.

Paul used the analogy of the articles in a large house, some of gold and silver for noble use, and others of wood and clay, for ignoble. Timothy is to clean himself, that he may be holy, useful and ready for any good work. Sin is the greatest enemy of usefulness in Christian ministry: sin, not lack of gifts or resources. Timothy must clean himself from personal sins ('the evil desires of youth' 2:22), and he must clean himself from sins of ministry ('foolish and stupid arguments' and quarrels 2:23). These sins of temperament and tongue are teachers' temptations. So Calvin warned against those who were always looking for grounds for a quarrel, and who 'lay snares around every word or syllable'.[7] Constant repentance and constant cleansing are the costs of good ministry: and they are a special challenge when the prevailing culture of the church is corrupt. And it is only when Timothy runs away from his evil desires that he can 'pursue righteousness, faith, love and peace' (2:22).

---

7   John Calvin, *Commentaries on The Epistles to Timothy, Titus and Philemon*, trans. W. Pringle, (reprint Grand Rapids, Baker, 1981, Calvin Translation Society vol xxi), p. 221

9. *Be 'kind to everyone, able to teach, not resentful' and gently instruct those who oppose you.*

How easy for those who want to guard the gospel to resent those who are wrong! How difficult to be kind to those who oppose us! Yet this will happen if we make ourselves clean: we are then prepared for *any good work*, even the difficult good work of winning people, not just arguments. For Timothy's ministry is not just to guard the gospel, but also to gently instruct his opponents, 'in the hope that God will grant them repentance leading to a knowledge of the truth...that they may escape from the trap of the devil...' (2:25).

10. *'Have nothing to do' with teachers and preachers who are totally corrupt (3:5).*

These corrupt teachers in Ephesus were formed by their loves: they loved themselves, money and pleasure; and had no love for God (3:2, 3). They had the form of godliness but denied its power (3:5), presumably in their lives and in their teaching. So Timothy had to distinguish between those whom he must gently instruct (2:25), and those he must avoid (3:5). The latter are obviously totally corrupt, and must be totally avoided. We need the same wisdom, for we live in the same 'terrible times', we live in the same 'last days' (3:1). We should not be surprised by corruption and false teaching in the church, for we have been well warned by the Lord Jesus and His apostles. Sadly, those teachers were still active in ministry in Ephesus, going from house to house, and preying on vulnerable people. They had depraved minds, like the Egyptian magicians who opposed Moses, and they too would be shown to be foolish (3:6-9).

11. *Follow Paul's example of ministry.*

Then, as now, there were many different models of Christian ministry, and it seems as if in most of Paul's churches, the predominant and powerful models were wrong. So Paul had to encourage churches not to be seduced or swayed by bad ministry (1 and 2 Corinthians, Galatians, Philippians). In those cases he set his own ministry as a model for churches, so here he did the same as a model for Timothy (and so also for those Timothy was training). Paul did not mention his success! Instead he wrote of his teaching, way of life, purpose, faith, patience, love, endurance, persecutions, and sufferings (3:10, 11). If we do not fill our minds and imaginations with good models of ministry, we will fill them with bad models. We are profoundly influenced by the ministry that others do, both in what we receive, and in what models of ministry we adopt. We too should look to Paul, and point others not only to his gospel, but also to his example of ministry.

12. *Be thoroughly equipped for every good work by the Scriptures.* As Timothy will be prepared to do any good work by repentance (2:21), so too he will be equipped for every good work by the Bible. He had known the Scriptures since childhood: those Scriptures, of course, were the Old Testament, and he was presumably taught by his Jewish mother and grandmother,[8] at the synagogue, and by Paul. Those Old Testament Scriptures 'are able to make you wise for salvation through faith in Christ Jesus' (3:15). Paul, following the example and teaching of the Lord Jesus Christ, taught that the message of salvation by faith in Jesus Christ is to be found in the Old Testament, as we see in Luke 24:25-27, 44-47. Then Paul explained that not only the Old Testament, but also the new Scriptures were inspired by God, and therefore useful (3:16, 17). For in 1 Timothy 5:18 he introduced a quotation from the gospel of Luke with the words, 'as Scripture says'; and Paul's own letters were referred to as 'Scripture' in 2 Peter 3:16. All the Scriptures are inspired and so useful. Useful for what? 'Teaching,

---

8   Timothy's father was a Gentile, see Acts 16:1-5

rebuking, correcting and training in righteousness' (3:16). And for what purpose? That the 'man of God', the Christian speaker of God's words (for 'man of God' was used in the Old Testament of a prophet), might be 'thoroughly equipped for every good work' (3:17). So while everyone benefits from the Scriptures, they have special power in training preachers and teachers. A firm grasp of the Bible is a fundamental requirement for preachers, because the Bible is the God-given means to prepare preachers. Not only, 'no Bible, no sermon', but also, 'no Bible, no preacher'. Ignorance of the Bible excludes people from preaching, for they will not be equipped by God to preach.

13. Preach the Word constantly, appropriately, patiently, and with careful instruction.

If Timothy and his friends have taken these instructions to heart, then they can be commissioned before God and before Christ to preach the Word. How will this the done? We find the answers in 4:2.

1. They must be always ready, looking for opportunities to proclaim the message, in public and in private, to many or to few, to believers or unbelievers, whether convenient or inconvenient: 'be prepared'.

2. They must not just preach a general message but vary their style according to which part of the message they are preaching and who they are preaching to. They should not just preach: they should 'correct, rebuke, encourage,' some of the many voices of the preacher.

3. They should preach 'with all patience'. They need all patience, and all patience in teaching, that is, with careful instruction. They will not do their ministry to serve themselves, because they want to preach, because they want to get this message off their chests,

to show their importance, and nor will they preach impatiently or angrily. They will need patience, because people will turn away from sound doctrine, and turn away from the truth (4:3, 4).

4. They will preach 'with careful instruction'. They should use the Scriptures, because they are useful for 'teaching, rebuking, correcting and training in righteousness' 3:16. The Scriptures are the means, not the end. They will use them to 'preach the Word'.

14. Complete your ministry.

It is a universal rule of ministry that it is easier to start than to finish, so the preacher is called to 'discharge all the duties of your ministry' (4:5), and to follow Paul: 'I have fought the good fight, I have finished the race, I have kept the faith' (4:7). And preachers will be able to do this, if they, like Paul, look for eternal rewards of grace, promised to all who long for Christ's appearing at His return (4:8). How else will we persevere, without the hope of Christ's return and the rewards of grace?

15. Be part of a gospel team, with a gospel passion for the world.

Paul gives news of his gospel team. There are encouragements of those who are doing well, and warnings of those who are not. There is the example of Paul, who even in his trial was proclaiming the Word, 'so that through me the message might be fully proclaimed, and all the nations might hear it' (4:17). The apostle to the nations spent a lot of time reforming and correcting the church, and training its leaders and teachers. He did so because of his confidence that through the church the world might hear of Jesus Christ and be saved. Timothy needed a big picture to see the significance of his daily ministry, as do all gospel teachers and preachers.[9] He must, in William Carey's words, expect great things of God and attempt great things for God.

CONCLUSION.

We miss the point if we think that all that Paul wanted Timothy to do was to 'preach the Word.' Paul told Timothy to make a major investment in training preachers and teachers of the gospel. There are more ministries of the Word than Sunday sermons.[10] In context, the issue was that of continuing gospel ministry in the post-apostolic age. However, the universal and general application is that leaders of churches today, like Timothy, must meet this challenge: ...'to provide long-term, intensive, closely watched and intimate training for the few, in order to provide adequately for the needs of the church for the future,'[11] and, through the same preachers, to bring the gospel to the world.

Of course, we also need to train preachers in the practicalities of preaching: skills in interpreting the Bible, biblical theology, understanding people, understanding congregations and their contexts, and public communication and persuasion. Yet skills without character are worth nothing.

If we look back over these fifteen instructions there are two striking observations. First, how easily ministers focus on their own sermons, and neglect training others to preach and teach. Secondly, different Christians emphasise different instructions, but Paul provides them all. We must not separate what Paul has joined together.

When John Calvin began his sermons on 2 Timothy, he said, 'as for me, I know I have profited, and do daily profit,

---

9   Paul's message in 2 Timothy echoed that of the Lord Jesus in Matthew 28:16-20

10   Peter Adam, *Speaking God's Words: A Practical Theology of Preaching*, (Leicester, Inter-Varsity Press, 1996), pp. 52-61

11   Christopher Green, *Finishing the Race: Reading 2 Timothy Today*, (Sydney, South, Aquila Press, 2000), p. 74

more by this Epistle, than by any other book of the scripture'.[12] He certainly heeded its message, and worked hard to raise up and train a new generation of gospel preachers and teachers. He did this as he preached, aware that in his congregation were those whom God would call to be preachers, and commended and explained the preaching ministry. He did this in the weekly 'Congregations' in which local ministers met for training and encouragement. He did this in writing his commentaries and publishing his sermons. He did this in founding the Geneva Academy, to provide basic training for ministers and others.[13]

In many places, the task of mentoring, training and equipping people for ministry is left to para-church organisations and colleges. The book of 2 Timothy is a resounding call for ministers of local churches to train preachers and teachers, to provide what the Puritans called 'nurseries of preachers.' May God raise up such Timothys for this ministry, that more faithful people may be well taught, trained, prepared and equipped to be preachers, that the gospel may be fully proclaimed, and all the nations might hear it.

---

12 John Calvin, *John Calvin's Sermons on Timothy and Titus*, (Edinburgh, The Banner of Truth Trust, 1983, facsimile of the 1579 translation), p. 659, with modernised language.

13 See Peter Adam, 'Preaching of a lively kind: Calvin's engaged expository preaching' in Mark D Thompson, ed., *Engaging with Calvin: Aspects of the Reformer's legacy for today*, (Nottingham, Apollos, 2009), pp. 13-41, and Peter Adam, 'Calvin's Preaching and Homiletic: Nine Engagements' Part 2, (Churchman, Vol. 124, No. 4, 2010), pp. 331-42

5

The Pastor as Evangelist

PAUL WILLIAMS

Philip Hacking has always taken seriously Paul's injunction to Timothy to 'Do the work of an evangelist'. In this chapter, the present Vicar of Christ Church, Fulwood, Paul Williams, underscores the primacy of this task in the pastoral ministry and how it might be worked out in today's setting, with the Good and Great Shepherd being set before us as the supreme role model.

There are many things I rejoice in as the Senior Pastor at Christ Church, Fulwood, but without question, one of the greatest privileges of holding this office is the legacy I have inherited. Following in the footsteps of a man who has been faithful in proclaiming the gospel, teaching the Word and visiting the flock is a huge blessing. Under God, the result of one man's faithful ministry is a church built on solid foundations. This is a gift to those who follow.

Philip Hacking, along with his wife Margaret (and the old adage is so evidently true with the Hackings – behind every good man there is a great woman) remain as passionate as ever to continue in gospel ministry. Today Philip preaches regularly around the country, he remains concerned for the lost and he still makes around a hundred pastoral visits in the parish each month!

Quite simply, Philip and Margaret are an inspiration. Oh, that I would be as passionate for the gospel should I still be walking planet earth in my eightieth year!

To follow such a remarkable man could be daunting, except the man (and his wife) give me unflinching, loyal support. Consequently, they are a delight to have around and are only a benefit to me in ministry. They liberally use their gift of encouragement to build me up and so I don't feel threatened by them or the remarkable ministry Philip exercised at Fulwood for over twenty-nine years. Rather, I find myself inspired by their passion to see people won for Christ and established in Christ.

Anyone who knows Philip knows that he is a man of conviction. And although I have never asked him (or heard him verbalise it), a look at his ministry shouts clearly that one of his strongest convictions is that the pastor should be about the work of evangelism. A conviction sadly not shared by all in pastoral ministry today.

KEEPING THE MAIN THING, THE MAIN THING.

A poor understanding of the role of the pastor has led to many inept platitudes being embraced by twenty-first century British congregations. Sentiments that could not be defended from the Scriptures are accepted, and even cherished, as godly wisdom. 'He's not a preacher, he's a pastor,' is one of the most obvious sayings that has been warmly recited among church families as an assessment of an acceptable approach to ministry. It is a cliché usually used when members of a local congregation appreciate a man's kindness in visiting, but don't care much for the way he preaches. Comments like that, from those who have not been well taught, can be excused. But I find myself less charitable towards church leaders who trot out theologically inept platitudes that have become an accepted part of the Christian subculture as if they were Holy Writ itself.

A classic example of misunderstanding the pastor's role is the church leader who justifies his lack of evangelistic activity by describing himself as 'a pastor and not an evangelist'. We know what he means, namely, he does not feel especially gifted when it comes to evangelism. He feels far more at home when caring for the flock. But the New Testament will not allow any church leader to adopt that approach to ministry, for quite simply the pastor *must* be about the work of evangelism.

Take, for instance, Paul's magnificent charge to Timothy at the end of his second letter. Virtually his last words to young Tim are, 'do the work of an evangelist' (2 Tim. 4:5) – and the gravitas of last words has been well documented.

If the call to the evangelistic task is virtually Paul's last word to his young protégé, the way he introduces that last word adds substantial weight to the charge: 'In the presence of God and of Christ Jesus, who will judge the living and the dead, and in view of his appearing and his kingdom, I give you this charge.' (2 Tim. 4:1).

The stakes could not be higher. One would be hard-pressed to find a more compelling or powerful beginning to a charge in the Bible.

In the presence of God the Father, and not forgetting the presence of the second person of the Trinity, God's Son, Christ Jesus, *and* remembering that He will judge all people, living and dead, *and* (as if that were not enough), having in view that this same Christ Jesus will appear and His Kingdom will come .... do the work of the evangelist.

For sure, the words which follow this majestic opening salvo, are a command to Timothy to do many things before Paul tells him to get on with the evangelistic task. But while this charge is more than, 'do the work of the evangelist', it certainly isn't less. How could it be when Paul has set it in this context?

Every man and woman and boy and girl who ever walked this blue/green planet is going to stand before God as their judge: the entailment? – Timothy, do the work of the evangelist.

Jesus Christ is going to appear and His Kingdom is going to be ushered in, in all its glory: the entailment? – Timothy, do the work of the evangelist.

In the presence of God and of His Christ, Timothy, persuade people to repent and believe: the entailment? – Timothy, do the work of the evangelist.

(For our purposes, considering the subject of this chapter, we can see from this majestic charge that it is inexcusable for a church leader to attempt to absent himself from the task of evangelism, because he is a pastor. Evangelism *is* the work of the pastor.)

With the pastoral epistles laying out for us a paradigm of church leadership post the apostolic era and with this imperious introduction to chapter 4 of 2 Timothy, whatever I feel about my primary gifting, as a pastor, if I have any concern for God's glory and the mission of Christ, and the good of people, I cannot, indeed I dare not, excuse myself from doing the work of the evangelist.

From these verses alone we can see that the pastor must be about the evangelistic task. But the biblical warrant for the pastor to be doing the work of the evangelist doesn't end there.

UNDER-SHEPHERDS, THE CHIEF SHEPHERD AND EVANGELISM

Having considered Paul's charge to Timothy, second, we turn to Peter's words to church leaders in Asia Minor. Peter describes elders as 'shepherds of God's flock' (1 Pet. 5:2). It's a lofty responsibility to be caring for God's sheep; to be feeding His lambs (Peter surely has the tripartite command of the risen Lord Jesus in mind in John 21 to feed His lambs, to take care of His sheep, to feed His sheep). It is a weighty undertaking. Every elder is to shepherd God's flock. But every elder must remember, he is caring for God's flock, not his own, and every elder must know he is under the authority of one infinitely greater than himself – namely, the Chief Shepherd (1 Pet. 5:4). What is more, the Chief Shepherd will appear and that future appearing should motivate the elders in their pastoral task. (Interestingly, Peter has his eye on the Parousia, just as Paul did in 2 Tim. 4).

So by describing elders as shepherds and Jesus as the Chief Shepherd, church leaders should look to Jesus as the model Shepherd. So, when it comes to pastoring, to shepherding the flock, the elder must look to the Chief Shepherd not only as his motivation for the task, but also to understand the method and the substance of shepherding. Jesus Christ is the example *par excellence* for every under-shepherd to follow. So, as we survey the ministry of the Chief Shepherd, the role and priorities of the under-shepherd will become clear.

One of the most well-trodden passages describing the activity of the Chief Shepherd is Luke chapter 15. In this most famous and loved parable we see the shepherd leaving the ninety-nine sheep who are all safely tucked up in the sheep pen, to look for the one lost sheep who is dangerously wandering around a Palestinian hillside. It's a favourite parable for the Sunday school, but a look at the immediate context opens up the passage for big boys and girls!

Now the tax collectors and 'sinners' were all gathering round to hear him. But the Pharisees and the teachers of the law muttered,

'This man welcomes sinners and eats with them'. (Luke 15:1-2)

It was the muttering criticism of the religious leaders of the day towards the action and ministry of Jesus that led Jesus to tell this most famous parable on this occasion. The Pharisees and teachers of the law were complaining about Jesus welcoming and eating with sinners and tax collectors. They abhorred Jesus as He went about the evangelistic task of befriending the most undesirable low life of society.

As a result, Jesus told the parable of the lost sheep to explain why He spent time with religious no-hopers who were so desperately lost and so very far from the Kingdom of God.

With that context before us, it is clear that Jesus is the shepherd in the parable. Here is the Chief Shepherd looking for lost sheep. Here is the Chief Shepherd explaining why he does the work of evangelism. Under-shepherds are to note and follow in the footsteps of the Chief Shepherd. Be about the work of the evangelist.

This parable should have left the Pharisees and teachers of the law (the under-shepherds of the day) walking away uncomfortably red in the face from the huge flush of embarrassment of ever having questioned Jesus' desire to spend time with such low-life. Of course, he spent time with these scoundrels for they were hopelessly lost – and Pharisees and teachers of the law should have spent time with them too.

Seeing the Chief Shepherd leaving the ninety-nine to go after the one demonstrates a priority for the under-shepherd.

Let's do the math (as our friends across the pond would say). If we had ninety-nine Christian friends and one unbelieving friend, we should spend time seeking the lost unbelieving friend. If Britain were to become 99 per cent Christian (and by that I mean 99 per cent real born-again committed Christian), just consider how full the churches would be. Yet this parable would scream at us, 'the work is not yet done, there's still 1 per cent wandering around, lost and in need of salvation. Go and find them, for every one matters!'

Even if our nation became overwhelmingly Christian, with our buildings bulging on a Sunday, it would still be incumbent upon us to go looking for the lost 1 per cent. That's quite a thought for the churches in Britain who consider themselves successful or large because they have a reasonably full building, amounting to several hundred attending their church on a Sunday.

What's more, this parable tells the pastor who has 297 people in the congregation and three unbelievers in his circle of contacts (do the math) to follow the example of the Chief Shepherd and go looking for the three unbelievers. To spend a disproportionate time with the three, eating with them, socialising with them, making every attempt to bring them into the fold, *and* leaving the 297 to carry on in Bible study groups and business meetings without him at times!

That is the way of the Chief Shepherd, and as under-shepherds we must follow in His footsteps – seeking the lost.

The task of the pastor, the elder, the shepherd of God's flock, is not only evangelism; it is more than evangelism, but it is certainly not less.

It was some years ago now, when I was working for another church, the staff team were discussing the priority of evangelism for the church leader, when a colleague made this most obvious yet gloriously insightful comment, 'No-one ever knocked on your door and asked you, "Will you tell me the gospel?" but Christians will knock on your door and demand all kinds of things from you all the time.' You don't have to be in gospel ministry for long to know the truth of that.

The under-shepherd will always have sheep appealing to him to visit them, to teach them, to organise church activities for them, to answer emails, to attend business meetings, to plan church services. Of course, I am not suggesting that those things do not need to be done, or that they should not be done by the elder, *BUT* (and it is a very big but), unbelievers, the lost, those right outside the Kingdom of God, will not asked to be saved. So, quite simply, if pastors do not have the conviction that a crucial part of their task is to be about the work of the evangelist, the sheer volume of demands (volume in both senses of the word – quantity of work and who shouts loudest) will dictate their workload and they will never get around to the evangelistic task.

Seeing the example of the Chief Shepherd in the parable of the lost sheep in Luke tells us to reach out to those right outside the Kingdom of God.

EVANGELISING THE 'INSIDERS'

The same parable in Matthew chapter 18 has a slightly different context. This time the setting is a concern for those who were once involved in the church community, but who have wandered off due to disputes with other Christians. This introduces another aspect to the evangelistic role of the under-shepherd – namely, to spend time with the disaffected. To go looking for those who have had connection with church and Christian things in the past, but who have since wandered off. What a difference we would see in church attendance if we could only draw alongside all those former churchgoers in our area. That too is the work of the shepherd in Matthew 18 and therefore, I suggest, an evangelistic task for the pastor to engage in.

This has been one of the concerns close to Philip Hacking's heart down through the years. With his meticulous card index system (and I would guess a structured and disciplined prayer life) Philip knows, remembers and has a concern for those who have been members of the congregation in the past and who now stay away, for one reason or another. His passion for them is evident when, at the end of a Sunday service, he comes bounding up to me like an excited Great Dane puppy dog to tell me with great enthusiasm about someone at church that morning, whom I only know as a newcomer, but whom he had contact with many years ago. His delight to see them back says it all!

That seeking out (dare I say 'sniffing out') the newcomers on a Sunday and then welcoming them, befriending them, introducing them to others demonstrates the concern that both Philip and Margaret have for people. If everyone in the congregation did the work they do on a Sunday we would have no need of any formal welcoming structures.

Having considered the parable of the lost sheep, in surveying the work of the Chief Shepherd, we cannot neglect a consideration of arguably the most famous of all the Shepherd references, John chapter 10 and verse 11, 'The good shepherd lays down his life for the sheep.'

Here is the missionary God, describing *the* work of saving men and women. The atoning work of the Good Shepherd dying on the cross is not something we are to do, or can do. However, this is the central work of the Good Shepherd; it tells us, as under-shepherds, to be about the work of the salvation of men and women.

The Good Shepherd laid down His life not only for the sheep of Israel, but also for the 'sheep that are not of this sheep pen' (John 10:16). Once again we see the task of evangelism very clearly to be a central role of the Chief Shepherd. It becomes more evident as we contrast the work of the Good Shepherd with the bad shepherds of Ezekiel chapter 34, which I believe is the backdrop to Jesus' words in John 10.

Through Ezekiel, the Lord accused the shepherds of Israel of neglecting the sheep in their care and taking care only of themselves. This is what we read in chapter 34:1-4:

> The word of the Lord came to me: 'Son of man, prophesy against the shepherds of Israel; prophesy and say to them: "This is what the Sovereign Lord says: Woe to the shepherds of Israel who only take care of themselves! Should not shepherds take care of the flock? You eat the curds, clothe yourselves with the wool and slaughter the choice animals, but you do not take care of the flock. You have not strengthened the weak or healed the sick or bound up the injured. *You have not brought back the strays or searched for the lost.* You have ruled them harshly and brutally."' (Italics mine).

There were many ways that the shepherds in Ezekiel's' day were errant but one reason the lord took issue with them was their failure to bring back the strays or search for the lost (v. 4).

Notably, after rebuking the bad shepherds, the Lord says,

"'For this is what the Sovereign LORD says: I myself will search for my sheep and look after them. As a shepherd looks after his scattered flock when he is with them, so will I look after my sheep. I will rescue them from all the places where they were scattered on a day of clouds and darkness. I will bring them out from the nations and gather them from the countries, and I will bring them into their own land. I will pasture them on the mountains of Israel, in the ravines and in all the settlements in the land. I will tend them in a good pasture, and the mountain heights of Israel will be their grazing land. There they will lie down in good grazing land, and there they will feed in a rich pasture on the mountains of Israel. I myself will tend my sheep and have them lie down, declares the Sovereign LORD. I will search for the lost and bring back the strays. I will bind up the injured and strengthen the weak, but the sleek and the strong I will destroy. I will shepherd the flock with justice.'" (Ezek. 34:11-16)

Wonderfully the Lord Himself promises to step in and shepherd His sheep. The promise of care and the Lord's concern for His people is marvellously heart-warming and reassuring. His care package is total. It is more than evangelistic, but note, it is not less. Indeed, seeking out the lost is where it begins in verse 11.

So, the Good Shepherd lays down His life to bring His sheep into His fold. He acted because the bad shepherds failed so spectacularly. Now he appoints under-shepherds to care for His flock, to follow in His footsteps. Searching for the sheep; rescuing them from all the places where they have been scattered; gathering them from far and wide; bringing them into the fold. Woe betide the under-shepherd who neglects this task, for he will be on his way towards imitating the bad shepherds of Ezekiel chapter 34 rather than following in the footsteps of the Good Shepherd.

We have seen, then, that the evangelistic task is part and parcel of the role of the elder. For a church leader to avoid the work of the evangelist on the premise that he is 'a pastor and not an evangelist' is to misunderstand one crucial aspect of the role of the pastor.

FROM PRINCIPLES TO PRACTICE
In practical terms I suggest three ways the pastor should live out this charge.

i) *The pastor must be personally evangelistic*
As with all aspects of Christian leadership ,evangelism must be modelled. The faithful pastor can never say, 'Don't do as I do, do as I say.'

The demands of Christian ministry are so great that elders must be intentional if they are to do this. Pastors need to carve out time in their diaries to spend with unbelievers. Pastors need to be intentional in blocking out time to 'hang out' with sinners and tax collectors. It won't just happen. But when it is modelled, the church family will catch on. When the pastor explains, 'Sorry, I can't lead your Bible study because I'm spending time with unbelievers' the flock will begin to believe him when he says that evangelism is a priority.

What's more, when the pastor spends time with un-believers it will revolutionise his teaching.

First, he will be rescued from any accusations of hypocrisy in this area. The fear of hypocrisy will always hamper the teaching of God's Word. Either the congregation will not take note when the pastor commands them to do something he is not doing himself. Or the pastor will not teach the commands of Scripture to avoid being labelled a hypocrite.

Second, if the pastor has been about personal evangelism, as he teaches the congregation about evangelism his teaching will be relevant. While the gospel remains the same, the big issues people are grappling with change from generation to generation and from area to area. By being personally evangelistic the pastor will be relevant in his teaching.

Third, when the pastor is doing personal evangelism his teaching the church family about evangelism will be realistic. He will know how hard evangelism is. In spending time with my unbelieving friends I know how difficult it is to turn conversations to things that matter and how difficult it is to persuade my friends that Jesus is relevant to them. Meeting with unbelievers regularly helps me when I'm speaking to the congregation to avoid the temptation to trot out trite formula and evangelistic techniques that will 'work'.

ii)   The pastor must train the congregation in evangelism
In Ephesians chapter 4, Paul tells us that the ascended and exalted Lord Jesus gave gifts to His church. One of those gifts is the gift of the evangelist (Eph. 4:11). He then explains why the gifts were given:

> It was he who gave some to be apostles, some to be prophets,
>
> some to be evangelists, and some to be pastors and teachers, to
>
> prepare God's people for works of service, so that the body of
>
> Christ may be built up ... (Eph. 4:11-12).

The gift of the evangelist was given to the church not only so that those endowed with that gift could bring people to repentance and faith, but also to prepare God's people for works of service. I presume that means that the evangelist is to prepare the people of God to be about the work of evangelism. And so, as Paul tells Timothy to do the work of the evangelist, a major aspect of that work will be to train God's people to do evangelism.

Pastors must run evangelism training courses; take members of the congregation on missions; instruct them in leading a Christianity Explored course or lead them in door-to-door work or open-air evangelism. Training others is an integral part of the work of the evangelist.

iii)   The pastor must organise the church to be evangelistic

As pastors, we can say that we are evangelistically concerned (and indeed we should say that), but it is as we are involved in personal evangelism and train the congregation in evangelism and as we plan evangelism into the life of the church that the church family will begin to believe that we are evangelistically concerned.

Subsequently, the pastor must organise the church to be evangelistic. That will mean planning regular, high-quality, low-cringe evangelistic events and services for the congregation to be able to bring their friends along to, and ensuring that a good evangelism course is run regularly as part of the programme. And, apart from a programme that says to people, 'This church is for the outsider', every Sunday should be outsider-friendly. By that I don't mean that we need to have 'seeker services' every week or that we need to tag on to the end of every sermon the ABC of becoming a Christian. What I do mean is that every Sunday we should be aware that outsiders may well be among us and so as we lead our meetings we should use language that can be understood; greet newcomers from the front; explain why we do what we do and what we're doing next; invite first-timers to something that will help them get integrated into the life of the church; and generally look out for those for whom walking into church has been a daunting and alien experience.

Christian ministry is busy and demanding. No-one is going to knock on your door and ask, 'What must I do to be saved?' There will always be a thousand and one things clamouring for our attention. The urgent is always the enemy of the important. So we must remember that while being a pastor is more than being about evangelism, it is never less.

The pastor must be about the work of the evangelist, for he is a shepherd, an under-shepherd, under the Chief Shepherd, and the Chief Shepherd is *the* great evangelist. He came from heaven to earth, seeking the lost, laying down His life for the sheep, humbling Himself, dying the most excruciating death, death on a cross.

6

The Pastor and Worship[1]

D. A. CARSON

Leading God's people in public worship is one of the main tasks of a pastor. This was something Philip always did with a due sense of propriety without ever being 'stuffy'. The sense that God is seated on His throne and yet close to His people was never far from Philip's mind. However, in recent years some have questioned the appropriateness of using the term 'worship' at all to describe what God's people do when they gather as a church. Others have restricted the term to one particular aspect of what happens in the gathering, namely 'praise'. In this extended chapter, Professor Don Carson carefully presents an exposition of what is to be understood by 'worship' and what are some of the implications for what Christians do when they gather on a regular basis which will be of special interest to the pastor.

WHAT IS 'WORSHIP'?

Robert Shaper asserts that worship, like love, is characterised by intuitive simplicity (everybody 'knows' what worship is, just as everyone 'knows' what love is) and philosophical complexity (the harder you press to unpack love or worship, the more difficult the task).[2] Worship embraces relationship, attitude, act, life. We may attempt the following definition:

---

1   This chapter is an edited version of 'Worship Under the Word', in *Worship by the Book*, (Zondervan, 2002, Ed., D.A.Carson)

2   Robert Shaper, *In His Presence* (Nashville: Thomas Nelson, 1984), p. 13.

Worship is the proper response of all moral, sentient beings to God, ascribing all honour and worth to their Creator-God precisely because he is worthy, delightfully so. This side of the Fall, *human worship* of God properly responds to the redemptive provisions that God has graciously made. While all true worship is God-centred, *Christian worship* is no less Christ-centred. Empowered by the Spirit and in line with the stipulations of the new covenant, it manifests itself in all our living, finding its impulse in the gospel, which restores our relationship with our Redeemer-God and therefore also with our fellow image-bearers, our co-worshippers. Such worship therefore manifests itself both in adoration and in action, both in the individual believer and in *corporate worship*, which is worship offered up in the context of the body of believers, who strive to align all the forms of their devout ascription of all worth to God with the panoply of new covenant mandates and examples that bring to fulfilment the glories of antecedent revelation and anticipate the consummation.

Doubtless this definition is too long and too complex. But it may provide a useful set of pegs on which to hang a brief exposition of the essentials of worship. This exposition is organised under an apostolic number of points of unequal weight that arise from the definition.

1. The first (and rather cumbersome) sentence of the definition asserts that worship is 'the proper response of all moral, sentient beings to God'. There are two purposes to this phrase. First, the inclusive 'all' reminds us that worship is not restricted to human beings alone. The angels worship; they are commanded to do so, and in a passage such as Revelation 4, they orchestrate the praise offered in heaven. Among other things, this means that worship cannot properly be defined as *necessarily* arising out of the gospel, for one of the

great mysteries of redemption is that in His wisdom God has provided a Redeemer for fallen human beings but not for fallen angels. The angels who orchestrate the praise of heaven do not offer their worship as a response born of their experience of redemption. For our part, when we offer our worship to God, we must see that this does not make us unique. The object of our worship, God Himself, is unique in that He alone is to be worshipped; we, the worshippers, are not.

Second, by speaking of worship as the proper response 'of moral, sentient beings', this definition excludes from worship rocks and hawks, cabbages and toads, a mote of dust dancing on a sunbeam. Of course, by understandable extension of the language, all creatures, sentient and otherwise, are exhorted to praise the Lord (e.g., Ps. 148). But they do not do so in conscious obedience; they do so because they are God's creatures and are constituted to reflect His glory and thus bring Him glory. In this extended sense all of the created order 'owns' its Lord. As all of it now participates in death and 'groans' in anticipation of the consummation (Rom. 8:22-23), so also on the last day it participates in the glorious transformation of the resurrection: our hope is a new heaven and a new earth. In this extended sense, all creation is God-oriented and 'ascribes' God's worth to God alone. But it is an *extended* sense. For our purposes, we will think of worship as something offered to God by 'all moral, sentient beings.'

2. Worship is a 'proper response' to God for at least four reasons. First of all, in both Testaments worship is repeatedly enjoined on the covenant people of God: they worship because worship is variously commanded and encouraged. God's people are to 'ascribe to the LORD the glory due his name. Bring an offering and come before him; worship the LORD in the splendour of his holiness' (1 Chron. 16:29). 'Come, let us bow down in worship, let us kneel before the LORD our Maker; for he is our God and we are the people of his pasture, the flock under his care' (Ps. 95:6-7). 'Worship

the LORD with gladness; come before him with joyful songs' (Ps. 100:2). When He was tempted to worship the devil, Jesus insisted, 'Worship the Lord your God, and serve him only' (Matt. 4:10). It follows that the worship of any other god is simply idolatry (Ps. 81:9; Isa. 46:6; Dan. 3:15, 28). It is a mark of terrible judgment when God gives a people over to the worship of false gods (Acts 7:42-43). In the courts of heaven, God has no rival. No homage is to be done to any other, even a glorious interpreter of truth: 'Worship God' and Him alone (Rev. 19:10).

Second, worship is a 'proper response' because it is grounded in the very character and attributes of God. If worship is repeatedly enjoined, often the link to the sheer greatness or majesty or splendour of God is made explicit. In other words, the 'worth' of God is frequently made explicit in the particular 'worth-ship' that is being considered. Sometimes this is comprehensive: 'Ascribe to the LORD *the glory due his name*' (1 Chron. 16:29; cf. Ps. 29:2) – that is, the glory that is His due, since in biblical thought God's name is the reflection of all that God is. That text goes on to exhort the reader to 'worship the Lord *in the splendour of his holiness.*' That is tantamount to saying that we are to worship the Lord in the splendour of all that makes God God. Like white light that shines through a prism and is broken into its colourful components, so this truth can be broken down into its many parts. Many elements contribute to the sheer 'Godness' that constitutes holiness in its purest form. Thus, people will speak of 'the glorious splendour of [his] majesty' (Ps. 145:3-5). If 2 Kings 17:39 commands the covenant community to 'worship the LORD your God,' it gives a reason: 'it is he who will deliver you from the hand of all your enemies.' But all of the focus is on God.

Third, one of the most striking elements of God's 'worth-ship,' and therefore one of the most striking reasons for worshipping him, is the fact that He alone is the Creator. Sometimes this is linked with the fact that he reigns over us. 'Come, let us bow down in worship,' the psalmist exhorts, 'let us kneel *before the* LORD *our Maker*' (the first element); '*for he is our God and we are the people of his pasture*' (the second element) (Ps. 95:6-7). If we are to worship the Lord with gladness (Ps. 100:2), it is for this reason: 'It is he who made us, and we are his; we are his people, the sheep of his pasture' (v. 3). Nowhere, perhaps, is this more powerfully expressed than in Revelation 4. Day and night the four living creatures never stop ascribing praise to God: 'Holy, holy, holy is the Lord God Almighty, who was, and is, and is to come' (4:8). Whenever they do so (and we have just been told that they never stop), the twenty-four elders 'fall down before him who sits on the throne, and worship him who lives for ever and ever' (4:10). Moreover, 'they lay their crowns before the throne' (4:10), an act that symbolises their unqualified recognition that they are dependent beings. Their worship is nothing other than recognising that God alone is worthy 'to receive glory and honour and power, *for you created all things and by your will they were created and have their being*' (4:11, italics added). Worship is the proper response of the creature to the Creator. Worship does not create something new; rather, it is a transparent response to what is, a recognition of our creaturely status before the CreatorHimself. [3]

Fourth, to speak of a 'proper response' to God calls us to reflect on what God Himself has disclosed of His own expectations. How does God want His people to respond to Him? Although God always demands faith and obedience, the precise outworking of faith and obedience may change across the years of redemptive history. Suppose that at some point in history God insisted that believers be required to build great monuments in His honour. For them, the building of such monuments would be part of their 'proper response' precisely because it would have been mandated by God.

---

3   This is the sort of theme that is often movingly treated by Marva J. Dawn, *A Royal 'Waste' of Time: The Splendor of Worshiping God and Being Church for the World* (Grand Rapids: Eerdmans, 1999). But because she does not set her discussion within the context of biblical theology (see below), she rather consistently reduces worship to what we have called 'corporate worship.'

Once the Mosaic covenant was in place, the people of Israel were mandated to go up to the central tabernacle/temple three times a year: this was part of their proper response. What this means for members of the new covenant is that our response to God in worship should begin by carefully and reflectively examining what God requires of us under the terms of this covenant. We should not begin by asking whether or not we *enjoy* 'worship', but by asking, 'What is it that God expects of us?' That will frame our proper response. To ask this question is also to take the first step in reformation. It demands self-examination, for we soon discover where we do *not* live up to what God expects. This side of the Fall, every age has characteristic sins. To find out what they are by listening attentively to what the Bible actually says about what God demands will have the effect of reforming every area of our lives, including our worship.

3. We worship our Creator-God 'precisely because He is worthy, *delightfully* so.' What ought to make worship delightful to us is not, in the first instance, its novelty or its aesthetic beauty, but its object: God Himself is delightfully wonderful, and we learn to delight in Him.

In an age increasingly suspicious of (linear) thought, there is much more respect for the 'feeling' of things – whether a film or a church service. It is disturbingly easy to plot surveys of people, especially young people, drifting from a church of excellent preaching and teaching to one with excellent music because, it is alleged, there is 'better worship' there. But we need to think carefully about this matter. Let us restrict ourselves for the moment to corporate worship. Although there are things that can be done to enhance corporate worship, there is a profound sense in which excellent worship cannot be attained merely by pursuing excellent worship. In the same way that, according to Jesus, you cannot find yourself until you lose yourself, so also you cannot find excellent corporate worship until you stop trying to find excellent corporate worship and pursue

God Himself. Despite the protestations, one sometimes wonders if we are beginning to worship worship rather than worship God. As a brother put it to me, it's a bit like those who begin by admiring the sunset and soon begin to admire themselves admiring the sunset.

This point is acknowledged in a praise chorus like 'Let's forget about ourselves, and magnify the Lord, and worship Him.' The trouble is that after you have sung this repetitious chorus three or four times, you are no farther ahead. The *way* you forget about yourself is by focusing on God – not by singing about doing it, but by doing it. There are far too few choruses and services and sermons that expand our vision of God – His attributes, His works, His character, His words. Some think that corporate worship is good because it is lively where it had been dull. But it may also be shallow where it is lively, leaving people dissatisfied and restless in a few months' time. Sheep lie down when they are well fed (cf. Ps. 23:2); they are more likely to be restless when they are hungry. 'Feed my sheep,' Jesus commanded Peter (John 21); and many sheep are unfed. If you wish to deepen the worship of the people of God, above all deepen their grasp of His ineffable majesty in His person and in all His works.

This is not an abstruse theological point divorced from our conduct and ethics. Nor is it an independent point, as if there were two independent mandates: first of all, worship God (because He deserves it), and then live rightly (because He says so). For worship, properly understood, shapes who we are. We become like whatever is our god. Peter Leithart's comments may not be nuanced, but they express something important:

> It is a fundamental truth of Scripture that we become like whatever or whomever we worship. When Israel worshipped the gods of the nations, she became like the nations – bloodthirsty, oppressive, full of deceit and violence (cf. Jer. 7). Romans 1 confirms this principle

by showing how idolaters are delivered over to sexual deviations and eventually to social and moral chaos. The same dynamic is at work today. Muslims worship Allah, a power rather than a person, and their politics reflects this commitment. Western humanists worship man, with the result that every degrading whim of the human heart is honoured and exalted and disseminated through the organs of mass media. Along these lines, Psalm 115:4-8 throws brilliant light on Old Covenant history and the significance of Jesus' ministry. After describing idols as figures that have every organ of sense but no sense, the Psalmist writes, 'Those who make them will become like them, and so will everyone who trusts in them.' By worshipping idols, human beings become speechless, blind, deaf, unfeeling, and crippled – but then these are precisely the afflictions that Jesus, in the Gospels, came to heal![4]

Pray, then, and work for a massive display of the glory and character and attributes of God. We do not expect the garage mechanic to expatiate on the wonders of his tools; we expect him to fix the car. He must know how to use his tools, but he must not lose sight of the goal. So we dare not focus on the mechanics of corporate worship and lose sight of the goal. We focus on God Himself, and thus we become more godly and learn to worship – and collaterally we learn to edify one another, forbear with one another, challenge one another.

Of course, the glories of God may be set forth in sermon, song, prayer or testimony. It is in this sense that the title of one of Mark Noll's essays is exactly right: 'We Are What We Sing' [5] What is clear is that if you try to enhance 'worship' simply by livening the

---

4   Peter Leithart, 'Transforming Worship' *Foundations* 38 (Spring 1997): 27.
5   *Christianity Today*, 12 July 1999, pp. 37-41.

tempo or updating the beat, you may not be enhancing worship at all. On the other hand, dry-as-dust sermons loaded with clichés and devoid of the presence of the living God mediated by the Word do little to enhance worship either.

What we must strive for is growing knowledge of God and delight in Him – not delight in worship per se, but delight in God. A place to begin might be to memorise Psalm 66. There is so much more to know about God than the light diet on offer in many churches; and genuine believers, when they are fed wholesome spiritual meals, soon delight all the more in God Himself. This also accounts for the importance of 'retelling' in the Bible (e.g., Ps. 75–76). Retelling the Bible's storyline brings to mind again and again something of God's character, past actions and words. It calls to mind God's great redemptive acts across the panorama of redemptive history. This perspective is frequently lost in contemporary worship, where there are very few elements calculated to make us remember the great turning points in the Bible. I am thinking not only of those bland 'services' in which even at Easter and Christmas we are deluged with the same sentimental choruses at the expense of hymns and anthems that tell the *Easter or Christmas story*, but also of the loss of hymns and songs *that told individual Bible stories* (e.g., 'Hushed Was the Evening Hymn'). Similarly, whatever else the Lord's Table is, it is a means appointed by the Lord Jesus to remember His death and its significance.[6] The Psalms frequently retell parts of Israel's history, especially the events surrounding the exodus, serving both as review and as incentive to praise. Paul recognises that writing 'the same things' may be a 'safeguard' for his readers (Phil. 3:1). Written reminders may stimulate readers to 'wholesome thinking' (2 Pet. 3:1), for Peter wants them 'to recall the words spoken in the past by the holy prophets and the command given by our Lord and Saviour' through the

---

6   cf. Tim Ralston, ' "Remember" and Worship: The Mandate and the Means,' *Reformation and Revival* 9/3 (2000): 77-89

apostles (3:2). In this he mirrors Old Testament exhortations, for there we are told that we must remember not only all that God has done for us, but every word that proceeds from the mouth of God, carefully passing them on to our children (Deut. 6, 8). All of this presupposes that retelling ought to prove formative, nurturing, stabilising, delightful.[7] Equally, it presupposes that even under the terms of the old covenant, everything that might be embraced by the term *worship* was more comprehensive than what was bound up with the ritual of tabernacle and temple.

Perhaps it is in this light that we ought to wrestle with the importance of repetition as a reinforcing pedagogical device. If mere traditionalism for the sake of aesthetics is suspect, surely the same is true of mere innovation for the sake of excitement. But there must be some ways of driving home the fundamentals of the faith. In godly repetition and retelling, we must plant deeply within our souls the glorious truths about God and about what He has done that we will otherwise soon forget.

4. 'This side of the Fall, *human worship* of God properly responds to the redemptive provisions that God has graciously made.' The brief glimpse afforded of human existence before the Fall (Gen. 2) captures a time when God's image-bearers delighted in the perfection of His creation and the pleasure of His presence precisely because they were perfectly oriented towards Him. No redemptive provisions had yet been disclosed, for none were needed. There was no need to exhort human beings to worship; their entire existence revolved around the God who had made them.

At the heart of the Fall is the self-love that destroys our God-centredness. Implicitly, of course, all failure to worship God is neither more nor less than idolatry. Because we are finite, we will inevitably worship something or someone.

---

7   cf. Eugene H. Merrill, 'Remembering: A Central Theme in Biblical Worship,' *JETS* 43 (2000): 27-36.

In *The Brothers Karamazov*, Dostoyevsky was not wrong to write, 'So long as man remains free he strives for nothing so incessantly and so painfully as to find someone to worship.' Yet because we are fallen, we gravitate to false gods: a god that is domesticated and manageable, perhaps a material god, perhaps an abstract god like power or pleasure, or a philosophical god like Marxism or democracy or postmodernism. But worship we will.

Worse yet, we stand guilty before God, for our Maker is also our Judge. That might have been the end of the story, but God progressively discloses His redemptive purposes. As He does so, He makes demands about what approach is acceptable to Him, what constitutes acceptable praise and prayer, what constitutes an acceptable *corporate* approach before Him. Thus, worship becomes enmeshed, by God's prescription, in ritual, sacrifice, detailed law, a sanctuary, a priestly system, and so forth. Three important points must be made here.

First, the changing and developing patterns of God's prescriptions for His people when they draw near to Him constitute a complex and subtle history.[8] The first human sin calls forth the first death, the death of an animal to hide the nakedness of the first image-bearers. Sacrifice soon becomes a deeply rooted component of worship. By the time of the Mosaic covenant, the peace offering (Lev. 17:11ff.) was the divinely prescribed means of maintaining a harmonious relationship between God and His covenant people. The sin offering (Lev. 4) dealt with sin as a barrier between the worshippers and God. This sin offering was a slaughtered bull, lamb or goat with which the worshipper had identified himself by laying his hands on its head. When the blood of the victim, signifying its life (Lev. 17: 11), was daubed on the horns of the altar, symbolising the presence of God, God and the worshippers

---

8   See the relevant sections of David Peterson, *Engaging with God*, Y. Hattori, 'Theology of Worship in the Old Testament,' in *Worship: Adoration and Action*, pp. 21-50.

were united in a renewed relationship. Under the terms of the pre-scribed covenantal relationship, there could no longer be acceptable worship apart from conforming to the demands of the sacrificial system. By this system, God had prescribed the means by which His rebellious image-bearers could approach Him. 'Worship was thus Israel's response to the covenant relationship and the means of ensuring its continuance.'[9]

There were many variations both before and after Sinai. In the patriarchal period, clans and individuals offered sacrifice in almost any location and without a priestly class. The Mosaic covenant prescribed that offerings be restricted to the tabernacle, a mobile sanctuary, and that they become an exclusive prerogative of the Levites; but both restrictions, especially the former, were often observed in the breach. With the construction of Solomon's temple, covenantal worship became more centralised, at least until the division of the kingdom. The high feasts brought pilgrims on to the roads by the thousands, going 'up' to Jerusalem, the city of the great king. Choirs were in attendance, and musical instruments contributed to these festal occasions. Worship was powerfully tied to cultus.

The division of the kingdom and the spiralling degeneration of both Israel and Judah soon broke up even this degree of uniformity. The exile dispersed the northern tribes to sites that made access to the temple impossible; in due course, exile reached the kingdom of Judah and witnessed the utter destruction of the temple. The revolution in thinking that accompanied this obliteration of the central reality of the cultus is shown in many Old Testament texts, not least in the vision of Ezekiel 8–11, where it is the exilic community – not the Jews remaining in Jerusalem who are about to be destroyed along with the temple – who constitute the true remnant, the people for whom God Himself will be a sanctuary (11:16). Such realities

---

9   J. G. Davies, 'Worship,' *A Dictionary of Biblical Tradition in English Literature*, ed. David Lyle Jeffrey (Grand Rapids: Eerdmans, 1992), p. 851.

relativise the temple and with it the covenantal structure inex-
tricably linked with it. The same effect is achieved by promises
of a new covenant (Jer. 31:31ff.; Ezek. 36:25-27). As the author
of Hebrews would later reason, the promise of a new covenant
made the old covenant obsolete in principle (Heb. 8:13). The
restoration of a diminished temple after the exile did not really
jeopardise these new anticipations, for neither the high-priest-
ly line of Zadok nor the Davidic kingdom was ever restored.

Thus, the first point to observe is that however enmeshed in
cultus, sacrifice, priestly service, covenantal prescription and major festivals the worship of Israel had become, that worship kept
changing its face across the two millennia from Abraham to Jesus.

Second, there is no reason to restrict all worship in ancient Israel to the cultus. The Psalms testify to a large scope
for individual praise and adoration, even if some of them are
addressed to a wide readership and even if some were intended for corporate use in temple services. The Old Testament provides ample evidence of individuals pouring out
their prayers before God, quite apart from the religion of the
cultus (e.g., Hannah, Daniel and Job).

Third, and most importantly, a remarkable shift takes
place with the coming of the Lord Jesus and the dawning
of the new covenant He introduces. Under the terms of the
new covenant, the Levitical priesthood has been replaced:
either we are all priests (i.e., intermediaries, 1 Peter), or
else Jesus alone is the high priest (Hebrews), but there is
no priestly caste or tribe. Jesus' body becomes the temple
(John 2:13-22); or, adapting the figure, the church is the temple (1 Cor. 3:16-17); or the individual Christian is the temple
(1 Cor. 6:19). No church building is ever designated the 'temple' (e.g., 'Temple Baptist Church').

The pattern of type/antitype is so thorough that
inevitably the way we think of worship must also change.
The language of worship, so bound up with the temple and
priestly system under the old covenant, has been radically
transformed by what Christ has done.

We see the change in a well-known passage like Romans 12:1-2. To offer our bodies as 'living sacrifices, holy and pleasing to God' is our 'spiritual act of worship'. In other words, Paul uses the worship language of the cultus, except that his use of the terminology transports us away from the cultus: what we offer is no longer a lamb or a bull but our bodies. We see the change again in another well-known passage. Jesus tells us we 'must worship in spirit and in truth' (John 4:24). This does not mean that we must worship 'spiritually' (as opposed to 'carnally'?) and 'truthfully' (as opposed to 'falsely'?). The context focuses our Lord's argument. Samaritans held that the appropriate location for worship was at the twin mountains, Gerizim and Ebal; Jews held that it was Jerusalem. By contrast, Jesus says that a time is now dawning 'when the true worshippers will worship the Father in spirit and truth.... God is spirit, and his worshippers must worship in spirit and in truth' (4:23-24). In the first instance, then, this utterance abolishes both Samaria's mountains and Jerusalem as the proper location for the corporate worship of the people of God. God is spirit, and He cannot be domesticated by mere location or mere temples, even if in the past He chose to disclose Himself in one such temple as a teaching device that anticipated what was coming. Moreover, in this book – in which Jesus appears as the *true* vine, the *true* manna, the *true* Shepherd, the *true* temple, the *true* Son – to worship God 'in spirit *and in truth*' is first and foremost a way of saying that we must worship God *by means of Christ*. In Him the reality has dawned and the shadows are being swept away (cf. Heb. 8:13). Christian worship is new covenant worship; it is gospel-inspired worship; it is Christ-centred worship; it is cross-focused worship. [10]

Elsewhere in the New Testament, we discover that Paul could think of evangelism as his *priestly* service (Rom. 15). Jesus is our Passover lamb (1 Cor. 5:7). We offer a sacrifice of praise (Heb. 13:15), not a sacrifice of sheep. Our worship is no longer

---

10 On all these points, Peterson, *Engaging with God*, is very good.

focused on a particular form or festival. It must be bound up with all we are and do as the blood-bought people of God's Messiah. We offer up *ourselves* as living sacrifices. Augustine was not far off the mark when he wrote, 'God is to be worshipped by faith, hope and love.' This is something we do all the time: under the terms of the new covenant, worship is no longer primarily focused in a cultus shaped by a liturgical calendar, but it is something in which we are continuously engaged.

To sum up: 'This side of the Fall, *human worship* of God properly responds to the redemptive provision that God has graciously made.' But because of the location of new covenant believers in the stream of redemptive history, the heart of what constitutes true worship changes its form rather radically. At a time when sacrificial and priestly structures anticipated the ultimate sacrifice and high priest, faithful participation in the corporate worship of the covenant community meant the temple with all its symbolism: sacrificial animals, high feasts, and so forth. This side of the supreme sacrifice, we no longer participate in the forms that pointed towards it; and the focus of worship language, priestly language, sacrificial language has been transmuted into a far more comprehensive arena, one that is far less oriented towards any notion of cultus.

5. Nevertheless, so that we do not err by exaggerating the differences between the forms of worship under the Mosaic covenant and under the new covenant, it is essential to recognise that '*all* true worship is God-centred.' It is *never* simply a matter of conforming to formal requirements. The Old Testament prophets offer many passages that excoriate all worship that is formally 'correct' while the worshipper's heart is set on idolatry (e.g., Ezek. 8). Isaiah thunders the Word of the Lord: 'The multitude of your sacrifices—what are they to me?' says the LORD. 'I have more than enough of burnt offerings, of rams and the fat of fattened animals; I have no pleasure in the blood of bulls and lambs and goats.... Stop bringing meaningless offerings!

Your incense is detestable to me. New Moons, Sabbaths and convocations—I cannot bear your evil assemblies.... When you spread out your hands in prayer, I will hide my eyes from you.... Take your evil deeds out of my sight! Stop doing wrong, learn to do right!' (Isa. 1:11-17). 'Without purity of heart their pretence of worship was indeed an abomination,' says Robert Rayburn. 'Even the divinely authorised ordinances themselves had become offensive to the God who had given them because of the way they had been abused.' [11]

This may clarify a point from Peterson[12] that can easily be turned towards a doubtful conclusion. Peterson rightly points out that the move from the old covenant to the new brings with it a transmutation of the language of the cultus. Under the new covenant the terminology of sacrifice, priest, temple, offering and the like is transformed. No longer is there a supreme site to which pilgrimages of the faithful must be made: we worship 'in spirit and in truth'. This transformation of language is inescapable and is tied to the shift from type to antitype, from promise to reality, from shadow to substance. But we must not therefore conclude that, apart from instances of individual worship, in the Old Testament the formal requirements of the cultus exhausted what was meant by public worship.

In any legal structure there has always been a hierarchy of priorities. Jesus Himself was quite prepared to deliver His judgment as to which was the greatest commandment in 'the Law': 'Love the Lord your God with all your heart and with all your soul and with all your mind' (Matt 22:37; cf. Deut. 6:5). It follows that the greatest sin, the most fundamental sin, is to *not* love the Lord our God with all of our heart and soul and mind. The connection with worship, as we have defined it, is transparent. We cannot ascribe to the

---

11   Robert G. Rayburn, *0 Come, Let Us Worship* (Grand Rapids: Baker Book House, 1980), p. 19.

12   David Peterson, *Engaging with God* (Leicester: Apollos, 1992)

Lord all the glory due His name if we are consumed by self-love or intoxicated by pitiful visions of our own greatness or independence. Still less are we properly worshipping the Lord if we formally adhere to the stipulations of covenantal sacrifice when our hearts are far from Him. To put the matter positively, worship is not merely a *formal* ascription of praise to God: it emerges from my whole being to this whole God, and therefore it reflects not only my understanding of God but my love for Him. 'Praise the LORD, O my soul; all my inmost being, praise his holy name' (Ps 103:1).

Thus, the transition from worship under the old covenant to worship under the new is not characterised by a move from the formal to the spiritual, or from the cultus to the spiritual, or from the cultus to all of life. For it has *always* been necessary to love God wholly; it has *always* been necessary to recognise the sheer holiness and transcendent power and glory and goodness of God and to adore Him for what He is. So we insist that '*all* true worship is God-centred.' The transition from worship under the old covenant to worship under the new is characterised by the covenantal stipulations and provisions of the two respective covenants. The way wholly loving God works out under the old covenant is in heartfelt obedience to the terms of that covenant – and that includes the primary place given to the cultus, with all its import and purpose in the stream of redemptive history; and the implications of this outworking include distinctions between the holy and the common, between holy space and common space, between holy time and common time, between holy food and common food. The way wholly loving God works out under the new covenant is in heartfelt obedience to the terms of that covenant – and here the language of the cultus has been transmuted to all of life, with the implication, not so much of a desacralisation of space and time and food, as with a sacralisation of all space and all time and all food: what God has declared holy let no-one declare unholy.

There is a further implication here that can only be mentioned, not explored. In theological analysis of work, it is a commonplace to say that work is a 'creation ordinance' (the terminology varies with the theological tradition). However corrosive and difficult work has become this side of the Fall (Gen. 3:17-19), work itself belongs to the initial paradise (Gen. 2:15), and it continues to be something we do as creatures in God's good creation. That is true, of course, but under the new covenant it is also inadequate. If everything, including our work, has been sacralised in the sense just specified, then work itself is part of our worship. Christians work not only as God's creatures in God's creation, but as redeemed men and women offering their time, their energy, their work, their whole lives, to God – loving Him with heart and mind and strength, understanding that whatever we do, we are to do to the glory of God.

This does not mean there is no place for corporate gathering under the new covenant, no corporate acknowledgment of God, no corporate worship – as we shall see. But in the light of the completed cross-work of the Lord Jesus Christ, the language of the cultus has necessarily changed, and with it our priorities in worship. What remains constant is the sheer God-centredness of it all.

6. *Christian* worship is no less Christ-centred than God-centred. The set purpose of the Father is that all should honour the Son even as they honour the Father (John 5:23). Since the eternal Word became flesh (John 1:14), since the fullness of the Deity lives in Christ in bodily form (Col. 2:9), since in the light of Jesus' astonishing obedience (even unto death!) God has exalted Him and given Him 'the name that is above every name, that at the name of Jesus every knee should bow, in heaven and on earth and under the earth' (Phil. 2:9-10), and since the resurrected Jesus quietly accepted Thomas's reverent and worshipping words, 'My Lord and my God!' (John 20:28), contemporary Christians follow the example of the first generation of believers and worship Jesus without hesitation.

Nowhere is the mandate to worship the Lord Jesus clearer than in the book of Revelation, from chapter 5 on. In Revelation 4, in apocalyptic metaphor, God is presented as the awesome, transcendent God of glory before whom even the highest orders of angels cover their faces. This sets the stage for the drama in chapter 5. There an angel issues a challenge to the entire universe: Who is able to approach the throne of such a terrifying God, take the book in his right hand, and slit the seven seals that bind it? In the symbolism of the time and of this genre of literature, this is a challenge to bring to pass all God's purposes for the universe, His purposes of both blessing and judgment. No one is found who is worthy to accomplish this task, and John the seer is driven to despair (5:4). Then someone is found: the Lion of the tribe of Judah, who is also the Lamb – simultaneously a kingly warrior and a slaughtered Lamb – emerges to take the scroll from the right hand of the Almighty and slit the seals. But instead of approaching the throne of this transcendent and frankly terrifying God, He stands in the very centre of the throne, one with Deity Himself (5:6). This sets off a mighty chorus of worship addressed to the Lamb, praising Him because He is *worthy* to take the scroll and open its seals (5:9). What makes Him uniquely qualified to bring to pass God's purposes for judgment and redemption is not simply the fact that He emerges from the very throne of God, but that He was slain, and by His blood He purchased men for God from every tribe and language and people and nation (5:9). In short, not only His person but His atoning work make Him uniquely qualified to bring to pass God's perfect purposes.

Thereafter in the book of Revelation, worship is addressed to 'him who sits on the throne and to the Lamb,' or some similar formulation. For in our era, Christian worship is no less Christ-centred than God-centred.

7. Christian worship is Trinitarian. This point deserves extensive reflection. One might usefully consider, for instance, a Trinitar-

ian biblical theology of prayer.[13] But for our purposes it will suffice to repeat some of the insights of James Torrance. He writes:

The [Trinitarian] view of worship is that it is the gift of participating through the Spirit in the incarnate Son's communion with the Father. That means participating in union with Christ, in what he has done for us once and for all, in his self-offering to the Father, in his life and death on the cross. It also means participating in what he is continuing to do for us in the presence of the Father and in his mission from the Father to the world. There is only one true Priest through whom and with whom we draw near to God our Father. There is only one Mediator between God and humanity. There is only one offering which is truly acceptable to God, and it is not ours. It is the offering by which he has sanctified for all time those who come to God by him (Heb. 2:11; 10:10, 14).... It takes seriously the New Testament teaching about the sole priesthood and headship of Christ, his self-offering for us to the Father and our life in union with Christ through the Spirit, with a vision of the Church which is his body.... So we are baptised in the name of the Father, Son and Holy Spirit into the community, the one body of Christ, which confesses faith in the one God, Father, Son and Holy Spirit, and which worships the Father through the Son in the Spirit.[14]

---

13   See, for instance, the important essay by Edmund P. Clowney, 'A Biblical Theology of Prayer,' in *Teach Us To Pray: Prayer in the Bible and the World*, ed. D. A. Carson (Carlisle: Paternoster Press, 1990), pp. 136-73.

14   James B. Torrance, *Worship, Community and the Triune God of Grace* (Downers Grove: InterVarsity Press, 1996), pp. 20-2. This book often proves very insightful, even though in my view Torrance sometimes attacks a Zwinglian view of the Lord's Supper that is little more than a straw man.

This is very helpful, especially if it is not taken to refer to what must pertain only at 11:00 a.m. on Sunday morning. The justifying, regenerating, redeeming work of our triune God transforms His people: that is the very essence of the new covenant. New covenant worship therefore finds its first impulse in this transforming gospel, 'which restores our relationship with our Redeemer-God and therefore with our fellow image-bearers, our co-worshippers.'

8. Christian worship embraces both adoration and action.[15] By referring to both, I do not mean to reintroduce a distinction between the sacred and the common (see section 4 above). It is not that we withdraw into 'adoration' and then advance into 'action,' with the former somehow gaining extra kudos for being the more spiritual or the more worshipful. We are to do everything to the glory of God. In offering our bodies as living sacrifices, which is our spiritual worship, we do with our bodies what He desires. Indeed, there may be something even more aggressive about this 'action.' As Miroslav Volf puts it, 'There is something profoundly hypocritical about praising God for God's mighty deeds of salvation and cooperating at the same time with the demons of destruction, whether by neglecting to do good or by actively doing evil. Only those who help the Jews may sing the Gregorian chant, Dietrich Bonhoeffer rightly said, in the context of Nazi Germany... Without action in the world, the adoration of God is empty and hypocritical, and degenerates into irresponsible and godless quietism.'[16] Conversely, Christian action in this world produces incentive to adore God (i.e., 1 Pet. 2:11-12).

On the other hand, *mere* activism is not a particularly godly alternative either; for like active evil, it may be impelled by

---

15   See especially the essay by Miroslav Volf, 'Reflections on a Christian Way of Being-in-the-World' in *Worship. Adoration and Action*, pp. 203-11, to which I am indebted for some elements of this section.

16   Ibid., p. 211.

mere lust for power, or mere commitment to a tradition (no matter how good the tradition), or mere altruism or reformist sentiment. To resort to periods of adoration, whether personal and individual or corporate, is not, however, to retreat to the classic sacred/profane division, but it is to grasp the New Testament recognition of the rhythms of life in this created order. Jesus Himself presupposes that there is a time and place for the individual to resort to a 'secret' place for prayer (Matt 6:6). The church itself, as we shall see, is to gather regularly.

In short, precisely because Christian worship is impelled by the gospel 'which restores our relationship with our Redeemer-God and therefore also with our fellow image-bearers, our co-worshippers,' precisely because the ultimate triumph of God is a reconciled universe (Col. 1:15-20), our worship must therefore manifest itself in both adoration and action.

9. Similarly, if the New Testament documents constitute our guide, our worship must manifest itself both in the individual believer and in 'corporate worship, which is offered up in the context of the body of believers,'

This corporate identity extends not only to other believers here and now with whom we happen to be identified but also to believers from all times and places. For the fundamental 'gathering' of the people of God is the gathering to *God*, 'to Mount Zion, to the heavenly Jerusalem, the city of the living God. You have come to thousands upon thousands of angels in joyful assembly, to the church of the firstborn, whose names are written in heaven. You have come *to God*, the judge of all men, to the spirits of righteous men made perfect, to Jesus the mediator of a new covenant, and to the sprinkled blood, that speaks a better word than the blood of Abel' (Heb 12:22-24; emphasis added). The local church is not so much a part of this church as the manifestation of it, the outcropping of it. Every church is simply the church.

Thus, whatever it is we do when we gather together – something still to be discussed – we do in the profound recognition that we believers constitute something much bigger than any one of us or even any empirical group of us. We are the church, the temple of God (1 Cor. 3:16-17).[17] One of the entailments of such a perspective is that, however much we seek to be contemporary for the sake of evangelistic outreach, there must also be a drive in us to align ourselves with the *whole* church in some deeply rooted and tangible ways. What it means to be the church was not invented in the last twenty years. The demands of corporate rootedness must be melded with the demands of living faithfully and bearing witness in a particular culture and age.

The New Testament speaks of the gathering or the coming together of the people of God in many contexts (e.g., Acts 4:31; 11:26; 14:27; 15:6, 30; 20:7-8; 1 Cor 5:4; 11:17, 33-34; 14:26).[18] 'The church in assembly not only provides encouragement to its members but also approaches God (Heb. 10:19-25),' writes Everett Ferguson.[19] But this could equally be put the opposite way: the church in assembly not only approaches God, but it provides encouragement to its members. Even in Ephesians 5:19 we speak 'to one another' when we sing; and in Colossians 3:16, the singing of 'psalms, hymns and spiritual songs' is in the context of teaching and admonishing one another – part of letting 'the word of Christ dwell in you richly.' This means that the purist model of addressing *only* God in our corporate worship is too restrictive. On the other hand, while one of the purposes of our singing should be mutual edification, that is rather different from making ourselves and our experience of worship the *topic* of our singing.

10. This body of believers strives 'to align all the forms of their devout ascription of all worth to God with the panoply of new

---

17   The context shows that in this passage the temple of God is *the church*, unlike 1 Corinthians 6:19-20, where in quite a different figurative usage the temple of God is the body of the individual Christian.

18   See the important work of Everett Ferguson, *The Church of Christ* (Grand Rapids: Eerdmans, 1996), esp. 231ff.

19   Ibid., p. 233

covenant mandates and examples.' This will be true in the arena of conduct, to which the apostle Paul devotes so much space. Again and again he exhorts his younger colleagues to help believers learn *how* to live and speak and conduct themselves.

But my focus here will be on the church in its gathered meetings. What does the New Testament mandate for such meetings, whether by prescription or description? Is it the case, under the terms of the new covenant, that it is *wrong* to say that our purpose in coming together (for instance, on Sunday morning) is for worship? Some, as we have seen, reply, 'Yes, it is clearly wrong.' Nor is this some newfangled iconoclasm. William Law, in his justly famous *A Serious Call to a Devout and Holy Life*, written more than two centuries ago, insists, 'There is not one command in all the Gospel for public worship.... The frequent attendance at it is never so much as mentioned in all the New Testament.' In the light of the New Testament's penchant for deploying all the old worship terminology in fresh ways, no longer bound up with temple and feast days but with all of Christian living, to say that we come together 'to worship' implies that we are *not* worshipping God the rest of the time. And that is so out of touch with New Testament emphases that we ought to abandon such a notion absolutely. We do not come together for worship, these people say; rather, we come together for instruction, or we come together for mutual edification.

Yet one wonders if this conclusion is justified. Of course, if we spend the week *without* worshipping God and think of Sunday morning as the time when we come together to offer God the worship we have been withholding all week (to set right the balance, as it were), then these critics are entirely correct. But would it not be better to say that the New Testament emphasis is that the people of God should worship Him in their individual lives and in their family lives and then, when they come together, worship him corporately?

In other words, worship becomes the category under which we order *everything* in our lives. Whatever we do, even if we are simply eating or drinking, whatever we say, in business or in the home or in church assemblies, we are to do all to the glory of God. That is worship. And when we come together, we engage in worship in a corporate fashion.

Some are uncomfortable with this analysis. They say that if worship is something that Christians should be doing all the time, then although it is formally true that Christians should be engaged in worship when they gather together, it is merely true in the same sense in which Christians should be engaged in breathing when they gather together. It is something they do all the time. But the analogy this makes between worship and breathing is misleading. We are not commanded to breathe; breathing is merely an autonomic function. But we are *commanded* to worship (e.g., Rev. 19:10). And although it is true that the technical language of worship in the Old Testament is transmuted in the New from the cultus to all of life, there are odd passages where the language also refers to the Christian assembly (e.g., *proskyneo* in 1 Cor. 14:25).

Moreover, just as in the light of the New Testament we dare not think we gather for worship because we have *not* been worshipping all week, so also it is folly to think that only part of the 'service' is worship – everything but the sermon, perhaps, or only the singing, or only singing and responses. The notion of a 'worship leader' who leads the 'worship' part of the service before the sermon (which, then, is no part of worship!) is so bizarre, from a New Testament perspective, as to be embarrassing.[20] Doesn't even experience teach us that sometimes our deepest desires and heart prayers to ascribe all worth to God well up during the powerful preaching of the Word of God? I know that 'worship leader' is merely a matter of semantics, a currently popular tag, but it is a popular tag that unwittingly skews people's expectations as to what worship is.

---

20 Scarcely less bizarre is the contention of some that we should distinguish between services for worship and services for teaching (e.g., Robert E. Webber, in a generally helpful book, *Worship Old and New* [Grand Rapids: Zondervan, 1982], pp. 125, 194).

At the very least, it is misleadingly restrictive.[21]

So what should we do, then, in corporate worship so understood? Although some might object to one or two of his locutions, Edmund Clowney provides one of the most succinct summaries of such evidence as the New Testament provides:

> The New Testament indicates, by precept and example, what the elements of [corporate] worship are. As in the synagogue, corporate prayer is offered (Acts 2:42; 1 Tim. 2:1; 1 Cor. 14:16); Scripture is read (1 Tim. 4:13; 1 Thess. 5:27; 2 Thess. 3:14; Col. 4:15, 16; 2 Pet. 3:15, 16) and expounded in preaching (1 Tim. 4:13; cf. Luke 4:20-21; 2 Tim. 3:15-17; 4:2). There is a direct shift from the synagogue to the gathering of the church (Acts 18:7, 11; cf. 19:8-10). The teaching of the word is also linked with table fellowship (Acts 2:42; 20:7, cf. vv. 20, 25, 28). The songs of the new covenant people both praise God and encourage one another (Eph. 5:19; Col. 3:16; 1 Cor. 14:15, 26; cf. 1 Tim. 3:16; Rev. 5:9-13; 11:17f, 15:3, 4). Giving to the poor is recognised as a spiritual service to God and a Christian form of 'sacrifice' (2 Cor. 9:11-15; Phil. 4:18; Heb. 13:16). The reception and

---

21 Perhaps this is the place to reflect on the fact that many contemporary 'worship leaders' have training in music but none in Bible, theology, history, or the like. When pressed as to the criteria by which they choose their music, many of these leaders finally admit that their criteria oscillate between personal preference and keeping the congregation reasonably happy – scarcely the most profound criteria in the world. They give little or no thought to covering the great themes of Scripture, or the great events of Scripture, or the range of personal response to God found in the Psalms (as opposed to covering the narrow themes of being upbeat in the midst of 'worship'), or the nature of biblical locutions (in one chorus the congregation manages to sing 'holy' thirty-six times, while three are enough for Isaiah and John of the Apocalypse), or the central historical traditions of the church, or anything else of weight. If such leaders operate on their own with little guidance or training or input from senior pastors, the situation commonly degenerates from the painful to the pitiful. On this and many other practical and theological points, see the wise and informed counsel of David Montgomery, *Sing a New Song: Choosing and Leading Praise in Today's Church* (Edinburgh: Rutherford House and Handsel Press, 2000).

distribution of gifts is related to the office of the deacon (Acts 6:1-6; Rom. 12:8, 13; cf. Rom. 16:1, 2; 2 Cor. 8:19-21; Acts 20:4; 1 Cor. 16:1-4) and to the gathering of believers (Acts 2:42; 5:12; 1 Cor. 16:2). The faith is also publicly confessed (1 Tim. 6:12; 1 Pet. 3:21; Heb. 13:15; cf. 1. Cor. 15:1-3). The people receive God's blessing (2 Cor. 13:14; Luke 24:50; cf. Num. 6:22, 27). The holy kiss of salutation is also commanded (Rom. 16:16; 1 Cor. 16:20; 2 Cor. 13:12; 1 Thess. 5:26; 1 Pet. 5:14). The people respond to praise and prayer with the saying of 'Amen' (1 Cor. 14:16; Rev. 5:14; cf. Rom. 1:25; 9:5; Eph. 3:21 etc.). The sacraments of baptism and the Lord's Supper are explicitly provided for. Confession is linked with baptism (1 Pet. 3:21); and a prayer of thanksgiving with the breaking of bread (1 Cor. 11:24).[22]

One might quibble over a few points. Some might say that explicit *permission* must be opened up for tongues as restricted by 1 Corinthians 14, for example. Still, Clowney's list is surely broadly right. But observe:

a. To compile such a list is already to recognise that there are some distinctive elements to what I have called 'corporate worship'. I am not sure that we would be wise to apply the expression 'corporate worship' to any and all activities in which groups of Christians faithfully engage – going to a football match, say, or shopping for groceries. Such activities doubtless fall under the 'do all to the glory of God' rubric and therefore properly belong to the ways in which we honour God; therefore, they do belong to worship in a broad sense. Yet the activities the New Testament describes when Christians gather together in assembly, nicely listed by Clowney, are more restrictive and more focused. Doubtless

---

22 Edmund P. Clowney, 'Presbyterian Worship,' *Worship: Adoration and Action*, ed. D. A. Carson, p. 117. cf. also Hughes Oliphant Old, *Themes and Variations for a Christian Doxology: Some Thoughts on the Theology of Worship* (Grand Rapids: Eerdmans, 1992); Michael B. Thompson, 'Romans 12:1-2 and Paul's Vision for Worship,' in *A Vision for the Church: Studies in Early Christian Ecclesiology*, ed. Markus N. A. Bockmuehl and Michael B. Thompson (Edinburgh: T & T Clark, 1998), esp. 129-30.

there can be some mutual edification going on when a group of Christians take a sewing class together, but in the light of what the New Testament pictures Christians doing when they assemble together, there is nevertheless something slightly skewed about calling a sewing class an activity of corporate worship. So there is a narrower sense of worship, it appears; and this narrower sense is bound up with corporate worship, with what the assembled church does in the pages of the New Testament. Yet it is precisely at this point that one must instantly insist that this narrower list of activities does *not* include all that the New Testament includes within the theological notion of worship in the broader sense. If one restricts the term *worship* to the list of church-assembly activities listed by Clowney, one loses essential elements of the dramatic transformation that occurs in the move from the old covenant to the new;[23] conversely, if one uses the term *worship* only in its broadest and theologically richest sense, then sooner or later one finds oneself looking for a term that embraces the particular activities of the gathered people of God described in the New Testament. For lack of a better alternative, I have chosen the term *corporate worship* – but I recognise the ambiguities inherent in it.

b. It is worth reflecting on how many of the items listed by Clowney are related, in one way or another, to the Word. The book of Psalms opens by declaring that the just person is the one who delights in the law of the Lord and meditates on it day and night (Ps. 1:2). Jesus asserts, in prayer, that what will sanctify His disciples is the Word (John 17:17). Doyle puts his finger on this integrating factor:

---

23 This, of course, is the use of the word worship found in most older studies or in recent studies that do not take into account the redemptive-historical developments within the canon. See, for example, D. E. Anne ('Worship, Early Christian,' in *Anchor Bible Dictionary* 6.973-89), who ties worship to such activities and responses as these: acclamation, awe, blessing, commemoration, confession, doxology, fear, hymn, invocation, offering, praise, prayer, prophecy, prostration, sacrifice, supplication and thanksgiving.

The characteristic response we are to make to God as he comes to us clothed in his promises, clothed with the gospel, is faith. In the context of the New Testament's vision of what church is to be, this faith most appropriately takes the form of confession. To each other we confess and testify to the greatness of God. We do this by the very activity of making God's Word the centre of our activities – by reading it, preaching it, making it the basis of exhortation, and even setting it to music in hymns and praise. The Spirit uses all this, we are assured, to build us up in Christ. Praise is integral to our activities in church, because it is another form of our response of faith. It is part of our whole life of worship, but only one part of it.[24]

What this also suggests, yet again, is that an approach to corporate worship that thinks of only *some* of the activities of assembled Christians, such as singing and praying, as worship, but not the ministry of the Word itself, is badly off base. Worse yet are formulations that are in danger of making 'worship' a substitute for the gospel. It is not uncommon to be told that 'worship leads us into the presence of God' or that 'worship takes us from the outer court into the inner court' or the like. There is a way of reading those statements sympathetically (as I shall note in a moment), but taken at face value they are simply untrue. Objectively, what brings us into the presence of God is the death and resurrection of the Lord Jesus. If we ascribe to worship (meaning, in this context, our corporate praise and adoration) something of this power, it will not be long before we think of such worship as being meritorious, or efficacious, or the like. The small corner of truth that such expressions hide (though this truth is poorly worded) is that when we come together and engage in the activities of corporate worship (including not only prayer and praise but the Lord's Supper and attentive listening to the Word, and the other

---

24   Robert Doyle, 'The One True Worshipper,' *The Briefing*, (29 April 1999), p. 8.

items included in Clowney's list), we encourage one another, we edify one another, and so we often *feel* encouraged and edified. As a result, we are renewed in our awareness of God's love and God's truth, and we are encouraged to respond with adoration and action. In this subjective sense, *all* of the activities of corporate worship may function to make us more aware of God's majesty, God's presence, God's love. But I doubt that it is helpful to speak of such matters in terms of worship 'leading us into the presence of God': not only is the term *worship* bearing a meaning too narrow to be useful, but the statement is in danger of conveying some profoundly untrue notions.

c. Although the *elements* Clowney lists are obviously the elements of corporate worship mentioned in the New Testament, there is no explicit mandate or model of a particular order or arrangement of these elements. Of course, this is not to deny that there may be better and worse arrangements. One might try to establish liturgical order that reflects the theology of conversion, or at least of general approach to God: confession of sin before assurance of grace, for instance. Nevertheless, the tendency in some traditions to nail everything down in great detail and claim that such stipulations are biblically sanctioned is to 'go beyond what is written' (to use the Pauline phrase, 1 Cor 4:6).

The New Testament does not provide us with officially sanctioned public 'services' so much as with examples of crucial elements. We do well to admit the limitations of our knowledge.

d. There is no mention of a lot of other things: drama, 'special' (performance) music, choirs, artistic dance, organ solos. Many churches are so steeped in these or other traditions that it would be unthinkable to have a Sunday morning service without, say, 'special music' – though there is not so much as a hint of this practice in the New Testament. [25]Some

---

25 By 'special music' I am including not only the solos and small groups that a slightly earlier generation of evangelical churches customarily presented but also the very substantial number of 'performance' items that current 'worship teams' normally include in services. These are often not seen by the teams themselves as 'special music' or 'performance music,' but, of course, that is what they are.

preferences are conditioned not only by the local church but by the traditions of the country in which it is located. The overwhelming majority of evangelical churches in America, especially outside the mainline denominations, offer perform-ance music almost every Sunday. The overwhelming majority of denominationally similar churches in Britain never have it.[26]

Occasionally attempts have been made to justify a 'bells and smells' approach to corporate worship on the basis of some of the imagery in the Book of Revelation. In Revelation 5, for instance, incense is wafted before God by the elders, and the incense is identified as 'the prayers of the saints'. Granted that this is an instance of the rich symbolism of the Apocalypse, does it not warrant us to introduce similarly symbol-laden realities as aids to corporate worship? But this reasoning is misguided on several fronts. So much of the symbolism of this book's apocalyptic is deeply rooted in the Old Testament world. In this case, it calls to mind passages such as Psalm 141:2: 'May my prayer be set before you like incense; may the lifting up of my hands be like the evening sacrifice.' In other words, the comparison is drawn between David's private prayers and the central institutions of the tabernacle (and later temple) – which is precisely what is done away with under the new covenant. One avoids the obvious hermeneutical quagmires by patiently asking the question, 'So far as our records go, did Christians in New Testament times use incense during corporate worship?'

---

26 There are many entailments to these cultural differences beyond the differ-ences in the corporate services themselves. For example, Britain, without much place for 'special music' in corporate worship, does not have to feed a market driven by the search for more 'special music'. Therefore, a great deal of intellectual and spiritual energy is devoted to writing songs that will be sung congregationally. This has resulted in a fairly wide production of new hymnody in more or less contemporary guise, some of it junk, some of it acceptable but scarcely enduring, and some of it frankly superb. By contrast, our addiction to 'special music' means that a great deal of creative energy goes into supplying products for that market. Whether it is good or bad, it is almost never usable by a congregation. The result is that far more of our congregational pieces are dated than in Britain, or are no more than repetitive choruses.

e. Historically, some branches of the church have argued that if God has not forbidden something, we are permitted to do it, and the church is permitted to regulate its affairs in these regards in order to establish good order (this is known as the Hooker Principle, after the Anglican divine, Richard Hooker). Others have argued that the only things we should do in public worship are those that find clear example or direct prescription in the New Testament, lest we drift from what is central or impose on our congregations things that their consciences might not be able to support (the Regulative Principle, a Presbyterian understanding).

To attempt even the most rudimentary evaluation of this debate would immediately double the length of this chapter. Besides, these matters will surface again in later chapters. But four preliminary observations may be helpful. First, historically speaking, both the Hooker Principle and the Regulative Principle have been understood and administered in both a stronger and a more attenuated way, with widely differing results. Some have appealed to Hooker to support changes far beyond the appropriateness of prescribing or forbidding vestments and the like; others have appealed to Hooker in defence of a church-ordered prayer book. Some have appealed to the Regulative Principle to ban all instruments from corporate worship and to sanction only the singing of psalms; others see it as a principle of freedom within limits: it recognises that we are not authorised to worship God 'as we please' and that our worship must be acceptable to God Himself and therefore in line with His Word. In short, both the Hooker Principle and the Regulative Principle are plagued by complex debates as to what they mean, today as well as historically.[27] For many of the protagonists, their interpretations are as certain, as immovable, and as inflexible as

---

27　For example, the Regulative Principle, well articulated by the Westminster divines, opposed the introduction of new *observances* in worship but does not deny culturally appropriate arrangements of the *circumstances* of worship – which has generated no little debate on what is meant by 'circumstances'. See the discussion in Clowney, 'Presbyterian Worship,' 117ff; and John M. Frame, *Worship in Spirit and Truth* (Phillipsburg: Presbyterian and Reformed, 1996), though on the latter, cf. the review by Leonard R. Payton in *Reformation and Revival* 6/3 (1997): pp. 227-35.

the Rock of Gibraltar. Second, it must be frankly admitted that both the Hooker Principle and the Regulative Principle have bred staunch traditionalists. Traditionalists who follow Hooker argue that according to this principle the church has the right to *regulate* certain matters, and endless innovation is a denial of that right. So stop tampering with the Prayer Book! Traditionalists who follow the Regulative Principle not only tend to adopt the simplest form of public worship but tie it to traditional forms of expression (e.g., they will always find fault with psalms set to contemporary music, preferring the metrical psalms sung centuries ago).[28] Third, both camps have also bred pastors who are remarkably contemporary, thoroughly evangelical in the best sense of that long suffering term, and innovative in their leading of corporate worship. In the Anglican tradition, for instance, one thinks of John Mason's duly authorised 'experimental service' in Sydney, which deserves circulation and evaluation among evangelical Anglicans.[29] In the Presbyterian tradition, one thinks of Tim Keller in New York (but here I will say little for fear of embarrassing a fellow contributor). Fourth, for all their differences, theologically rich and serious services from both camps often have more common *content* than either side usually acknowledges.

f.   There is no single passage in the New Testament that establishes a paradigm for corporate worship. Not a few writers appeal to 1 Corinthians 14. Yet the priorities of that chapter are set by Paul's agenda at that point, dealing with *charismata* that have gained too prominent a place in public meetings. There is no mention of the Lord's Supper and no mention of public teaching by a pastor/elder even though other passages in Paul show

---

28   On these and related points, see John Frame, *Contemporary Worship Music: A Biblical Defense* (Phillipsburg: Presbyterian and Reformed, 1997). See also Lee Irons, 'Exclusive Psalmody or New Covenant Hymnody?' at http://members.aol.com/ ironslee/private/Psalmody.htm.

29   John Mason, *A Service for Today's Church* (Mosman: St Clement's Anglican Church, 1997).

that such elements played an important role in the corporate meetings of churches overseen by the apostle.

g. First Corinthians 14 lays considerable stress on intelligibility. The issue for Paul, of course, is tongues and prophecy: his concern is to establish guidelines that keep undisciplined enthusiasm in check. Frame[30] applies the importance of intelligibility to the music that is chosen. Although that is scarcely what the apostle had in mind, I doubt that he would have been displeased by the application. Nevertheless, there are complementary principles to bear in mind. Paul speaks of 'psalms, hymns, and spiritual songs.' We may debate what is the full range of musical styles to which this expression refers, but psalms are certainly included – whether they are judged intelligible for our biblically illiterate generation or not. Corporate meetings of the church, however much God is worshipped in them, have the collateral responsibility of educating, informing, and transforming the minds of those who attend, of training the people of God in righteousness, of expanding their horizons not only so that they better know God (and therefore better worship Him) but so that they better grasp the dimensions of the church that He has redeemed by the death of His Son (and therefore better worship Him) – and that means, surely, some sort of exposure to more than the narrow slice of church that subsists in one particular subculture. The importance of intelligibility (in music, let us say) must therefore be juxtaposed with the responsibility to expand the limited horizons of one narrow tradition.[31] Incidentally, the punch of this observation

---

30 *Worship in Spirit and Truth*, passim.

31 One wishes, for instance, that more leaders were aware of a work such as Andrew Wilson-Dickson, *The Story of Christian Music: From Gregorian Chant to Black Gospel. An Illustrated Guide to All the Major Traditions of Music in Worship* (Minneapolis: Fortress Press, 1996). This is not to suggest that every church should try to incorporate every tradition: there is neither adequate time for, nor wisdom in, such a goal. But if we are to transcend our own cultural confines, we ought to be making a significant attempt to learn the traditions of brothers and sisters in Christ outside our own heritage.

applies both to churches trying to be so contemporary that they project the impression that the church was invented yesterday and to churches locked into a traditional slice that is no less narrow but rather more dated.

11. Numerous matters cry out for articulation in greater detail – the various functions of the Lord's Supper in the New Testament, for example. But the primary focus of this section is to demonstrate and illustrate ways in which the body of believers in corporate worship strives 'to align all the forms of their devout ascription of all worth to God with the panoply of new covenant mandates and examples.'

Properly understood, this takes place 'to bring to fulfilment the glories of antecedent revelation.' In other words, the richest conformity to new covenant stipulation is not some Marcion-like rejection of the Old Testament but the fruit of a biblical-theological reading of Scripture that learns how the parts of written revelation interlock along the path of the Bible's plotline. The result is a greater grasp of what God has revealed and, ideally, a deeper and richer worship of the God who has so wonderfully revealed Himself.

12. At the same time, such worship is an 'anticipation of the consummation'. The climax of the massive theme of worship in the book of Revelation lies in chapters 21–22. The New Jerusalem is built like a cube – and the only cube of which we hear in antecedent Scripture is the Most Holy Place. In other words, the entire city is constantly and unqualifiedly basking in the unshielded glory of the presence of God. There is no temple in that city, for the Lord God and the Lamb are its temple. God's people will see His face. [32]

---

32 cf. N. T. Wright, *For All God's Worth: True Worship and the Calling of the Church* (Grand Rapids: Eerdmans, 1997), 7: 'The great multitude in Revelation which no man can number aren't playing cricket. They aren't going shopping. They are *worshipping.* Sounds boring? If so, it shows how impoverished our idea of worship has become. At the centre of that worship stands a passage like Isaiah 33: your eyes will see the king in his beauty ... the LORD is our judge, the LORD is our ruler, the LORD is our king; he will save us. Worship is the central characteristic of the heavenly life; and that worship is focused on the God we know in and as Jesus.'

But we must conduct ourselves here in the anticipation of this end. Biblically faithful worship is orientated to the end. Even the Lord's Supper is 'until He comes' and thus always an expectation of that coming, a renewal of vows in the light of that coming. As Larry Hurtado has put it:

> More specifically, Christian worship could be re-enlivened and enriched by remembering the larger picture of God's purposes, which extend beyond our own immediate setting and time to take in all human history and which promise a future victory over evil and a consummation of redeeming grace. Apart from a hope in God's triumph over evil, apart from a confidence that Jesus really is the divinely appointed Lord in whom all things are to find their meaning, Christian acclamation of Jesus as Lord is a stupid thing, refuted and mocked by the powerful, negative realities of our creaturehood: the political and economic tyrannies, religious and irreligious forces, and social and cultural developments that make Christian faith seem trivial and our worship little more than a quaint avocation.[33]

SOME PRACTICAL CONCLUSIONS
The brief list in this concluding section is suggestive rather than comprehensive.

1. If the line of argument in this chapter is biblically faithful, we ought to avoid common misunderstandings of worship. Ferguson identifies four of them: an external or mechanical interpretation of worship, an individualistic interpretation, an emotional uplift interpretation and a performance interpretation.[34] We might add

---

33   Larry W. Hurtado, *At the Origins of Christian Worship: The Context and Character of Earliest Christian Devotion* (Grand Rapids: Eerdmans, 1999), 116.

34   Ferguson, *The Church of Christ*, pp. 227-9

interpretations that restrict worship to experiences of cultus and, conversely, interpretations of worship that are so comprehensive that no place whatsoever is left for corporate worship.

2. Hindrances to excellent corporate worship are of various sorts. For convenience, they may be broken into two kinds. On the one hand, corporate worship may be stultified by church members who never pray at home, who come to church waiting to be entertained, who are inwardly marking a scorecard instead of participating in worship, who love mere tradition (or mere innovation!) more than truth, who are so busy that their minds are cluttered with the press of the urgent, who are nurturing secret bitterness and resentments in the dark recesses of their minds.

On the other hand, corporate worship may be poor primarily because of those who are leading. There are two overlapping but distinguishable components. The first is what is actually said and done. That is a huge area that demands detailed consideration, some of which is provided in later chapters. But the second component, though less easily measurable, is no less important. Some who publicly lead the corporate meetings of the people of God merely perform; others are engrossed in the worship of God. Some merely sing; some put on a great show of being involved; but others transparently worship God.

It is worth pausing over this word 'transparently'. By asserting that 'others transparently worship God', I am indicating that to some extent we can observe how well we are being served by those who lead corporate worship: their conduct is 'transparent'. The way they lead must in the first instance be marked by faithfulness to the Word of God: that is certainly observable, in particular to those who know their Bibles well. But the way they lead can be measured not only in terms of formal content but also in terms of heart attitudes that inevitably manifest themselves in talk, body language, focus and style. Some pray with strings of evangelical clichés; some show off with orotund phrasings, others pray to God out of profound personal knowledge and bring the congregation along with them.[35] Some preach without punch; others speak as if delivering the oracles of God.

What is at stake is authenticity. Sooner or later Christians tire of public meetings that are profoundly inauthentic, regardless of how well (or poorly) arranged, directed, performed. We long to meet, corporately, with the living and majestic God and to offer Him the praise that is His due.

3. The question of authenticity in corporate worship intersects with some urgent questions of contemporary evangelism. *First*, one of the passions that shapes the corporate meetings of many churches (especially in the 'seeker-sensitive' tradition) is the concern for evangelism, the concern to tear down barriers that prevent particular people groups from coming and hearing the gospel. The 'homogeneous unit' principle, at one time associated with particular tribes, has now been extended to generations: busters cannot be effectively evangelised with boomers, and so forth. But somewhere along the line we must evaluate what place we are reserving in our corporate life for tearing down the barriers that the world erects – barriers between Jew and Gentile, blacks and whites, boomers and busters. How does our corporate life reflect the one new humanity that the New Testament envisages? Is there not some need for Christians from highly different backgrounds to come together and recite one creed, read from one Scripture, and jointly sing shared songs, thereby crossing race gaps, gender gaps and generation gaps, standing in a shared lineage that reaches back through centuries and is finally grounded in the Word? This does not mean that everything has to be old-fashioned and stodgy. It *does* mean that those in the Reformed tradition

---

35 I am referring now, of course, not to a particular style, but to a Spirit-anointed authenticity that in large part transcends matters of style.

(for instance) do well to wonder now and then what would happen if John Calvin were an 'Xer.'[36]

Second, one of the most compelling witnesses to the truth of the gospel is a church that is authentic in its worship – and here I use the word *worship* in the most comprehensive sense but certainly including corporate worship. A congregation so concerned not to cause offence that it manages to entertain and amuse but never to *worship God* either in the way it lives or in its corporate life carries little credibility to a burned-out postmodern generation that rejects linear thought yet hungers for integrity of relationships. Because we are concerned with the truth of the gospel, we must teach and explain; because we are not simply educating people but seeking to communicate the glorious gospel of Christ, the authenticity of our own relationship with Him, grounded in personal faith and in an awareness not only of sins forgiven and of eternal life but also of the sheer glory and majesty of our Maker and Redeemer, carries an enormous weight.

4. Not every public service can fruitfully integrate everything that the New Testament exemplifies of corporate meetings. Not every meeting will gather around the Lord's Supper, not every meeting will allow for the varied voices of 1 Corinthians 14, and so forth. But that means that, in order to preserve the comprehensiveness of New Testament church life, we need to plan for different sorts of meetings.

5. In every tradition of corporate worship, there are many ways in which a leader may greatly diminish authentic, godly, biblically faithful worship. Those in more liturgical traditions may so greatly rely on established forms that instead of leading the congregation in thoughtful worship of the living God, the entire exercise becomes mechanical and dry, even though the forms are well-loved and well-known

---

36   That line comes from Scot Sherman, 'If John Calvin Were an "Xer".... *Worship in the Reformed Tradition,' regeneration* 3/1 (Winter 1997): pp. 22-5.

expressions that are historically rooted and theologically rich. (Consider the pastor who, right in the middle of holy communion, interrupts his flow to tell the warden to shut a window.) Those in less liturgical traditions may retreat into comfortable but largely boring clichés: the freedom and creativity that is the strength of the 'free church' tradition is squandered where careful planning, prayer and thought have not gone into the preparation of a public meeting. Indeed, such planning may borrow from many traditions. I recently attended a Christmas service in a Reformed Baptist church in which there were not only the traditional Christmas Scripture readings and Christmas carols, but the corporate reading, from the prepared bulletin, of the Nicene Creed, the prayer of confession from Martin Bucer's Strasbourg Liturgy, and a prayer of thanksgiving from the Middleburg Liturgy of the English Puritans.

6. Small ironies are to be found amongst Evangelicals in their practice. Sometimes churches that have the strongest denominational heritage of liturgies and prayer books, aware of the dangers of mere rote, and newly alive to the demands of biblical theology, become the vanguard that warns us against mere traditionalism. Knowing how Old Testament terminology has so often been abused when it has been unthinkingly applied to the church, they become nervous about using the term 'sanctuary' when referring to the biggest room in the church building and will never speak of a 'service'. Conversely, churches from the most independent traditions, aware of the dangers of open-ended subjectivism and spectacularly undisciplined corporate meetings, and newly alive to the glories of public worship as a reflection of entire lives devoted to the living God, incorporate increasing solemnity, liturgical responses, corporate readings, and the like. They do not hesitate to use terms like 'sanctuary' and 'service' – not because they associate such terms with either Old Testament structures

of thought or with sacramentarianism, but (rightly or wrongly) out of respect for tradition.[37]

But perhaps the most intriguing irony is how much the best of the corporate meetings of *both* traditions, matters of terminology aside, resemble each other in what is actually said and done. Nowadays, the actual shape of a Sunday morning 'service' (meeting?) varies more within denominations (from the seeker-sensitive party to the charismatic party to the more Reformed party) than *across* denominations when comparing similar parties. For those (like the writers of this volume) committed to 'worship under the Word', minor differences in terminology and strategy surface here and there, while the fundamental priorities are remarkably similar, as is also the shape of their Sunday morning meetings.

7. Not long ago, after I had spoken on the subject of biblical worship at a large metropolitan church, one of the elders wrote to me to ask how I would try to get across my main points to children (fourth to sixth-graders, approximately ages ten to twelve). He was referring in particular to things I had said about Romans 12:1-2. I responded by saying that kids of that age do not absorb abstract ideas very easily unless they are lived out and identified. The Christian home, or the Christian parent who obviously delights in corporate worship, in thoughtful evangelism, in self-effacing and self-sacrificing decisions within the home, in sacrificial giving for the poor and the needy and the lost – and who then explains to the child that these decisions and actions are part of grati-

---

37 One correspondent pressed further and asked what would happen if we could somehow put all our histories and traditions to one side and begin from scratch, and then tried to label and speak of our corporate life, judging only by the terminology and theology of the New Testament. I take his point – but that is precisely what we cannot do. All of us speak and think and interact within a historical context, a context that needs reforming by the Word but that cannot be ignored. Moreover, I wonder if my interlocutor would like to construct all of his theology without benefit of historical insight, good and bad.

tude and worship to the sovereign God who has loved us so much that He gave His own Son to pay the price of our sin – will have far more impact on the child's notion of genuine worship than all the lecturing and classroom instruction in the world. Somewhere along the line it is important not only to explain that genuine worship is nothing more than loving God with heart and soul and mind and strength and loving our neighbours as ourselves, but also to show what a statement like that means in the concrete decisions of life. How utterly different will that child's thinking be than that of the child who is reared in a home where secularism rules all week but where people go to church on Sunday to 'worship' for half an hour before the sermon. 'Come, let us bow down in worship, let us kneel before the LORD our Maker; for he is our God and we are the people of his pasture, the flock under his care. Today, if you hear his voice, do not harden your hearts' (Ps. 95:6-8).

7

The Pastor and Baptism

A Sacrament of the Covenant of Grace[1]

J.I. PACKER

*Philip Hacking was ordained into a church which practices infant bap-
tism. Over a ministry extending many decades Philip has baptised hun-
dreds of children of believing parents. This was done in good conscience
grounded in solid theology. Today many Evangelicals starting out in
the ordained ministry seem to be less certain. Here Dr J.I. Packer lays
the groundwork for a Reformed theology of infant baptism as a sacrament of the covenant of grace.*

'Such words as stretch, in large characters, from one end of
the chart to the other', said Dupin, 'escape observation by
dint of being excessively obvious.'[2] Some things, in fact, are
too big to be seen. The case of God's covenant with sinners
well illustrates this paradoxical truism. The covenant is
the comprehensive soteriological idea of the Bible. It is
the presupposition, sometimes explicit, always implicit,
of everything that is taught from Genesis to Revelation
concerning redemption and religion, church and sacraments,
and the meaning and goal of history. It integrates these
doctrines into a single unified structure, sets them in their

---

1   This originally appeared as 'Baptism: A Sacrament of the Covenant of
     Grace', in *Churchman* 69/2 1955
2   E. A. Poe, *The Purloined Letter*

true mutual relations and enables the theologian to view them from a proper theocentric standpoint. It is thus the key to biblical theology. Since the apostolic age, however, theologians have generally overlooked it. Only within Reformed Christendom has its centrality received adequate recognition, and there not universally. The Church of England is a Reformed Church; but its seventeenth-century leaders deliberately cut themselves off from the broad stream of Reformed thought, and as a result 'covenant theology' is scarcely known today within the Anglican Communion, even among evangelicals. Perkins, Preston, Sibbes and Bishop Downame, the pioneer Anglican covenant theologians, are forgotten; More and Cross[3] do not even mention them. Usher's Irish Articles and the Westminster Confession, the most explicitly covenantal of all the Reformed creeds, were drawn up by theologians of the Church of England to amplify and make explicit the teaching of the Thirty-Nine Articles,[4] but they have never been treated as part of the Anglican heritage. Among modern evangelicals, Bishop Moule stands almost alone in giving prominence to the covenant idea.[5] The seventeenth-century recoil from the Augustinianism of the

---

3   More and Cross, *Anglicanism: the thought and practice of the Church of England, illustrated from the religious literature of the seventeenth century* S.P.C.K.; Reprinted edition (1962)

4   It is a simple matter of fact that all the English clergymen who sat in the Westminster Assembly were episcopally ordained; most were incumbents at the time; and some conformed in 1662. On their theological ideals, cf. P. Schaff, *History of the Creeds*, p. 761: '(the Westminster Confession) kept in the track of the English Articles of religion, which the Assembly was at first directed to revise, and with which it was essentially agreed. It wished to carry on that line of development which was begun ... by the framers of the Lambeth Articles (1595), and which was continued by Archbishop Usher in the Irish Articles (1615). It was a Calvinistic completion and sharper logical statement of the doctrinal system of the Thirty-Nine Articles.'

5   cf. *Outlines of Christian Doctrine* (1889). pp. 40 ff., 102, and Girdlestone-Moule-Drury, *English Church Teaching* (1897), pp. 55 ff. 'If we would get a right view of Christian life and worship, we need a right view of the COVENANTS' (p. 55).

Reformers on to the semi-Pelagian slippery slope has led to great theological impoverishment. The doctrines of the Church, the Sacraments and the work of the Holy Spirit, have suffered most; and the lost key to their meaning will not be recovered until covenant theology comes into its own in the Church of England. The following article is an essay in the kind of reconstructive work which the writer believes to be urgently needed. It is an attempt to expound the main features of the doctrine of Christian baptism in the light of the covenant idea.

THE COVENANT OF GRACE
We shall briefly examine three topics: (i) the nature of the covenant relationship between God and sinners; (ii) the unity and continuity of God's covenant under its successive editions; (iii) the place of children in that covenant.

The Nature of the Covenant
In the Ancient Near East, any personal bond entered upon by mutual agreement constituted a covenant. The Bible refers to covenants between individuals (1 Sam. 18:3), husband and wife (Mal. 2:14), tribes (Exod. 23: 32), kings (1 Kings 20: 34), king and people (2 Kings 11: 4). Such engagements were normally sealed by a token act in which both parties joined, such as an exchange of gifts (Gen. 21:27), a handshake (Ezek. 17:18), a meal together (Gen. 26:27 ff.) or eating salt (Num. 18: 19, 2 Chron. 13: 5). The essence of the covenant was the relationship which it inaugurated rather than the obligations, if any, that were specified at the time of its making. Covenant obligations were derivative; what was fundamental was the covenant relationship itself. For this reason the word 'contract', which in ordinary speech means simply the acceptance of specific and limited obligations towards each other by parties not otherwise related, does not adequately represent the biblical idea. In the Bible, covenant obligations are limited only by the character of the covenant relation; within that relation they are unlimited. Buber usefully distin-

guishes a covenant between equals, which he terms 'a covenant of brotherhood' from a covenant between unequal parties, such as that which David imposed on the northern tribes (2 Sam. 5:3). Of such a covenant, he writes: 'the relation of overlordship and service, into which the two parties enter, is the decisive factor... I classify this kind of *berith* as the Royal Covenant. It is this kind which YHVH makes with Israel'.[6]

God sums up the terms of His covenant in the words: '*I will be your God, and you shall be my people*'. This covenant 'slogan' is the comprehensive promise which comprises all particular promises; it is related to them as a pantechnicon [Ed: a large moving van] to all that is packed inside it.[7] In these words the covenant was promulgated to Abraham and his seed (Gen. 17: 8-9) and reaffirmed to Moses (Exod. 6:7), and to Israel through Moses (Exod. 29:45, cf. 19: 3-6; Lev. 26: 12), at the time of the Exodus. They were quoted by Jeremiah as expressing the core of the Sinaitic covenant (Jer. 7: 23, cf. Hosea 1:9 ff., 2:23); and also as epitomising the new covenant to which he looked forward, which was to consist in, not a new relation between the people and God, but a more perfect realisation of the old one (Jer. 24:7; 31:1, 33; 32:38; so too Ezek. 11:20; 14:11; 36:28; 37:23, 27 and Zech. 8:8, cf. 13:9). The New Testament proclaims the fulfilment of Jeremiah's prophecy in the Christian church (Heb. 8: 10, cf. 2 Cor. 6: 16), and looks forward to the final realisation of covenant eschatology, and thereby the consummation of the covenant relationship, in the world to come. 'Then I saw a new heaven and a new earth, for the first heaven and the first earth had passed away, and there was no longer any sea. I saw the Holy City, the new

---

6   M. Buber, *Moses*, p. 103

7   cf. Richard Sibbes' comment: 'there is no phrase in Scripture, that hath so much in so little as this. ... All other particular promises in the covenant of grace are members of this. ... This is the first and fundamental promise ... the life and soul of all the promises ...' (*Works*, ed. Grosart, vi. 8). And Calvin: 'These words the prophets habitually expound as comprehending both life, and salvation, and the whole sum of blessedness ... again and again the prophets proclaim that nothing further is needed to bring us the wealth of all blessings and assurance of salvation, if only the Lord is a God to us (*Inst.* II. x. 8).

Jerusalem, coming down out of heaven from God, prepared as a bride beautifully dressed for her husband. And I heard a loud voice from the throne saying, 'Now the dwelling of God is with men, and he will live with them. They will be his people, and God himself will be with them and be their God.' (Rev. 21: 1-3, quoting Ezek. 37: 27 and Lev. 26: 11, 12).

From these passages the character of the relationship becomes clear. Grace and promise on God's side, and faith and hope on man's side, are its keynotes. God inaugurates it by confronting sinners with the announcement that they shall be His and He will be theirs. By designating Himself *their God*, He invites them to enter into union and communion with Himself, assures them that their sins shall be forgiven and forgotten, and promises freely to bestow upon them all that He has to give – in a word, to give them Himself, as a bridegroom gives himself to his bride. By calling them *His people*, He binds them to unconditional and unlimited obedience. His covenant word, 'I will, and you shall,' requires a twofold response: faith, which embraces the covenant and expresses itself in trustful obedience, and hope, which longs and lives for the promised unfolding of the covenant relationship in this world and beyond.

The Bible knows no other basis for religion than God's covenant. Sinners have no natural claim on God's mercy by virtue of being men, as the older Arminians taught; they may not presume on the universal Fatherhood of God, as modern Arminians have supposed; they have no warrant whatsoever for saying 'my God' until God has first said to them 'My people'. The gospel promises, which the church is under orders to proclaim to the world, are to be understood as *covenant* promises, through which God in Christ summons those who before were not a people to become 'His people' (Rom. 9:25, 1 Pet. 2: 10, both quoting Hosea 2:23) and offers Himself to them as 'their God'.

The Unity of the Covenant

What has been said has already shown that God's covenant is substantially the same today as when it was first revealed to

Abraham. Since Christ's coming its implications for blessing have been more clearly known and more of its blessings have become available here and now, but this has in no way affected the character of the relationship itself. Article VII explicitly safeguards this point against Anabaptist denial: 'The Old Testament is not contrary to the New; for in both the Old and New Testament everlasting life is offered to mankind by Christ.... Wherefore they are not to be heard, which feign that the Fathers did look only for transitory promises. ...' The new Marcionism here condemned is still taught by 'dispensationalists' and during the past century has been widely accepted; but the Bible is emphatic that God has never made more than one covenant with fallen man. Two passages out of many must suffice for proof of this: (1) In Galatians 3, Paul takes for granted (i) that God has only ever made one covenant of blessing with sinners: namely, that made with Abraham and his seed; (ii) that the only way of securing blessings from Him is to be one of Abraham's seed and so a legatee under this covenant (vv. 7-9, 29); and (iii) that this covenant conveys, not primarily material benefits (which are not even mentioned in the context) but the spiritual privileges of a present acceptance and family relationship with God (justification and adoption, vv. 8, 26), and a consequent title to the inheritance laid up for God's people (v. 29, 4:7). On this basis he argues to show that the Mosaic law, so far from annulling the covenant promises (v. 17-18) or opening an alternative way of salvation apart from them (v. 21), was promulgated for the sole purpose of impelling sinners to faith in them (vv. 22-24); and that Gentiles become Abraham's seed and beneficiaries under the covenant, not by practising works of law, but by following Abraham's faith (vv. 6-14, 26-29). (2) The Epistle to the Hebrews takes it for granted that from the dawn of history till now God's covenant has always been the same thing: a summons to trustful, obedient fellowship with God in this world together with a promise of reward in 'a better country, that is an heavenly' at the end of this pilgrimage. The whole eleventh chapter shows this, as does the assertion that the oath with which God confirmed His promise to Abraham was intended to strengthen not merely Abraham's faith but also that of Christian believers, who are heirs of the same promise (6:13-18). In chapters 7–10, the writer contrasts the two systems that God has revealed for the implementing of that part of the covenant promise which concerned communion with Him on earth: the Mosaic, which bore from the outset the marks of its own imperfection and provisional character, and the Christian, which has now replaced it. We must not be misled by the fact that he speaks of two 'covenants', the first and the second, the old and the new: this is simply a reflection of Old Testament usage, in which the word 'covenant' acquired an institutional significance and became 'the formula designating the entire structure and content of the religion of Israel'.[8] The two 'covenants' are two successive systems, the first typifying the second, for the realisation of the selfsame covenant privilege – present fellowship between God's people and Himself. So far from throwing doubt on the unity and continuity of the covenant promise, the contrast thus presupposes and confirms it.[9]

Children and the Covenant

God entailed His covenant upon Abraham *and his seed* (Gen. 17:7-8), and accordingly required the circumcision

---

8 G. Vos, in Hastings' *DCG*, l. 373, col. 2

9 Limitations of space preclude any treatment of the passages in which Paul opposes the Mosaic law to the gospel, describing it as a covenant of works which brings bondage and death (cf. Gal. 4:21 ff., 2 Cor. 3, etc.). It must suffice to say that these passages are arguments *ad hominem*, in which he accepts *pro tempore* the evaluation of the Law as a self-sufficient covenant of life which Judaism by its rejection of Christ had given it, and devotes himself simply to proving that those who treat it as such will find that it leads to death, for they will in fact break it and thus incur its curse. The ease with which he slips into this line of thought reflects his years of controversy in Jewish synagogues. We have already seen that in his own view the Law was not given to be a covenant of life at all.

of all his male descendants at the first convenient moment (i.e., when eight days old) as 'a token of the covenant' (v. 11) between Himself and them. The covenant thus confirmed the solidarity of the family, making it a spiritual as well as a social and economic unit. Abraham's descendants were henceforth born into a covenant relation with God, and were by virtue of their parentage heirs of the promises pertaining to that relation. They could repudiate the covenant at age by unbelief, and forfeit their inheritance by refusing to claim it; but until they thus 'contracted out' and renounced their hereditary rights, God was and would remain 'their God'.

Abraham, his son, and his male retainers, were all marked with the covenant sign, as a token of their reception into covenant status (vv. 23-27). Thus they became the foundation members of a community which has continued from that day to this without a break – the *visible church*, the fellowship which professes to embrace and live under God's covenant.

When on the day of Pentecost Peter announced that the long-awaited Messianic kingdom and outpouring of the Spirit had at last begun, he took pains to make it clear that the status of children in the covenant had not been in any way affected by the dawning of the New Age. 'The promise (sc., of a complete and final remission of all sins and the present gift of the Spirit) is to you *and to your children*' (Acts 2:39). The blessings of the New Age, like every other good thing which the covenant relationship involved, would belong by hereditary right to the children of those who by faith received these gifts for themselves. Similarly, in 1 Cor. 7:14 Paul assured his Gentile readers that the 'birth-privilege' of Abraham's lineal seed was now extended to their own children. The fact that one of his parents was a Christian constituted a child 'holy' (*hagios*): that is to say, if one parent was *hagios*, i.e. related to God in covenant (the word implies this), the child was born into that same status. 'Since the wall of partition is broken down, the same covenant of salvation which was made with Abraham and his posterity is communicated to us' (Calvin, *ad loc.*). We conclude, then, that the covenant status and privilege of believers' children has been unaffected by the transition from the Mosaic to the Christian era.

We have not exhausted the doctrine of the covenant. We have not even mentioned its objective basis in God's election and Christ's mediatorial ministry, nor the Holy Spirit's work in conveying its benefits to the individual with and by the Word; we have only hinted at the doctrine of the church, the covenant community, and we have by no means fully defined the relation between the 'Old' and 'New' covenants. But we have said enough to lay the foundation for a study of the initiatory sacraments of the covenant, and to these we now turn.

BAPTISM

We saw that in Old Testament times covenants between man and man were normally ratified by a symbolic action in which both parties joined. God's covenant with Abraham and his seed was sealed in the same way, by the rite of circumcision. The covenant sign was changed to baptism when the Mosaic economy gave way to the Christian (cf. Matt. 28:19). Accordingly, the New Testament, while attributing to both signs the same significance, treats circumcision as the sign of a bygone economy, to which Christians may not return. Circumcision marked the pre-Christian era of waiting and hoping; baptism proclaims the fulfilment of Old Testament hopes in the coming of Christ, and by its symbolism bears witness to the objective ground of the bestowal of all covenant blessings, now for the first time made known: namely, union with Christ in the death and resurrection to which His own representative baptism in Jordan had testified and committed Him.

The Bible accords to each of these rites, as administered to adults, a threefold significance: (i) They assure the believer of his covenant status and hope. God instituted circumcision as 'a token of the covenant' between Himself and Abraham (Gen. 17: 11). Paul merely interprets this statement when he calls the rite 'a sign or seal of the righteousness which he had by faith' (Rom.4:11, RSV.); for justification, which to Paul meant both non-imputation of sins (v. 7-8) and acceptance by God as a son and heir (Gal. 3:24-26), is the first and fundamental covenant blessing and the pledge of all the rest (cf. Rom. 5: 9-10). Similarly, Paul appeals to baptism as a God-given proof of the covenant status of Gentile believers. To a church inclined to suppose that covenant status could only be gained by circumcision, he wrote: 'You are all sons of God through faith in Christ Jesus, for all of you who were baptised into Christ have clothed yourselves with Christ (i.e., baptism sealed and declared your union with Him).... If you belong to Christ, then you are Abraham's seed (sc., in Him), and heirs according to the promise.'(Gal. 3:26-9) Because both signs assure the believer that God is in very truth 'his God', the mere possession of them has always tempted hypocrites to suppose that He must be 'their God' too. We find Paul exploding such groundless optimism, however, with reference both to circumcision (Rom. 2:25-9) and to baptism (1 Cor. 10: 1 ff.).

(ii) They visibly represent to the recipients the blessings, obligations and character of the covenant which they seal. Both witness to the remission of sins and *justification* (cf. Rom. 4:11; Acts 2:38; 22:16). Both, again, signify *regeneration*. Circumcision is taken in the Old Testament to represent God's gracious work of renewing and purifying the heart (Deut. 30:6). This, Paul affirms (Col. 2: 11-12) is the 'circumcision made without hands', 'the circumcision of Christ,' which God effects by uniting believers to Christ in His death and resurrection: a union which baptism symbolises. Again, the symbolism of each sign summons its recipients to a new life of holiness. Circumcision told the Jew that he must purify his heart (Deut. 10:16, Jer. 4:4); baptism tells the Christian that he must die to sin and rise to righteousness (Rom. 6:1-13). Moreover, both are eschatological symbols, sealing God's covenant promise (cf. Ezek. 36: 26-28) that He will work in His people the new obedience to which He binds them (Deut. 30:6, Rom. 6:5); thus the symbols oblige and encourage their recipients to hope in God for *sanctification* and *glorification*. Finally, we must note that the manner of their administration bears witness to the gracious character of the covenant. As in its conclusion it is God who acts, confronting the sinner with His word of promise and command for acceptance or rejection, so in its sealing the candidate is passive, merely accepting what his Creator imposes, while God acts through the officiant to mark him out as His own. Nobody in the Bible baptises or circumcises himself. Both sacraments thus proclaim the gracious initiative of God.

(iii) As ceremonies of initiation, they admit to membership of the visible covenant community, to which one may not belong without them. In Genesis 17: 14, God enacts that 'Any uncircumcised male, who has not been circumcised in the flesh, will be cut off from his people; he has broken my covenant'. Accordingly, we find that when the covenant sign was changed converts were received into the visible church by baptism immediately upon their professing faith (Acts 2:41; 16:33, etc.). The New Testament nowhere suggests any relaxation of God's categorical demand that all church members should be marked with the covenant sign.

Two corollaries may be briefly drawn from what has been said.

(1) The ground and necessity of baptising the infants of Christian parents now becomes clear. The *ground* of the practice is the fact that from the moment of birth these children share their parents' covenant status. The covenant sign, therefore, has the same significance when administered to them as it

has for adult converts: it does not create, but confirms and attests a status and relationship which is already theirs on other grounds. The adult enjoys it by reason of his own faith; the Christian's child, by reason of his parentage. The child possesses the thing signified; he has, therefore, a right to the sign which confirms him in possession of it. The necessity of the practice derives from the fact that when God announced the covenant of grace to Abraham He commanded that all his male descendants, as members of the covenant, should be marked with the covenant sign in infancy and thus be formally admitted to junior membership of the church. As we saw, the New Testament teaches that the covenant sign has since been altered, the sphere of the covenant extended to cover the whole Gentile world and the blessings of the church on earth increased; but it nowhere suggests that God has changed the rule which He originally laid down concerning infant church membership. If ever there was a speaking silence, it is the silence of the New Testament at this point. It can mean only one thing: that the *status quo ante* remains. The proof-text for the baptism of Christians' children is thus Genesis 17:10: 'This is my covenant with you and your descendants after you, the covenant you are to keep: Every male among you shall be circumcised'. Since God spoke these words to Abraham, baptism has replaced circumcision as the covenant sign and the distinction between male and female has ceased to be relevant to the possession and sealing of covenant status;[10] the command therefore to the Christian church now reads: 'Every infant among you shall be baptised.' Infant baptism is thus the will of God. It

---

10 In the Old Testament church, women were counted as partakers of the covenant, and so as circumcised, by virtue of their marital or blood relationship to male covenant members. This appears from the fact that women ate the Passover, which no uncircumcised person shall eat (Exod. 12:48); and that the circumcising of all the males is spoken of as the circumcising of 'all the people' (Josh. 5:8). But in the New Testament women are baptised on their own profession of faith just as men are (Acts 16:15). cf. Galatians 3:28.

is not merely legitimate; it is obligatory. Christians' children are to be enrolled as junior church members by means of the regular ceremony of admission. There is nothing in the Bible more certain than this. There is no Scriptural warrant *at all* for infant baptism if the continuity of the covenant be denied; but, once it is admitted, infant baptism is so unassailably established as to make further argument superfluous.

(2) It is now clear also what conception should be formed of the *efficacy* and *use* of baptism. Baptism is the word of the covenant made visible and seeking admission to the mind through 'eye-gate', and it is a means of grace, as is the word preached and heard, because it is a means to *faith*. God designed and uses it to confirm faith in those who have it and to awaken faith in those baptised as infants (cf. Art. XXV). In the latter case, of course, the intended effect is conditional upon the meaning of the sacrament being explained to the child. 'Faith comes by hearing'; and a sacrament that is never explained is of necessity inefficacious. Rightly understood, however, baptism has a lifelong efficacy and use, as an assurance and an incentive. 'As often as we fall,' wrote Calvin, 'we should recall our baptism, and thereby fortify our mind, so that it may be sure and certain of the remission of our sins' (*Inst.* IV. xv.3). And the thought of the promises and obligations which baptism sealed as his should constantly spur the Christian to faith, obedience, hope and love. We may conclude by quoting further from Calvin's masterly exposition of the right use and true benefit of this covenant sacrament: 'We should receive it as from the hand of its author,' he writes: 'we ought to be firmly convinced that it is he himself who speaks to us through the sign; he who washes and cleanses us, and puts out of mind our failings; he who makes us partakers of his death, destroys the kingdom of Satan and breaks the power of sin; he who, moreover, makes us one with himself, so that, clothed with him, we are accounted children of God. We should be as

certain, I say, that he brings these benefits to our souls, as we are that we see our bodies washed, immersed, and surrounded by water ... it is a most certain rule concerning sacraments, that in the material objects we should discern spiritual benefits, just as if they were actually set before our eyes. ... Not that these gracious gifts are so bound up with and tied to the sacrament as to be conferred upon us by its own efficacy; the fact is simply that by this token the Lord declares to us that it is his will and pleasure to bestow them all upon us. Nor is it with an empty spectacle that he feeds our gaze; but he leads us to the actual object signified, and effectively fulfils in us that which he represents before us' (*Inst.* IV. xv. 14).

8

The Pastor and Church Planting

FRANK RETIEF

While at Christ Church, Fulwood, Philip Hacking was never directly involved in church planting, although he did encourage local church planting initiatives. It can also be said that he left a legacy which has enabled Christ Church to plant several times over. Frank Retief, who himself is a 'long-stay' pastor like Philip Hacking, and who also like Philip was blessed to experience remarkable church growth, shares his own experience and reflections on this important subject.

I have nothing new to add to the current discussion on evangelism and church planting. It is true that my wife and I planted a church in Cape Town and were instrumental from that church in assisting with the establishment of many other churches, but the truth is that we were utterly clueless in those days and feel even in these days bewildered by the many resources, programmes, personnel and methodologies in regard to church planting today. Even now, looking back over the many years, we wonder why things worked out at all when by all the law of averages, nothing should have. So after all the activities, rushing about, planning and discussions that took place in our early years, we stand ultimately in awe at the grace of God and convinced that God calls His church into being often in spite of us and not because of us.

The only reason I agreed to write this chapter was because of the kindness and prompting of my dear friend Melvin Tinker and my respect for him and, of course, overwhelming respect for Philip Hacking.

I have decided that the best way for me to express myself on the matter of the ministry and churchplanting is simply to tell our own story. After all, that's all I have to go on. So here goes.

In spite of our own early ineptitude I remain so very grateful for the joy and privilege of seeing not one, but several churches started from scratch. With no knowledge, training, nor in those long-ago days, any manuals or dossiers to help us, I nevertheless had several things working for me. Firstly, I had a great wife who was totally given to ministry. Beulah is gentle, uncritical and wonderfully hospitable, so our home was always full of people. Secondly, God granted us unshakeable faith in the gospel. We really believed that the message would result in converts. We expected people to be converted. Thirdly, the Holy Spirit was with us, which is a very good thing indeed. What pity God had on our early, clumsy attempts to evangelise and witness. How easily the whole thing could have been derailed by unwise actions, utterances or plans. You, gentle reader, can have no idea of how raw and ignorant we were!

New churches are being planted all over. Many people establish churches virtually on each other's doorsteps and if these churches are indeed repositories of the gospel, I rejoice. There are enough unsaved people in any community for all these churches. But I have noticed that evangelical churches which adhere to a Reformation theology sometimes appear hesitant and reluctant, not only in church planting, but also in general evangelistic zeal, courage and activity, and seem sometimes to lack the in-your-face zeal of many of their counterparts.

But while some of us continue to struggle with the idea of church planting, the cults, sects and other religions just do it. Note the increase in Kingdom Halls, mosques and temples around the place, as well as school halls, factory shops and industrial buildings being turned into churches of various shapes, sizes and ethnic diversities.

I am grateful to God for the new churches that have been planted in my part of the world and also admire the new leaders for these churches that have been raised up. But amongst these churches there are increasing danger signs because many of the new leaders have no track record in pastoral work, no mentoring abilities and no theological training. God can use anyone and often does use clueless people to accomplish His plans, but I think that church planting is better accomplished when certain basic criteria are in place.

My wife Beulah and I had been married for seven months and were happily settled into a curacy when I was told to pack my bags and head from Durban to Cape Town to a suburb called Kenilworth, and there we were to establish a new congregation in some run-down old buildings which our denomination had purchased. In the 1960s South Africa was in the grip of apartheid politics and Kenilworth was one of its victims. Kenilworth had been a working-class, mixed-race community until people of colour were told to move. One can only imagine the upheaval and heartache involved. When Beulah and I arrived the suburb was in sad decay. Many of the original residents had not moved. Huge building projects for new trendy apartments were under way and the place was in a state of transition. The old buildings we were given were in an unbelievable state of dereliction.

But we were glad to be back. Kenilworth was very familiar to us. Beulah grew up in the region and we did all our courting there. We knew the place well. Furthermore, we were too young, inexperienced and too clueless to be nervous. We thought it perfectly normal to try to gather people around us and try to win them for Christ.

Beulah and I did what we were best at, at that stage – working with children. Soon we had children's clubs and Sunday schools operating. We then moved to church services. We had worked hard to clean up the decrepit buildings, and twenty-two adults came to our first adult church service. Eight of them were friends and well-wishers from our mother church, the rest formed our core adult group of contacts.

For the following thirty years we threw ourselves with abandon into this new work. Nothing was too much trouble. From door-to-door work, to special events, to creative leaflets and handouts, to music, church fairs and regular evangelistic exercises. Our main aim in all these activities was to see people converted, and by God's grace that is exactly what happened.

Four years after we started we had a congregation of about 250 people. We decided to hire a larger local venue for evangelistic meetings. In a wonderful way God met with us and we went through a period of remarkable conversions and special blessings.

We had such remarkable blessing in our evangelistic efforts that we ended up hiring the largest venues in Cape Town and going to the most unlikely places to evangelise. We let nothing stand in our way. We seemed to have been given a courage beyond ourselves, a blatancy and cheekiness in our requests for venues, a direct, take-all-consequences attitude in our preaching and presentation. We took no arguments but demanded that all people bow the knee to the Lord Jesus Christ.

After two years of this special evangelistic activity we had large crowds from all over the city and indeed from the rest of the country areas as well. When we moved from the hired venues back to our own building, people were unable to fit into our church in spite of several rebuilding projects and it soon became apparent to us that we would need to split off sections of the congregation. We did this by identifying people who were attending our church from new growing suburbs. We called for a special meeting with them and asked them to partner with us in an effort to establish a church where they were living. We asked for a home where we could start. Then we moved to nearby schools while actively seeking out land that we could purchase. Afterwards we raised funds for building.

Not once did we have the money to buy the land, and the congregation had to make it a matter of fervent prayer. To this day I do not know where we got the money, although our denomination helped us out from time to time, nor do I know how anything was accomplished. No-one was experienced in these matters, and I was personally overwhelmed by the numbers of people attending our church and the need to provide services for them in their own areas where they lived. We were flying by the seat of our pants. However, we had a hand in establishing about twenty churches in this manner. We always provided first for the children, then looked for space to accommodate all other people and activities. We hired people as we went along – pastors, counsellors, children's workers, youth workers, administrators – and not once did we have the money in the bank to pay them the salary we promised them. Yet we were able to support them all.

Looking back on my own experience, there are some things that now stand out in sharp relief to me which were not always evident at the time.

But I first need to pause at this point and admit to feeling like a great fraud in telling this story. I always fear it will come across as prescriptive when it is not meant to be so or that it will appear as self-promotion when it is not. We truly experienced an unusual era in the life of our church. It was exhausting, baffling, nerve-racking at times but it was overwhelmingly exhilarating. I often think about the man who is battling away in a plant somewhere where this kind of success or experience eludes him. Is his work any less valuable? Absolutely not!

In our case we enjoyed a period of great unique blessing. The Holy Spirit was among us and WE DO NOT CONTROL

THAT. But it happened. It was our experience, which is why I am rather reluctant to talk about church growth and evangelism. I really know nothing about it except the unusual way we experienced it. Our blessing does not correspond to the experience of many other faithful men and women labouring away at a church plant and seeing little for their effort, or experiencing only slow growth. I admire them. They are heroes and should never give up the fight. The little book by McKinley[1] is a great tonic for church planters and describes an experience the opposite of mine and probably more realistic for others.

We were also blessed to be part of a small Anglican denomination which was large-hearted and visionary. The trustees of our denomination got behind several of our efforts and have consistently encouraged church planting by making funds available ever since. Sometimes these funds came by way of an outright grant but more often it was by enabling us to borrow money at a greatly reduced interest rate.

There were three things I was sure of when we started our own church plant. The first was that hell and judgment were ultimate realities. The second was that heaven was the final destination of all true believers, and the third was that the crucified and risen Christ made the difference between the two. Thus we were seized with a sense of urgency in our talking with people and our teaching and preaching. Everything we did was done with the consciousness that an eternal soul was at stake. So although we made many mistakes along the way our mistakes were mistakes of zeal rather than spiritual lethargy or reluctance.

We were very fortunate to be provided with a building right from the outset. It wasn't much of a building but it was a start. As our congregation grew we were able to buy up property around us that formed part of the 'decayed and

---

1   Mike McKinley, *Church Planting Is for Wimps: How God Uses Messed-up People to Plant Ordinary Churches That Do Extraordinary Things* (Crossway Books, 2010).

condemned' buildings in our area. We bought fairly cheaply and dolled them up.

I often have heard people say that they do not need a building if they can use hired premises. Some have told me they would rather put their money into staff or missions. This is most laudable but it is in my view a basic mistake. Any enterprise needs a physical headquarters. Even the early churches met in the temple before they met in homes – and eventually caves. At least the cave was a place with a roof! We all need somewhere to meet. If you continue with hired premises perpetually, several things are bound to happen.

a. Your lease is only as good as your relationship with the owner. If the building is old or your relationship changes, you could have a problem.

b. You put a cap on your growth. If you are in a school and are using school rooms or classrooms, it is only a matter of time before a teacher becomes unhappy, or the Sunday school children themselves grow up to be unhappy. When children are very small it may be fine, but sooner or later the venue will fall into disfavour with the youth.

c. If you stay in hired premises, you are making a statement about your permanency. You are saying 'Hi everybody, come to us. See! We are meeting in this lovely school hall. The school is very good to us, but we don't know how long we will be able to meet here, but come and join us anyway!' Now, certain people may be willing to go along with you but eventually thinking people will say, 'This place is going nowhere. I'm out of here.'

Parents want to know that the church is there to stay; that it can be depended on; and that the premises are reasonable. They want to drive down the street and say to a friend 'That's my church!' Besides, the ongoing life of the church, if the church is doing the job well, deserves its own premises sooner or later.

I am aware that for some churches there may be no option but the rented space they occupy. We had that very problem with several of our church plants. Looking for a venue of our own became a great headache. But when the decision to stay in rented premises becomes the philosophy of ministry I think it is a mistake.

d. You will become more of a witness in the community when you signal to them that you are here to stay, by eventually buying a building or venue. This is, of course, dependent on circumstances and I do not mean to downplay the provision of at least a school. Our churches have met in schools and sometimes in Seventh-Day Adventists churches – but we always had the goal to move to our own premises.

This brings me back to the mother church. A church that is involved in church planting has to be willing to pay the price for that enterprise.

Firstly, it's a shock the Sunday after you have planted a church, to discover the empty pews back in the mother church. Unless you are convinced of the need to win people for Christ in the place you planted, you can quickly fall into panic.

Secondly, your finances will take a hammering for a while because the new church will put their money into a new bank account yet the mother church will hopefully supervise these matters, at least for a while, and make sure that the man put in charge of the plant is paid. So finance can be rocky initially, and the devil is quick enough to zero in on that and can make it the cause of friction. Watch out! Do not lose heart. The empty pews will soon be full again.

Thirdly, the new church plant may need help with its administration. The mother church cannot leave it to flounder. New leadership needs help, and new wardens and elders need to understand what their job is. Church leaders do not learn by osmosis! They need to be taught what it means to be a leader.

The dynamic that lies behind building a church, revitalising a church or planting a church is *Evangelism*. This word has lost much of its meaning these days. Who today speaks about 'winning souls'? We sometimes shudder when we hear that kind of talk. We are far more into 'holistic' ministry, concerned about bodies as well as souls. And so we should be. Therefore, churches fall over themselves today to show compassion for the poor and it seems we lose all credibility if we are not seen in some way to be involved socially both at home and abroad.

At least that is the way it is where I live. We have huge poverty issues in South Africa which is a very unequal society. There are many shanty townships and, as the world knows, HIV AIDS is a pandemic. So to feed the hungry, visit the sick, provide for the poor, minister in prisons as well as care for child-headed families – not to mention the crime victims that abound – is all part of normally healthy church work.

Here too I realise that different parts of the world have different problems but for us here in South Africa there is never a day when a sincere Christian needs to wake up in the morning and say, 'I have nothing to do today.' South Africa is full of opportunities to do gospel work.

But having said that, I submit that sometimes overwhelming, in-your-face needs can be so hard to bear emotionally that the work of 'saving souls' may become trite, sidelined and irrelevant.

We must be on guard. We should help all we can to display the love of Christ but we must never forget that the sufferers have souls that need to be saved. One of our churches in Pinetown, in the province of Kwazulu/Natal, once bought a house which took in sixteen men at a time who were in the last stages of full-blown AIDS. They usually had about two weeks to live. They were cared for and eventually died with dignity. But the church also hired a full-time African pastor who could speak the language, whose sole job day after day was to go from bed to bed to talk to the men about their souls, their faith in Christ and their eternal destiny.

That work has now grown into a state-of-the-art ministry to children who were orphaned by AIDS. It is called Lily of the Valley and can be checked out on the web.

Yes, we must not forget people have souls. Didn't Someone say 'What good is it for a man to gain the whole world, yet forfeit his soul? Or what can a man give in exchange for his soul?' Therefore I submit that it is indeed people's souls that must be saved. Jesus seemed to think so. (Mark 8:37)

If we are evangelicals we must be evangelistic as well. We cannot merely pay lip service to evangelism. If there is indeed a judgment to come and a place of final, dreadful separation from God – if it is true that faith in Christ makes the difference – we must be urgent, sincere and winsome to unbelievers. If there is no such judgment or hell, then why bother? But if there is, how can any minister not feel the weight of that upon him? Thus church planting comes out of a prior dynamic to evangelise.

Not only so but surely an evangelistic burden touches the hearts of all in the pews. The whole congregation picks up the cue from the pulpit. The intuition to evangelise catches on. Soon everybody in the pew is asking other people whether they are Christians. The leadership of the church sets them an example and a new vibe is created in the church. Evangelism done carefully, zealously, with humility and love, creates a happy congregation. They take fresh joy when the cross is preached. They embrace Christ all over again when His glory, especially in His suffering, is set before them. Now their spontaneous love, joy and zeal accompanies <u>a church plant out of a mother church</u> which models that.

In regard to evangelism J.I. Packer quotes Harry Boer as showing that 'the mainspring of evangelism among Christians was the naturalness of sharing Christ with one's neighbour out of sheer inner excitement over the new life of hope one had found.' This is exactly true. We should pray that God would raise up new converts who will be overwhelmed by their conversion and full of joy, as opposed to 'new converts' who are filled with doubt about what happened to them and need a six-week course to explain it to them.

Of course, I know very well not all our churches are planted like that. There are a million ways in which a church may be planted. I have often met, talked to, or been in churches planted by one zealous African man with no backing from anybody. Furthermore, anybody with a computer will sooner or later receive emails from someone in a Third-World country eliciting funds for some ministry they have started. Although we would be very careful before we responded, it is nevertheless an indication of how far and wide the gospel is spreading in our time, often without the help of any outsider and in all sorts of communities. But usually in my experience churches are planted by a mother church and all sorts of responsibilities follow.

For anyone engaging in church planting, evangelism or even in the ordinary routine of daily ministry in a local church, we should always remember that Jesus is presented to us in the Gospels as the One who is calling out from His own Jewish community a new people who will believe in Him as the Messiah and the redeeming Lord. Jesus said in John 12:32, 'But I, when I am lifted up from the earth, will draw all men to myself.'

Jesus also said in John 6:44 'No-one can come to me unless the Father who sent me draws him, and I will raise him up at the last day.'

And in Acts, Saul of Tarsus is confronted by none other than this same Jesus the crucified, risen and enthroned Lord who calls Paul to Himself and gives him his new instructions.

Furthermore, it doesn't take much reading in Acts to discover that the new believers were not only those who were the Lord's disciples, or who belonged to 'The Way' (Acts 9:2, 31), but are also presented as the community of the Holy Spirit. The Holy Spirit moved amongst them, filled them with joy and enabled them to witness to the gospel. The story of Stephen illustrates this truth (Acts 6:5 ff).

J.I. Packer writes that the 'Holy Spirit's true work is to lead sinners to Christ and through Christ to God; to make individual believers Christlike in love, humility, righteousness and patience....'. David Wells goes on to say that taking the Holy Spirit seriously means that Christians 'must rediscover the naturalness of three things that modern believers in the West rarely see as natural, namely worship, evangelism and suffering'.[2] And I would add spontaneous joy!

This is a great relief to all engaged in ministry today. To attempt to plant a church in a new area and to preach the Gospel is simply to be the voice of Christ who calls people to Himself. When this dawned on me it gave me greater liberty in preaching and in being definite about the great Christian basics, because I knew that God would save those whom God had given to Christ. I assumed that everyone would be among the elect of God. We do the preaching, witnessing and teaching, and God does the electing and the saving.

CONVERSIONS TRUE AND FALSE
However amongst the early conversions, both in my own church and also in the daughter churches with which we were involved, I soon discovered that all was not gold that glitters, as not all people were truly converted to Christ, even though they said 'Lord! Lord!' Even in the experience of the early church they had false conversions and needed both discernment and protection. Take, for instance, the two ac-

---

2   David F. Wells, *God the Evangelist: How the Holy Spirit Works to Bring Men and Women to Faith* (Paternoster, 1997), p. 13.

counts in Acts chapter 8 of two different conversions. One was Simon the Sorcerer who, '....himself believed and was baptised' (v. 13). Yet when confronted by the apostle Peter he was told '......your heart is not right before God' (v. 21). All of us in ministry have had experiences of this nature that have disappointed us. But then there is the account of the Ethiopian eunuch who said 'How can I understand (the Scriptures) unless someone explains it to me?' Whereupon Philip obliged and 'began at the very passage of Scripture (Isa. 53) and told him of the good news about Jesus (v. 35), and 'he went on his way rejoicing' (v. 39).

The true and the false often confront us side by side as we do gospel work and special grace is needed when planting new churches, to recognise this fact.

The fact is it would do us all the world of good to remember that often 'conversions' are not conversions to Christ but it may be conversion to something else. For instance, someone may be 'converted' to the minister, the church, the music, the vibe of the church, or to some sentimental resonance with their own culture – but not to Christ.

Sometimes that conversion can be a step towards a real, true, final conversion to Christ as in the case of C.S. Lewis. He describes his conversion in his book, *Surprised by Joy*.[3] The oft-quoted words are at the end of chapter 14 where he describes himself as being 'the most dejected and reluctant convert in all England'. But many people omit the opening words of his next chapter:

'It must be understood that the conversion recorded in the last chapter was only to Theism, pure and simple, not to Christianity. I knew nothing yet about the Incarnation. The God to whom I surrendered was sheerly non-human.'

---

3   C.S. Lewis, *Surprised by Joy* (Collins, 2012), pp. 266-7

For Lewis it was a step in the right direction but it was not the final thing. And so it may be with many of the people with whom we work.

On the other hand, their 'conversion' may not be real at all and as time goes by 'the devil takes away the word from their heart', or they have no root as they are choked by life's worries, riches and pleasures – to quote Luke 8:12-14. Their conversion evaporates into thin air.

So church planting requires patience, discernment and evidence. We need the power and the presence of the Holy Spirit and a true commitment to the gospel of Christ.

We may be disappointed but we should not be shocked. After all we remember the sad events in Genesis chapter 3. The world is fallen, it is in darkness. It is hostile to God, at enmity with Him. The world lies in the arms of the evil one. We should not be shocked by false conversions. They will happen. Very great power is needed to turn a man or woman, teenager, even an impressionable child to Christ. Greater power than any of us can produce. A great supernatural power has to be exercised upon people to awaken them spiritually and to release them from the grip of Satan and sin.

A missionary friend of ours serves in Sendai, Japan. During the recent earthquake and tsunami his car was wrenched from his hands by the water while he was trying to secure it with ropes. He and his wife worked hard amongst the survivors bringing relief, love and friendship. He also kept witnessing to Christ. He wrote in his newsletter, 'In spite of the earthquake and the tsunami the people remain spiritually unaffected. It takes a power greater than an earthquake to awaken sleeping souls.'

STATEMENTS OF FAITH

All new churches need to be instructed in what Christians believe. If the church is planted by a mother church that is part of a congregation that has established creeds and statements of faith, the battle is half won. Over a period of time the leader needs to instruct the new people in what they stand for. The need for clarity in biblical matters is illustrated by Paul's appeal to the elders in Jerusalem after constant battling with those who undermined the gospel of grace alone (Acts 15). A clear and authoritative foundation needs to be laid. Be sure that in every new baby church there will be somebody who will challenge the status quo. If the new church's belief system is not in place it can cause much heartache. If the person in charge of the plant is not clear or does not give a strong lead, the new church could be in for a rocky ride. Hence the need not only for clarity of creeds but also strong and, if possible, theologically trained men. Instructed leadership who will be able to lead the congregation through water that may occasionally be very troubled is a huge need in many a church.

GENERAL METHODOLOGY
In my view the best form of church planting is that in which a mother church plants a daughter church or several daughter churches in a responsible and committed manner. This is sure to happen if there is a generally strong evangelistic vision and fervour in the church. But I realise only too well that it often does not work out that way. Currently my daughter and son-in-law are in a Scandinavian country trying to plant a new church in a dormitory town. They are laypeople and the going is hard. There are no churches in the town that take even the remotest interest in them and what they are trying to do. There is no clear gospel focus for miles around. There are no older people or clergy who clearly understand their plans or motives. In addition they both need to work to keep the family going and also need time to raise their two children.

Ideally they need a mother church to adopt them, but there is none. So they labour on in prayer and hard work, often discouraged but not giving up. Fortunately in their case they have many good friends in other places who take a real interest in them, and they can occasionally visit England and its many conferences, which helps to refresh them. But what of those who do not have even that relief? There is no simple answer. There must be a heavy dependence on the Holy Spirit and an ongoing commitment to preach the word of the gospel.

So to conclude, my own experiences of church planting have been happy ones. Furthermore, some of our daughter churches have planted their own churches. I think the mother/daughter way is the best way forward.

But for many people that option does not exist. Nor do they see immediate blessing as we were privileged to do. These church planters should be treated as heroes. They should be encouraged and supported and if possible adopted by some church. In one instance, my church offered to assist a Baptist church and helped it to form a new church. In my view church planting arises out of a committed and spontaneous sense of love for Christ and belief that people without Christ are eternally lost. People in churches who are convinced of these things will immediately begin to witness and evangelise. Out of that, new churches will be born.

When a church is born there needs to be constant mentoring and support. The new church will need good leadership, financial help and a philosophy of ministry that includes on its agenda a building of its own. The mother church must also provide wise leaders to protect the new church from bad people and wrong decisions. The minister and leadership of the mother church should be generous in spirit and unaffected by large chunks of Sunday congregations going with the new plant. The mother church's own ministry will soon fill those pews again.

Those who start the plant should be godly, committed and courageous. All these things grow as time goes by but there must be a measure of it with which to begin.

I have nothing more to add. I am sure there are a million new churches out there whose pattern of development is completely different to what I have outlined in this chapter. Still, this is my story, and I'm sticking to it!

9

The Pastor and Church Growth

DAVID HOLLOWAY

During his long pastorate at Christ Church, Fulwood, Philip Hacking saw remarkable growth. By the time he retired, his church membership was over 1,000. His ministry took place within the context of the Church of England parish system, although many attended Christ Church from well beyond the local parish. What is more, Philip was committed to the growth of the church nationally and worldwide. The former was in part expressed through his chairmanship of Reform, an evangelical movement within the Church of England and its aim of winning the nation for Christ through the reform of the Church of England. Philip's commitment to worldwide Christianity was evident in the many missions he led abroad. In this chapter, David Holloway, who also under God has seen church growth in Newcastle-upon-Tyne, considers what church growth means in the twenty-first century in today's Anglican context. Lessons are drawn from Scripture and history, with a challenge for pastors to seek 'deep change'.

INTRODUCTION

I am assuming that any pastor concerned for the growth of the church will agree with the importance of having a church that has a vision for what God wants to do through them, a church which is biblical, prayerful, led well by the pastor who shares his leadership with others, and is sensitive to its community and culture. Many books have been written about all those general aspects of growing churches. In this chapter I want to deal specifically with some Anglican issues of church growth.

First, what should an Anglican pastor understand about 'the church' that he wants to see growing?

THE CHURCH AND THE THIRTY-NINE ARTICLES
In the Church of England he is committed by law to a Church that doctrinally is clear over fundamentals. The *Church of England (Worship and Doctrine) Measure 1974* underlines as the 'canon of canons', Canon A5. This says:

> The doctrine of the Church of England is grounded in the holy
>
> Scriptures, and in such teachings of the ancient Fathers and
>
> Councils of the Church as are agreeable to the said Scriptures. In
>
> particular such doctrine is to be found in the Thirty-Nine Articles
>
> of Religion, the Book of Common Prayer, and the Ordinal.

After the Bible, therefore, attention must be paid to the Thirty-Nine Articles of Religion where the Church is defined in Article XIX and which, as all the articles, has both an English and a Latin version. Entitled *Of the Church*, Article XIX says:

> The visible Church of Christ is a congregation of faithful men, in
>
> the which the pure word of God is preached, and the Sacraments
>
> be duly administered according to Christ's ordinance in all those
>
> things that of necessity are requisite to the same. As the Church
>
> of *Jerusalem, Alexandria*, and *Antioch*, have erred; so also the Church

of *Rome* hath erred, not only in their living and manner of Ceremo-

nies but also in matters of Faith.'

But what does the article mean by a 'congregation'? Does it refer to a parish congregation or, as some like to think, to the diocese corporately? In the sixteenth century, the Latin '*con-gregatio*' could refer either to the whole body of the faithful or to a particular local assembly or society of believers. So, what is the meaning here in Article XIX?

In the Latin version, Article XIX has the Latin *coetus* (lit-erally 'a coming together') for 'congregation' and not *congre-gatio*. This means that Article XIX is *not* a verbatim repeat of the Lutheran Augsburg Confession on which it seems to be based. For the Augsburg Confession uses the Latin *congrega-tio* (and there it means 'the *whole* body of the faithful').

Article XIX also has to be read in the light of both the An-glican *Homily for Whitsunday* and the contemporary *Reformatio Legum*. The former – the *Homily* – speaks of 'the true church' and says it is 'an universal congregation ... of God's faithful *and elect* people'. The latter – the *Reformatio Legum* – speaks of the 'visible church' and says it is 'that coming together of *all* faithful men'.

Article XIX, therefore, is in contrast to the homily as it cannot be understood as referring to the pure or 'true church' of the homily. That is because Article XXVI tells us that 'in the visible church of Christ the evil be ever mingled with the good'. And most significant of all, Article XIX omits 'univer-sal' (of the *Homily*) before 'congregation'. It also omits the 'all' (of the *Reformatio Legum*) before 'faithful' and it uses the indefinite and not the definite article (in the English form of the Article) – 'the visible Church of Christ is *a* congregation of faithful men.'

The conclusion, therefore, has to be that in Article XIX 'a congregation' refers to an actual group 'coming together' (a *coetus*) to hear 'the pure Word of God' preached and baptism and Holy Communion 'duly' celebrated 'according to Christ's ordinance'. This is a *local congregation* and not a diocese or province. At the end of the sixteenth century, Richard Hooker can therefore write that for 'convenience' churches are 'limited' into 'several *congregations* termed *parishes*' (*Laws of Ecclesiastical Polity*, Book 5.lxxx.2).

However, Article XIX does recognise the reality of the *connection* between visible local churches (or congregations) and a wider communion. It can speak of the Churches of *Jerusalem, Alexandria, Antioch* and *Rome* which at this time themselves had wider connections or communions.

But the *local church, not the connection, is at the heart of the Anglican understanding of the church here on earth*, and when possible we, surely, want to see it growing.

THE BOOK OF COMMON PRAYER AND THE ORDINAL
Our doctrine of the church also must come from the theology of the Book of Common Prayer. There our Anglican forefathers in the sixteenth century distinguished the church visible from the church 'mystical'. In *The Communion* service you hear about 'the mystical body of thy Son, which is the blessed company of all faithful people'. 'Mystical' is a better word than 'invisible' as true believers are visible in their lifetime here on earth. We could, therefore, do worse than follow Hooker who, with his brilliant precision, gives us this advice as a simple Anglican understanding of the church:

> 'For lack of diligent observing the difference, first between the Church of God mystical and visible, then between the visible sound and corrupted, sometimes more, sometimes less, the oversights are neither few nor light that have been committed' (3.i.9).

But in addition to the Book of Common Prayer, the Ordinal (attached to the BCP) is important for understanding the Church of England's ministry and how it is a connectional church. For while its fundamental doctrinal connection is through Canon A5, its practical connection is (or should be) facilitated by a bishop.

In the sixteenth and seventeenth centuries there was a major debate over episcopacy. Cranmer's intention was to be as eirenic (or comprehensive) as possible without sacrificing fundamentals. So in the Ordinal the episcopate is not stated to be essential to Church order, but it is spoken of as a given fact. It must be noted that the Ordinal does not commit the Church of England to 'three orders' but 'these Orders of Ministers in Christ's Church; Bishops, Priests, and Deacons' (*The Preface* to the Ordinal).

It is clear from details in the services and their rubrics that the Ordinal follows the Catholic understanding of two orders, with bishops being part of the presbyterate. In the *Making of Deacons*, the Ordinal requires a sermon to be preached on 'how necessary that Order is in the Church of Christ'. Similarly there is the same requirement for the *Ordering of Priests* (or Presbyters) and it is described as 'the Order and Ministry of Priesthood'. But in the case of bishops there is no requirement for a sermon on 'how necessary that Order is in the Church of Christ'. Theirs is simply an 'order of this realm'. They were particularly necessary, however, for Protestant Tudor monarchs as supportive prelates. Of course, things are very different today; yet there is no great desire to abandon episcopacy.

The consensus in Anglicanism is that good bishops are for the '*bene esse*' (the *well* being), not the '*esse*', (being) of the Church. In the Lambeth Quadrilateral, which gives Anglican 'minima' for intercommunion, the fourth clause requires ...

... the Historic Episcopate, locally adapted in the methods of its administration to the varying needs of the nations and peoples called of God into the Unity of His Church.

Therefore, in the Anglican tradition there seems to be a consensus that prefers Church senior leadership to be in the form of individuals, who are accountable, rather than committees which are less accountable. But that individual must, of course, subscribe to Canon A5.

STRUCTURAL CHANGE

However, many are currently saying that there has to be a radical reform of the episcopate, together with decentralisation so that local churches can evangelise more effectively. The *Reform Covenant* speaks of ...

> ... the urgent need for decentralisation at national, diocesan and deanery level, and the need radically to reform the present shape of episcopacy and pastoral discipline, to enable local churches to evangelise more effectively.

More precisely what is really being wanted is a 'federal' structure rather than a decentralised one. As Charles Handy puts it:

> In decentralised structures the centre is still in command but has delegated a range of tasks to the periphery. In federalist constitutions, the centre is the residuary body, doing things which the parts cannot or do not want to do – delegation the other way round.

In *voluntary* non-profit organisations, such as all churches became following the Act of Toleration in 1689, the centre finds it hard to enforce its will. The way to function efficiently, in such organisations, is 'federally' with a bishop being a focus of unity. But where there are bishops who violate Canon A5, for example by denying the virginal conception of Jesus and his Empty Tomb and by legitimating homosexual sex, they cannot provide that unifying focus. For there will be significant groups of clergy and congregations who are seeking to uphold Canon

A5 and who probably will represent the majority of attenders at Anglican churches in England (certainly worldwide). Such dysfunctional situations are not the way to growth.

As a way forward in restructuring the episcopate, the American Mission in the Americas (AMiA) has experiment-ed with episcopal 'affinity' networks chosen by congrega-tions. Another model is that of the Church of England in South Africa (CESA). That Church has clergy working in parishes who, as bishops, have authority to ordain. These sorts of option, surely, should be explored in England.

Before moving on, one final comment needs to be made on the Anglican doctrine of the church.

Regarding church growth another distinction made by Hooker in 1.xv.2 is very important. There he says that the church is 'both a *society* and a *society supernatural*'. So within however 'sound' (or not so sound) a local or national church, there must also be made a distinction between the church as a 'society' and the church as a 'society supernatural'.

As a society it shares a similar social nature and similar social possibilities in terms of human functioning as other organisations (outside the church) of the same size and structure. So you have here a parallel between Christian groups and Christian individuals. When people are converted to Christ they do not cease to be human individuals with the laws governing created human existence suddenly suspended. They should be progressively living humanly more as God intended. Similarly, believers corporately do not suddenly find the basic laws of human association suddenly suspended for their Christian societies. Rather when they form a society which is also a 'society supernatural', they now have new resources for living corporately and socially more as God intended.

CHURCH GROWTH BASICS

But how are we to aim for the growth of the church under-stood in these 'Anglican' terms?

The Bible makes it clear that God gives His people growth. That means we must pray for Him, by His Holy Spirit, to be working for growth. But it is not God working alone. We are to work together with Him. The Old Testament is crystal clear: Psalm 127:1 says that 'unless the Lord builds the house, its builders labour in vain'. This does not mean that when the Lord is building for His people, the human builders have a holiday! It means they now no longer work 'in vain'.

Similarly in the New Testament Paul is clear regarding the church at Corinth. He says that he 'planted the seed, Apollos watered it, but God made it grow' (1 Cor. 3:6). However, Paul was aware that there could be two sorts of building work in which Christians would be engaged. Some would be solid ('using gold, silver, costly stones') but some would be burnt to the ground (being made of 'wood, hay or straw'). He then added, but 'if it is burned up, he [*the human builder*] will suffer loss; he himself will be saved, but only as one escaping through the flames.' (1 Cor. 3:15).

And all that is assuming the building was built on the right foundation: 'for no-one can lay any foundation other than the one already laid, which is Jesus Christ' (1 Cor. 3:5-15). That is a challenging and sobering passage. One thing it means is that for church growth and in church planting the foundation needs to be correct, remembered, affirmed and reaffirmed.

The modern study of church growth thinking started with a missionary in India named Donald McGavran, and was developed in the United States at Fuller Theological Seminary in the second half of the twentieth century. McGavran's new thinking came to prominence in the 1930s with a book that was an analytical study of church growth in central India. In McGavran's dedication to the book, now entitled *Church Growth and Group Conversion*[1], he wrote this:

---

1   Donald A. McGavran, *Church Growth and Group Conversion*, (Gabriel Resources, 1973).

Dedicated to those men and women who labour for the growth of the churches, discarding theories of church growth which do not work and learning and practicing productive patterns which actually disciple the peoples and increase the Household of God.

Many years later, Arthur Glasser, at the time Dean of Fuller's School of World Mission, said the verbs in that dedication summarised McGavran's thinking in this way:

Labour! – The work of church growth is not readily accomplished without much thought, much pain and much prayer.

Discard! – All theories of church growth which have not produced results should be cast aside in the desire to be faithful to God.

Learn! – Be open to the insights of those whom God has singularly used in many parts of the world to produce church growth.

Practise! – Be willing to apply, under God, those patterns of church growth He has already been pleased to use to gather His people to Himself in great numbers.'

However, McGavran in his older age wrote (together with Win Arn) a simple book entitled, *Back to Basics in Church Growth*.[2] The basics, he argued, mean an 'unshakable conviction' in the uniqueness and finality of Jesus Christ. He was aware that we live in a pluralistic world. But 'it is of this pluralistic world that Jesus is Lord'. McGavran was conscious that 'the conviction that Jesus rules over pluralism is being steadily eroded by the main currents of modern life.' Hence, 'church growth' teaching that ignores

2   Donald McGavran and Win Arn, *Back to Basics in Church Growth* (Tyndale House, 1981).

the fundamental foundation will be worse than 'wood, hay
or straw'. His conclusion was that

> Church growth rises from theological roots, from Christian cer-
> tainty. People of unshakable conviction can profitably employ
> many insights from the social sciences and from communication
> and management, but without certainty all human resources sud-
> denly become mere methods. Without certainty all the swords of
> the church suddenly become wooden. The absolute certainty of
> the early church (so well proclaimed by Scripture, probably for
> just such an age as this, in which relativism is enshrined in the
> contemporary ethos) must be recaptured if the church is to be
> healthy and to fulfil its God-given function.

That certainty with regard to 'the uniqueness of Jesus (He
has no competitors) and the finality (He has no successors)'
has been described so well by John Stott:

> It is not the uniqueness of 'Christianity' as a system that we
> defend, but the uniqueness of Christ. He is unique in his
> incarnation (which is quite different from the a-historical and
> plural 'avatars' of Hinduism); in his atonement (dying once for all
> for our sins); in his resurrection (breaking the power of death);
> and in his gift of the Spirit (to indwell and transform us).

To make this assertion of the uniqueness and finality of Jesus
Christ as the 'Doctrine of Doctrines' for church growth,
follows the instincts of our Anglican forefathers. For they
preceded Article XIX *Of the Church*, with Article XVIII *Of
obtaining eternal Salvation only by the Name of Christ*:

They also are to be had accursed that presume to say, That every

man shall be saved by the Law or Sect which he professeth, so

that he be diligent to frame his life according to that Law, and the

light of Nature. For holy Scripture doth set out unto us only the

Name of Jesus Christ, whereby men must be saved.

So for an Anglican pastor the Anglican tradition of 'moderation' does not mean a refusal to express any certainties. Rather, as Oliver O'Donovan has put it: 'Anglican moderation is the policy of reserving strong statement and conviction for the few things which really deserve them.'

Given, therefore, such an understanding of the Church with such a foundation, what today particularly needs to be said about church growth for a pastor in the Church of England?

Most of the current studies of church growth relate to modern churches. This is most necessary. But we can also learn from church growth in history. I suggest two periods may be of help for the current situation in the Church of England today.

One is the very first period of church growth on our own islands – the period A.D. 400-700. So what happened then? The story, in brief, goes something like this.

CHURCH GROWTH A.D. 400-700

By the early 400s the Roman legions had left Britain to defend the Empire nearer home against barbarian invaders. This left the situation in Britain without Roman organisation and so fluid politically and religiously. There was now, therefore, a challenge for the few Christians that remained in the country. The challenge was met by fifth century evangelistic monks. They were people God used for church growth in these islands when invading Angles, Saxons and Jutes had driven Christians west and north to the Celtic regions of the West and Scotland.

But this new period of evangelisation started not in England but in Celtic Ireland with Patrick (390-461). A son of British Christians, he was kidnapped as a teenager by Irish slave traders to work as a shepherd in Ireland where in God's providence he was soundly converted. After managing to escape, he spent a period of monastic training on the Continent before going back to Ireland in 432. Now as a missionary bishop he travelled throughout the land, preaching, teaching and baptising new converts, against great odds and often in great danger. But before his death Ireland had become significantly a Christian country.

Patrick was an amazing church planter and evangelist. He established many churches, schools and monasteries (or minster churches – large churches with a wide ministry). He influenced Irish kings and argued for the abolition of slavery. He, indeed, was a man committed to 'godly living, church growth and changing Ireland'. Here are his own words: 'In the light, therefore, of our faith in the Trinity I must make this choice: regardless of the danger, I must make known the gift of God and everlasting consolation. Without fear and frankly I must spread everywhere the name of God so that after my decease I may leave a bequest to my brethren and sons whom I have baptised in the Lord – so many thousands of people.'

We need to note that Ireland was *not* part of the Roman Empire. It, therefore, lacked Roman administration and its organisational mirror image in the administration of the church. This allowed Patrick's Celtic Christianity to develop independently. How different this development was is disputed. But this much seems clear. Without a Roman diocesan and parochial system, abbots of monasteries had great authority (even over bishops); Celtic monks as a simple fact shaved their heads differently to Roman monks (this becoming a symbol of difference – like surplices were at the Reformation in the Church of England); and there was a practical difference over the date for Easter. However, the crucial difference was that while Roman monasticism was a tradition more of withdrawal, the Celtic monastic tradition was to encourage church growth, church planting and missionary work in the wider world and unimpeded by a Roman parochial system.

Indeed, a wider Celtic missionary movement was launched from Ireland in 563. That was when Columba, a Celtic monk, founded a monastery on Iona, an island off the west coast of Scotland. This became a centre for evangelising Scotland and northern England. Scotland soon saw many believers, as did many places in England. Monasteries were planted which in turn were new evangelistic centres. Even Continental mission work proceeded from Iona when Columbanus, a young monk with twelve assistants, went to the Continent, where having founded many other monasteries, he ended up in Italy and in his seventies founded the monastery at Bobbio.

But in 597, thirty-four years later, there was also a new Italian, or Roman, missionary initiative for Britain. It began small with Pope Gregory (590-604) sending a team under Augustine (not to be confused with the great Augustine, Bishop of Hippo) to the south of England. He was to establish diocesan structures and with provincial archbishoprics in London and York following the pattern of government left by the Roman legions nearly two centuries earlier. The Pope's desire was to organise and centralise the Christianity that was re-emerging. Augustine was not, however, the most robust of men. He wrote back before leaving Gaul saying his party were afraid! 'They were appalled', he said, 'at the idea of going to a barbarous, fierce and pagan nation,' to which Gregory replied to the effect, 'keep calm and carry on!'

In the event Augustine had a significant response with many converts. Bishoprics in London and Rochester were established, but in 616 a pagan East Saxon king succeeded a friendly Christian king and the Bishops of London and Rochester had to flee across the Channel. But Paulinus, who had joined Augustine's team, was able to go to York in 625 when he worked with King Edwin of Northumbria (through his Christian wife, Ethelburg). He, too, saw a number of conversions further north in (modern) Northumberland. Sadly, this work of Paulinus was also short-lived. With Edwin's death in 633 the Mercians gained control of Northumbria and re-established paganism as the kingdom's official religion. Paulinus had to flee south. So by the early 630s, forty years after its start, the Italian mission to Kent humanly appears to have been unsuccessful. But in God's timing that was when there was to be a new Celtic mission to England.

CELTIC CHURCH GROWTH AND MINSTER CHURCHES

This mission came from Iona to Lindisfarne, an island off the coast, just south of Berwick upon Tweed. Only a year or two after Edwin's death, a Christian Northumbrian king, named Oswald, gained power. He immediately invited not a missionary from Paulinus' Roman connection but from Celtic Iona to re-evangelise the north. After a short visit by someone unsuitable, Aidan came and in 635 founded the monastery on Lindisfarne. This island then became the centre for Christianity in Britain. People went from Lindisfarne not only evangelising Northumbria but many other parts of England. This resulted in a great advance of the Christian faith. So the Celtic mission took over where the Roman mission had failed and the converts seemed to have stood firm. There were no more widespread lapses into paganism. Nor was Lindisfarne only an evangelistic centre; it also became a centre for education and scholarship with the world-famous *Lindisfarne Gospels* being completed at the monastery in early eighth century.

The strength of the Celtic mission was centred on monasteries (or minster churches) under abbots rather than bishops, with evangelistic teams going out from the monasteries which were not regulated by any diocesan or parish structures. However, it seems the Pope, or those of the Roman connection in the south, had worries over a lack of practical conformity (with the presenting problems being the date for Easter and the tonsure of monks).

According to the historian Bede (672/673-735), a Northumbrian pro-Roman monk, matters came to a head at the Synod of Whitby in 664 (convened by King Oswy of Northumbria). At this synod the Roman tradition won the day. But faith and politics were so closely entwined at this stage that the King no doubt had his own political interests. One issue must have been the fundamental difference between the Celtic versus Roman way of evangelism. As John Finney puts it: 'The Roman pattern was to set up a skeleton organisation and then evangelise. The Celtic pattern was to gather the people and then set up an appropriate framework for them.'

According to Bede, the clinching argument at the synod was 'is Columba ... to take precedence before the most blessed Prince of the Apostles?' And Matthew 16:18 was quoted. This, in those days, was a knockdown argument. Indeed, King Oswy concluded: 'Peter is the guardian of the gates of heaven, and I shall not contradict him ... otherwise, when I come to the gates of heaven, he who holds the keys may not be willing to open them!'

Things then changed but only gradually. In the providence of God good came from both traditions with, undoubtedly, faults and deficiencies on both sides. But with society so unstable and people too often on the move as they were displaced through invasion or war, there was something to be said for the Celtic method and for the comment that the Celts looked after people while the Romans looked after geographical areas. Be that as it may, the fact is that after Whitby, the Roman diocesan and parish system was now on its way.

THE TERRITORIAL PARISH

Theodore (d. 690), who became Archbishop of Canterbury in 668, is said to have been the main advocate for the territorial parish system. However, establishing a parish system was a slow process and was hardly established by the time of the Norman Conquest. It was a valuable tool for collecting money for those with the power to collect it!

As a structure in the modern world it has been valuable Christianly in some situations (as, for example, currently in the south Sudan). In Britain it could work as long as there was 'one' church for the whole land; compulsion could ensure allegiance; modern urbanisation had yet to occur; and telephones and the motor car had not been invented. But it has gradually proved a liability following 'no compulsion' (through the Act of Toleration 1689) when rights were given to free churchmen; Catholic emancipation in 1829; modern urbanisation (soon after); the advent of phones and cars; and especially when, after 1960, the Church of England became seriously divided doctrinally and declined numerically. That is why in England many are now arguing the time has come to try again a Celtic model of church order and evangelism – the minster model.

Churches like Holy Trinity Brompton clearly are operating as 'minster model' churches, but so are other less well-known churches. Undoubtedly more should be so operating in urban areas.

It is a fact that urbanisation is likely to increase, world-wide and in Britain. Interestingly, David Martin, the sociologist, has written that ...

> At the cutting edge of modernity the megacity may well be complemented by the megachurch, which in the range of functions it includes almost harbingers a return to the medieval Church. Megachurches are emerging in Latin America as well as in North

America (and Korea) and are even found in Eastern Europe. Only Western Europe so far lacks them.

In urban areas (not in rural areas, where there are different problems) the parish system is still operated on the basis of a Christendom model of 'one church'. Yet people now in a pluralistic society have social networks that do not depend on where they sleep but on many other factors.

Modern communications and transport have radically changed socialisation. So a church in an urban area has a ministry area now not only of a twenty-minute walk away but a twenty-minute car drive away. Nor is that just for large churches but for smaller churches. In England the parish system cannot be abandoned in terms of duties (for example, for weddings and funerals). But a parish has lost its rights to a monopoly once churches of other denominations are in its parish and when many laypeople in its parish choose to attend another parish church or a church of another denomination or not attend any church at all.

Currently there is, on average, one Church of England clergy-person to 5,000 English citizens. Of that number, 4,700 – according to the last English Church Census of 2005 – will not be in *any* church, let alone a congregation of the Church of England, on a Sunday. It is, therefore, truly sad when some clergy claim 'no-go' areas to prevent others evangelising those 4,700.

Of course, there are negatives in the erosion of the parish system. But we do not live in the past, however much we wish we could. The positives are that urban areas, as in Celtic times, have become once again mission areas. Of course, the conurbations are different. Exactly one size will not fit all. But we need to pray and work for the development of minster churches having a church-planting and church extension vision; and we need to pray for and train more men to staff such extension. Far from draining smaller churches, there is evidence that such programmes long term stimulate growth in smaller churches that are biblically faithful (as Canon A5 requires us all to be).

There surely is much to learn from the period of the early growth of the church in Britain and Ireland to encourage us all to evangelise.

CHURCH GROWTH 1800-1950 AND WILLIAM CAREY'S CHALLENGE

There also seems much to learn from another period of church growth from 1800-1950, a mere 150 years, compared to the 300 years from Patrick to Theodore. This is the period of modern missions that began with William Carey in 1793.

In 1800 (it has been estimated) 1 per cent of Protestant Christians lived in Asia, Africa and Latin America. By 1900 this number had grown to 10 per cent. Today, at least 67 per cent of all active Protestant Christians live in countries formerly considered 'mission fields'. And the church has been growing in many areas such as Korea, sub-Saharan Africa and China. Only 200 years ago, Protestant Christianity was almost exclusively Western. Now Protestants are strongest in Asia, Africa and Latin America. The modern missionary movement has, indeed, turned the world upside down.

It is, therefore, not surprising that in the 1800s almost all the cross-cultural missionaries came from the West. But now there are cross-cultural missionaries going out from Asia, Africa and Latin America. In the 1970s there were 3,400. In the 1990s it was 48,000. Now it will be more.

Under God, the catalyst for this remarkable period of world history was William Carey. We need to note three things about Carey.

First, he had to challenge existing tradition.

In Catholic and Protestant Europe there had been (and still is) a tradition against 'going out' to evangelise. But how can this be when you think about the Great Commission of

Jesus at the end of Matthew's Gospel? The risen Jesus Christ is there reported as saying:

> All authority in heaven and on earth has been given to me. There-fore go and make disciples of all nations, baptising them in the name of the Father and of the Son and of the Holy Spirit, and teach-ing them to obey everything I have commanded you. And surely I am with you always, to the very end of the age (Matt. 28.18-20).

The answer is that many in Europe at this time did not think the Commission any longer relevant. They thought it was binding only on the Apostles. Here is Luther writing two centuries earlier than Carey:

> that the Apostles entered strange houses and preached was be-cause they had a command and were for this purpose appointed, called and sent, namely that they should preach everywhere, as Christ had said, 'Go into all the world and preach the gospel to every creature.' After that, however, no-one again received such a general apostolic command, but every bishop or pastor has *his own particular parish.*

And here is Calvin in his commentary on 1 Corinthians 12:28:

> For the Lord created the Apostles, that they might spread the gospel throughout the whole world, and he did not assign to each of them *certain limits or parishes,* but would have them, wherever they went, to discharge the office of ambassadors among all na-tions and languages. In this respect there is a difference between them and pastors, who are, in a manner, tied to their particular

churches. For the pastor has not a commission to preach the gospel over the whole world, but to take care of the church that has been committed to his charge.

Of course, these men believed the gospel should spread somehow. Indeed, they saw the ripple effect of persecution and dispersal. As people were persecuted, Christians would share their faith in new situations. But there was no planned strategy for the conversion of men and women through 'going out'. Christian workers were confined to their parishes. So when Wesley and Whitefield and their followers treated 'the world as the parish' and went around Britain preaching and evangelising in other people's parishes, we can understand the opposition.

However, then came William Carey – a simple Baptist shoemaker. On 30 May 1792 he was preaching to a group of ministers in Nottingham. He challenged them with this slogan: *'expect great things (from God); attempt great things (for God)'* – visionary words that encouraged the faith that, in God's strength, motored an amazing century and a half of Christian missionary work.

He then in the same year (1792) published his booklet, *An enquiry into the obligations of Christians to use means for the conversion of the heathen*, which referred to the Great Commission of Jesus to go into all the world making disciples. The first section of Carey's booklet was entitled, 'An Enquiry whether the Commission given by our Lord to his disciples be not still binding on us.' Carey was horrified at the lack of zeal and concern for the pagan world in his own generation. So he took direct issue with ...

... an opinion existing in the minds of some, that because the Apostles were extraordinary officers and have no proper successors, and because many things which were right for them to do would be unwarranted for us, therefore it may not be immediately binding

on us to execute the Commission, though it was so upon them.

Carey was insistent. Christ's command was as binding on men in his day as it was on the apostles in their day. Otherwise the command to baptise should be seen as restricted to the apostles, and the promise of the presence of Jesus 'to the very end of the age' should also not apply to us.

So Carey challenged a tradition and legacy of 'non-evangelism' (a tradition that, it seems, is still with many of us and is deep-rooted in Europe with its Roman parochial system).

WILLIAM CAREY PLANNING AND 'BREAKING THE RULES.'

Secondly, William Carey realised that Christians do have to take initiatives in evangelism.

Carey believed in the use of 'means'. The title of his little booklet was 'An enquiry into the obligations of Christians to use *means* for the conversion of the heathen.' Christians do have to plan, think and strategise for getting the gospel out. There are some who think that all you have to do in an age of confusion and denial is simply 'preach the truth'. That is vital. But it is obvious from the Acts of the Apostles that Paul was led by the Holy Spirit, through the advice of other church leaders at his 'minster church' of Antioch, to be strategic as well as faithful. He went, for example, to key urban areas to start his mission work. We have no evidence that he just sat back passively waiting for something to happen or for spiritual voices to tell him about the next move. It is more reasonable, in the light of his teaching, to think he believed that the Holy Spirit worked as he prayed and planned, and not just when he had 'immediate' supernatural experiences.

Thirdly, Carey upheld the law but when necessary risked prison by (carefully) breaking the rules – the rules when the local authorities were forbidding evangelism.

Following in the footsteps of Peter and the apostles, he realised that there are times when it is right to obey God rather than the authorities (Acts 4:27). The British East India Company had authority in India (where Carey was wanting to work) at the end of the eighteenth century. But they did not want missionaries evangelising local people. They seem to have thought that this might upset the Indians and be bad for business! Carey, therefore, had to enter the country as an 'illegal alien'. Here is the account of his arrival in India after many months at sea (it comes from Timothy George's biography of William Carey):

> Every one on board was anxious for landfall. Yet no-one in the missionary party had a permit to enter the country. Before disembarking the commander of every vessel was required to submit an affidavit stating that he carried no contraband or unlicensed passengers. To avoid this danger, the missionaries, with the connivance of Captain Christmas, transferred to a small fishing boat, called a *pansi*, which carried them from the mouth of the estuary up the Hooghly River towards Calcutta. On November 14 the *Calcutta Gazette* announced the arrival of the *Kron Princessa Maria* – her only cargo, 'Sundries'. Three days before, the missionaries had slipped into the vast city unnoticed and unmolested by the company officials.

So began an amazing period of church growth and world evangelism not only through Carey's work (in particular as a linguist) in India but as others followed his example. There soon was an explosion of mission agencies: the London Missionary Society (1795); the Scottish and Glasgow Missionary Societies (1796); the Church Missionary Society (1799); the Religious Tract Society (1799); and the British and Foreign Bible Society (1804).

Of course, there were contextual factors for Carey's success. There were the spiritual movements in the eighteenth century in Germany (von Zinzendorf and the Moravian movement); in America (Jonathan Edwards and the Great Awakening); and in England (Wesley and Whitefield and the evangelical revival). There was also the political fact that the East India Company's commercial work, although it could be negative for missionaries at first, meant that Britain was able to exercise more and more control in India and eventually able to incorporate nearly all of the country into the British Empire, which could be supportive of Christian mission.

LESSONS FOR TODAY

But what are the lessons for today's pastor in the Church of England from these two remarkable periods of Christian expansion, one earlier, one later, as he thinks about church growth and in the light of the Anglican understanding of the Church?

First, he needs to remember that Jesus calls him and his people to be 'fishers of men' and not just 'shepherds of sheep'. And personally he should remember those words of Colossians 1:28-29 for his philosophy of ministry, as they were for Paul's and as they seem to have been for Patrick's and for Carey's:

We proclaim him [*Jesus Christ, God's unique and final revelation – the Saviour and Lord*], admonishing [*being negative when necessary*] and teaching [*instructing positively*] everyone [*not just some*] with all wisdom [*therefore, the whole gospel not just parts of the truth*], so that we may present everyone perfect [*or mature*] in Christ. To this end I labour [*the word means hard work – late nights and early mornings*], struggling [*there will be conflict, but all this is*] with all his energy, which so powerfully works in me [*it is, indeed, possible*].

Secondly, the pastor needs to remember that church work is to be team work. Ephesians 4 is important for this. This chapter presupposes that there will be conflict but we must be humble and always work for unity as much as we can. There will be heretical teaching, as Paul later told the Ephesian elders, and people wanting to destroy the church from within through their teaching (Acts 20:29-30). But growth depends not just on faithfulness to the truth. Growth comes through every member ministry leading people to a unity in Christ. 'Then (Eph. 4:14-16) ...

> ... we will no longer be infants, tossed back and forth by the waves, and blown here and there by every wind of teaching and by the cunning and craftiness of men in their deceitful scheming. Instead, speaking the truth in love, we will in all things grow up into him who is the Head, that is, Christ. From him the whole body, joined and held together by every supporting ligament, grows and builds itself up in love, *as each part does its work*.

Each part doing its work is the practical 'basics' of church growth.

Thirdly, the Celtic experience and the experience of Carey illustrate the truth of revitalisation theory. This says that revitalisation movements (be they Christian or of some other philosophy or religion) need first leaders who clearly articulate the cultural crisis – in our case a religious crisis. But then many will opt for 'reaction' – a belief that the existing cultural forms, which include for us structures, can deliver a solution to the problems. Revitalisation, however, comes from 'transformation' not reaction. As Stewart Hoover writes:

> Revitalisation moves beyond reaction only when these movements include adherents who are willing to experiment with *new* cultural forms.

Certainly modern church music is a new 'cultural form', as are televised sermons in multi-site churches. But a federalising of the Church would be a more significant cultural shift. Already a significant shift is where churches are thinking 'outside the box' and planting proprietary chapels that are Anglican but, where necessary, not part of the diocesan or parish system. Nor are these 'independent' churches. They are retaining or wanting to retain links with Anglicanism understood in terms of Canon A5 and they are formally or informally connected with churches that are part of the parish system.

'DEEP CHANGE' AND CONCLUSION

Fourth, there has to be 'deep change'. Deep change is a management category and can refer to companies experiencing cases of 'slow death'. Such would seem to be the experience, not of the church of God, but of parts of the Church of England at present. In his book *Deep Change*[3], Robert Quinn identifies three strategies for confronting 'slow death'. First, there is 'peace and pay'; you just 'don't rock the boat'. But as Quinn says, 'when people do this, they are coping with slow death by choosing slow death.' Secondly, there is 'active exit'; this is when people 'jump ship' to work elsewhere. Thirdly, and the only effective solution, is 'deep change'. Such a deep change agent needs to be prepared for three things: one, to take significant risks; two, to 'build the bridge as you walk it' – there cannot be a foolproof business plan, but certain immediate, necessary steps are clear; and, thirdly, (like Carey) they are prepared to 'break the rules' – for it is some of the internal rules of the company that often are strangling the company to death. As Quinn says:

> Usually the organisation can be renewed, energised or made
>
> effective only if some leader is willing to take some big risks

---

3   Robert E. Quinn, *Deep Change: Discovering the Leader Within* (Jossey Bass, 1996).

stepping outside the well-defined boundaries. When this happens, the organisation is lured, pushed, or pulled into unknown territory. The resulting journey through the unknown is a terrifying experience.

That is what happens in a secular organisation. But with God we need not be terrified or afraid of the future when we step out in faith for Him, like Patrick and Carey did.

So let me conclude with some words of Hebrews to encourage boldness. They are highly relevant in the world of the twenty-first century with its threats of gay marriage and economic collapse. For these words of encouragement not to fear are in the context of warnings against sexual immorality and greed. These are warnings to be heeded by all those concerned for the growth of the Church of England along with other churches in need of deep change to combat 'slow death':

> Marriage should be honoured by all, and the marriage bed kept pure, for God will judge the adulterer and all the sexually immoral. Keep your lives free from the love of money and be content with what you have, because God has said, 'Never will I leave you; never will I forsake you.' So we say with confidence, 'The Lord is my helper; I will not be afraid. What can man do to me? (Heb. 13:4-6).

AN APPENDIX BY IAN GARRETT

My colleague at Jesmond Parish Church was given the title Church Growth in a sermon series, while I was writing this chapter. Each church is different. It was preached specifically for JPC but may be helpful for other churches, nevertheless – hence this addition as an appendix

GROW THE CHURCH – SUMMARY OF A SERMON BY IAN GARRETT (7/8/11)

[You'll need to look up the Bible references in italics throughout.]

Our vision for JPC is that under God, in one generation, we will grow to be a church of 5,000 with another 5,000 in churches planted from us – locally and around the world. So let's think Biblically about church growth:

1. CHURCH GROWTH IS WHAT *GOD* IS DOING

Talk of church growth can provoke negative reactions – partly because, often, it's not been our experience; partly because it sounds wrongly ambitious and dismissive of small churches; and partly because of the suspicion that it's basically an American idea – 'big is best' thinking, that's not for us. But church growth is *God's* idea. Read: Luke 24.45-47. The first part of God's plan in v46 has already happened; the second part in v47, God is still working on today – he's working to call more people from all nations to turn to Jesus as Lord. But he works through us – read *Acts 1.8*, where the risen Jesus says, "I will be at work by my Spirit – moving people to respond to me. But I'll work *through your witness*.' Then read Acts 2.41, 47 ('about 3,000 were added to their number... the Lord added to their number daily those who were being saved') and you see that church growth is what God is doing. So we're not to think of ourselves working *for* God, with God sitting passively on the sidelines. We're to think of God as the one ultimately doing the work – in peoples' hearts, in circumstances, in providing all the resources we need – but working *through us*, his *co-workers*.

And that should foster expectancy in us. So our '5,000 plus 5,000' vision came of asking, 'What do we believe – realistically – that God could do through us?' Now a numerical vision like that *isn't a prediction*. It's a faith-stretching but realistic idea of where we *could* be – if we work at being church as the New Testament sees church – *and God* works in and through us. And part of the value of a vision is that it shapes our praying and planning: if we only envisage the year ahead, we won't pray and plan for much more than is happening now. But if we envisage '5,000 plus 5,000' then we have to start praying and planning for how we might get there (God-willing) – eg, how we're going to develop dozens of ordained ministers from among our own number; how we're going to acquire more property to accommodate multiple congregations; and so on. And since the Lord has given us signs that he *could* do something like we're envisaging (he's doubled JPC in the last sixteen years; in the last four, we've seen a church plant grow to 250), shouldn't we expect much?

2. THREE KINDS OF GROWTH – AND HOW WE NEED TO CO-OPERATE

a) God is growing the numbers *in his church and we need to co-operate*
This is 'conversion-growth' (Eg, read Acts 2.47). Now that *wasn't* the early church's experience all the time. For example, read Acts 18.1-6, where Paul got a *very* negative reaction to his initial witness in Corinth – which tends to dampen our expectancy about how many people might come to faith. But read Acts 18.9-11: the Lord tells Paul to *keep* witnessing, 'because I have many people in this city' – meaning, 'because there are many people I plan to bring to faith *through you*.' So we're not to base our expectancy about the numbers who might come to faith on what we've seen so far or what seems likely, but on the thought that there are many people in this

city whom God plans to bring to faith in himself *through us*. So we need to work at our *individual* witness, but also at our corporate witness as we develop, and invite people to, a growing range of evangelistic events.

b) God is growing the maturity of his church and we need to co-operate

Read Ephesians 4.11-16. So the Lord wants not just *numerical* growth but *spiritual* growth, *maturity*: 1) *the individual* maturity of *each of us* knowing and trusting and reflecting Christ more; and 2) the *corporate* maturity of *us as a church* – corporately trusting in Christ more, as we face big steps forward; corporately reflecting Christ more in real commitment to one another; *corporately* working as a body in which everyone uses their gifts maximally, doing the ministries they should. So size doesn't *equal* maturity – for example, Christians feeling they're just 'passengers' in a church shows corporate *immaturity*. But size isn't the *enemy* of maturity – because in *any* sized church, the key to doing Ephesians 4.16 is developing *small groups* and sub-congregations. And if you wonder whether it wouldn't be better for us to be, say, four churches of 250 in different parts of the city, the answer is: partly that, in God's sovereignty, we're not – *he's* done what he's done and given us this strategic position; and partly that big churches have advantages and opportunities that small churches don't: like enabling specialised ministries, and good peer groups for children's and youth work, and training for ministry; and church-planting.

c) God is growing the reach of his church and we need to co-operate

Time permitting, we could have looked in Acts at the Lord sending out missionaries and church-planters, as well as moving Christians around through force of circumstances. And he still wants us to be exporting both the gospel and gospel-minded people. And he does that as students and young professionals regularly move on from us; he does that as we send and support mission partners; he did it with those who left to plant Holy Trinity Gateshead – and we pray he'll do that again and again. So if you belong to JPC, are you not just on board, but on board *for growth* – and willing to pay the price of growth in prayer, in time, in hard work, in serious giving, and in everything else it takes?

10

The Pastor and Student Ministry

John Risbridger

Over the course of many years, Philip Hacking was a familiar figure in the student world, speaking at Christian Union meetings and leading University Missions up and down the country. Christ Church, Fulwood, was, and still is a popular church amongst students. John Risbridger – himself a pastor at a large church which has a key student ministry in Southampton and former head of student ministry at the UCCF – gives a carefully reasoned presentation of the key role local churches and pastors can have in supporting effective student ministry which is vital for the future (and present) spiritual well-being of our churches.

My closest connection with Philip Hacking is our shared love for and involvement in the Keswick Convention, an annual Bible teaching conference based in the beautiful town of Keswick in the English Lake District. It is hard to overestimate the significance of Philip's visionary leadership in Keswick, which helped transform the convention into the large, contemporary, family event which it is today, drawing crowds of around 13,000 people each summer.

However, my first encounter with Philip was not in Keswick but in Nottingham University, where I was an undergraduate student in the 1980s. Today most University Christian Unions meet on a midweek evening but in those days we met on a Saturday night – with little or no thought for the church pastors who cheerfully came to open the Scriptures to us, travelled back late at night and still had to be up and ready for eight o'clock communion the next morning! Philip was among those servant-hearted pastors to whom I am (retrospectively!) so grateful, who made the journey from Sheffield to Nottingham and back that Saturday evening, in order to bring God's Word to us.

But why is it that many of the most able pastors and Bible teachers in a generation are willing to invest so significantly (and sometimes sacrificially) in student ministry?

WHY BOTHER WITH STUDENTS?

Personal gratitude

There are numerous reasons why people may look back on their student years with a sense of nostalgia and thankfulness: the experience of forming lifelong friendships, the opportunity to meet a future marriage partner, the freedom to establish a personal adult identity away from the family environment, the stimulus of acquiring understanding and skills which open many life opportunities, not to mention late-night discussions (with plentiful toast and coffee!), parties with friends and those long, long summers after exams!

However, many Christians also look back on student life as the time when they came to faith in Christ, or when a relatively unformed childhood faith began to blossom into maturity of conviction and character. My own experience of student life in Nottingham was immensely enriching. In my first weeks of university I met people from countries of which I had never even heard I met Bible-believing Christians from backgrounds of which I had no understanding; I began drinking in and being deeply formed by the rich Bible-teaching ministry of Peter Lewis at Cornerstone Evangelical Church; and I found myself plunged into a vibrant Christian

Union in which my peers were deeply prayerful, committed to evangelism and enthusiastic in their faith. It was a high-octane combination of experiences through which it would have been hard *not* to grow as a Christian!

Many Christian leaders look back with deep gratitude on such experiences and, for many, that gratitude (doubtless along with a modest dose of nostalgia!) is a significant part of what motivates their continuing involvement in student ministry.

Strategic opportunity

However, the motivation for student ministry is about much more than sentiment and nostalgia – or even personal gratitude!

Students represent the future. They embody the potential of a rising generation. To minister to students is to minister to the people who will shape and lead the world of tomorrow, whether in business, politics, academia, health and social care, the arts, or in society more generally. Time invested in students during their three years of undergraduate study has the potential to produce a significant return over decades to come.

Students also represent the nations. According to the UK Council for International Student Affairs, some 306,000 international students studied in the UK in 2008/9.[1] Of these students over two-thirds come from outside the EU so that UK universities today are truly global communities. History demonstrates that, among this vast number of individuals, there will be future world leaders and opinion formers (Bill Clinton, Robert Mugabe and Mahatma Gandhi all studied in British universities). This is clearly a huge and strategic opportunity for our nation but it is also a strategic opportunity for the church as key people from nations which are otherwise very difficult to reach, come and live on our doorstep.

For many pastors, however, it is the opportunity to nurture the future leaders of tomorrow's (global) church which

---

1   See http://www.ukcisa.org.uk/files/pdf/about/international_education_facts_figures.pdf

is prized above all. Among the students in our congregations are many of tomorrow's vicars and pastors, elders and church wardens, mission partners and evangelists, home group and missional-community leaders. For many, their experience of church and Christian Union life in student years will be seminal. The biblical understanding, doctrinal convictions and ministry skills they acquire in university years will often provide the essential foundation for years of mission and ministry to come.

Rewarding ministry

Student ministry is fun! Their creativity is energising. Their convictions are freshly formed and deeply felt. Their passion for God is refreshing. Their readiness to try something new is endlessly challenging. Their enthusiasm for prayer is infectious. Their practical commitment to evangelising their peers is often way ahead of most adult church members. If you preach to students they ask you questions! Sometimes they will challenge you! Some will become Christians! Some will become future members of your church. Some will stay in touch for years. Some will become friends for life!

Sectional interests

It is important (if slightly uncomfortable) to acknowledge that the very factors which make student ministry so strategic and rewarding also tend to make it fertile ground for any number of intra-evangelical disputes and agendas. The reasons are obvious: if we can win the hearts of students for our particular churchmanship, our particular denomination, our particular brand of worship culture, preaching style or church-growth methodology, then we can help secure the future of our 'tribe'. This is a regrettable but (in my view) undeniable aspect of student evangelicalism today, that we would all do well to guard against. Failure to do so runs the risk that student ministry becomes a kind of turf war between competing evangelical interest groups when the wider interests of the gospel are best served by retaining a proper focus on united mission and essential biblical discipleship.

WHY SHOULD THE LOCAL CHURCH BOTHER WITH STUDENTS?

The title of this chapter is 'The Pastor and Student Ministry', but does the local church pastor *have* a significant role in student ministry in fact? The answer is not quite so obvious as it may at first seem.

This is not the place for a full discussion of the role of so-called 'para-church' agencies in Christian mission. However, it has been widely recognised that the flexibility, focus and vision of such agencies has frequently enabled them to lead the way in establishing fruitful mission strategies to engage particular groups of people which the local church has struggled to reach[2]. This is unquestionably the case in student ministry in the UK in which the Universities and Colleges Christian Fellowship (UCCF, formerly the Intervarsity Fellowship), and the Navigators and Friends International (formerly International Student Christian Services) have played a pivotal role over decades[3].

While most evangelicals would welcome, unequivocally, the contribution of these agencies, their strength has sometimes left local churches uncertain as to whether they have a role in student ministry and, if so, what it is. As a result, some pastors have effectively seen their role in student ministry as limited to seeking to welcome students into their

---

2   For example see R. D.Winter, 'The Two Structures of God's Redemptive Mission' in *Perspectives on the World Christian Movement ,a Reader: Revised Edition*, ed. Ralph D. Winter and Steven C. Hawthorne (Pasadena, California: William Carey Library: 1992), cited on the website of UCCF.

3   In more recent years a number of other agencies (for example Fusion, Alpha for Students, Church Student Ministries and 9.38, to name but a few) have also had considerable focus on student ministry, with varying models for interaction with the local churches.

Sunday services, while leaving other aspects of student ministry to the local Christian Union or Navigator group.

There is, however, a growing consensus (shared increasingly by agencies such as those mentioned above) that it is appropriate for local churches to adopt a more proactive stance towards student ministry.

Welcoming the stranger

Students are visitors to our cities. They are away from home and parents for the first time. They may feel very vulnerable. They are facing unfamiliar pressures. They often feel lonely and lost in the crowd. Biblical injunctions to welcome the stranger[4] would surely suggest that it is right for local churches to recognise a responsibility to be actively involved.

Furthermore, many churches send their young people away to university fearing for their survival as Christians (these fears are often deepened by the largely unsubstantiated claims about shocking rates of students 'falling away') and longing that they should find a supportive and sound spiritual home in their university city. As pastors of churches in student cities, we are familiar with this experience as we send our own young people away. We are all very glad when such young people find spiritual encouragement among their peers in the university, but are we not equally concerned to see them welcomed into the care and support of a local church?

Making the most of the opportunity

It only takes a year or two of more active investment in student ministry for pastors of local churches to become convinced of the strategic nature of this opportunity. I think of students in our own church in recent years who have gone on to become significant leaders in our church, mission partners, godly and missional figures in their workplaces and

---

4   Matthew 25:31-46, Job 31:32, Hebrews 13:2

significant workers in student ministry in other cities. If, as I have already argued, student ministry really is so strategic then surely it is simply too important for local churches to hand over to others, leaving themselves as little more than bystanders.

God's commitment to the local church

However, the most important rationale for active involvement of churches in student ministry is not merely pragmatic; it is theological. Christ has been given 'as head over all things to the church' (Eph. 1:22, ESV). The cross unites a divided humanity in loving relationships in the church such that through the church, 'the manifold wisdom of God should be made known to the rulers and authorities in the heavenly realms'[5]. It is the church which Christ loves and for which He gave Himself up on the cross (Eph. 5:25). The primary evangelism strategy of the New Testament (exemplified most clearly in the ministry and mission of the apostle Paul) is church-planting. It is for the 'building up of the church' that the Holy Spirit gives his gifts (1 Cor. 14:1-12). It is 'among the lamp stands' (representing local churches) that the risen and glorified Christ walks in Revelation 1.

As we shall see, some have attempted to apply this argument in such a way as to rule out the contribution of agencies other than local churches. In my judgment this is an unnecessary step. However, it does seem to me that the New Testament emphasis on the local church is such that the full integration of students into local churches should be a priority which is wholeheartedly embraced by both the churches themselves and the other evangelical agencies working among students in a city.

---

5   Ephesians 3:10, cf Ephesians 2:11-21. Some may object that the references are to the universal or eschatological church. However, the argument depends on the visibility (and prophetic significance) of real relationships between real people, so that the nature of the eschatological church is to be seen in microcosm in the life of the local church.

Teaching students to love the church

If it is true that 'Christ loved the church and gave Himself up for her' it must be the case that those who seek to follow Him as His disciples will also learn to love the church and give themselves sacrificially for her health and growth. The New Testament norm is that it is the local church which provides the primary foundation for Christian life and Christian service, and even most of the New Testament examples of ministry outside the local church have a clear aim of planting or building the churches, not of establishing structures which are parallel to them. Therefore, if we want to prepare our students for *lifelong* ministry and service we need to prepare them for service *in and through the local church.* So we will not serve our students well if we give them the message either that the church is an optional extra for them or that the church is only a provider of spiritual services to consume as they see fit. Rather we need to teach students to love the church – and we can only do this by welcoming and including them in our church community as fully as possible.

STUDENT MINISTRY AND THE LOCAL CHURCH: A COMPLEMENTARY VISION OF SERVICE AND SUPPORT

Some models of student ministry take a *minimalist view* of the role of the local church in which the primary initiative rests with various 'campus-based' ministries. Some models of student ministry take a *maximalist view* of the role of the local church in which campus-based ministries are effectively sidelined, or at least marginalised. I shall argue instead for a *complementary view* of the role of the local church in student ministry.

Contextualised mission

First, students themselves are the ones who are best placed for mission in the student world. They know the culture, they speak the language, they have the relationships and they are part of the community. Local Christian leaders should therefore pause for thought before they assume that 'they know best' how to do mission on their local campuses. The student leaders of campus-based ministries often display great passion and real insight in their efforts to reach their own communities with the gospel and this is surely something that local churches should value and support.

Second, we need to recognise the sensitivities in our universities to issues of pluralism and extremism. The possibility of radicalisation of students by external voices of religious extremism remains a real concern[6]. In such a context it is hardly surprising that university authorities are cautious about giving access to external groups. The presence of student-led, Christian groups at the heart of university life is therefore tremendously important to the future of gospel witness among students. It is little short of scandalous when the ambitions of a local church lead to the weakening of such groups.

Third, given the transitory nature of the student community, it is difficult to see what a truly 'indigenous church planting model' would look like (even if we grant that this would be in some sense the ideal). Students generally spend a maximum of one year in a hall of residence. They usually spend only three years as active members of the university community. The establishing of a heterogeneous, multi-generational community, with mature and truly indigenous pastoral oversight and leadership will be all but impossible in most instances. Even in a situation where a chaplain, or a leader from a local church, is given access to lead an on-campus group, the result may be very fruitful but it will still fall short of New Testament norms for the local church (and

---

6   As recently as 6th June 2011 the Daily Mail reported that officials in the Home Office have identified forty university campuses where 'there may be particular risk of radicalisation or recruitment on campus' http.//www. dailymail.co.uk/news/article-1394625/40-UK-universities-breeding-grounds-terror.html#ixzz1RDvF4lnp

it may change overnight when the leader moves on or no longer has the same level of access).

All of these contextual factors suggest a continuing and significant role for on-campus ministries wherever possible. However, there are other factors to consider alongside these.

In reality, student leadership in the universities of twenty-first-century Britain will rarely be comparable to that of the post-war generation in which students were a small, elite group of whom a significant number were studying after experience of active military service. Student leadership in the twenty-first century will generally need much more input and support if it is still to be effective.

Furthermore, while the model of student-led, campus-based ministries remains significant for full-time residential students (especially those living in university halls of residence) it may well leave large swathes of part-time and non-residential students largely untouched. Indeed, even in a fairly traditional university setting, most students are only in hall for one year and will therefore have only a very short time as part of a CU small group, working together as a small community to reach people within their community for Jesus.

All of these factors suggest that, even when student-led campus-based ministries are strong, there is a crucial role for the local church both in supporting the leaders of those ministries and in engaging directly in various aspects of evangelism and disciple-making among students.

Church and 'para church'

Many discussions about the interaction between the local church and campus-based ministries come down to questions about the nature of the church[7]. Some argue

---

7   For a very thorough, theological analysis of this issue see the article 'What is a church, what is a CU' on the UCCF website – http://www.uccf.org.uk/resources/what-is-a-church-what-is-a-cu.htm

that wherever Christians meet around the Word of God, there you have the church. On this basis they argue that if a campus-based ministry exists it is a church (by definition) and therefore it should be led and structured as a church. Others include much more in their definition of a church (in some cases including the functioning of all the spiritual gifts and the presence of 'apostolic' oversight) and argue that, since campus-based ministries can rarely fit such definitions, they ought not to exist at all.

It seems better to recognise that campus-based ministries should be seen as belonging within the wider church (rather than being seen or being allowed to function as 'para-church') but that, given the nature of the community they serve, they are not able to function as a local church in the full New Testament sense[8]. On this basis students should be encouraged to see their primary 'spiritual home' as being within the local church, while being encouraged to be committed to their Christian Union (or other similar group) as a kind of mission team or (to use a contemporary 'buzz' phrase) missional community, complementing the role of the local church, in which students from various local churches come together for mission within their university.

---

8   *Calvin* - 'Wherever we see the word of God purely preached and heard and the sacraments administered according to Christ's institution, there it is not to be doubted a church of God exists.' (Institutes 4.1.9)

Luther - the church is 'the congregation of saints in which the gospel is rightly taught and the sacraments rightly administered.' (Lutheran Confession of 1530).

Along with word and sacrament the Reformers also spoke of the importance of church discipline as a mark of the church. Following their lead, reformed theology has classically recognised these three marks of a true church:

True preaching of the Word
Proper observance of the sacraments
Faithful exercise of church discipline.

A strong case can be made from Ephesians that an additional mark of the church is the bringing together of diverse strands of human society in unity and love.

Prayerful and practical support to campus-based ministries
This complementary vision of the relationship between the local church and campus-based ministries helps to free us from any sense of competition and enables us to embrace campus-based mission with enthusiasm. As a minimum, this should include public encouragement to students to get involved and prayerful support for them in their mission. A special focus in a church service leading up to a campus 'events week' (what we used to call a university mission!), with interviews, prayer and relevant teaching, can be an enormous encouragement to the students (and often, I have found, to the rest of the church too). In addition there are opportunities to give financial support for local staff workers and for the costs of outreach events, to offer the church's teaching and training resources where possible, to provide advice to student leaders (through local advisory teams or through mentoring relationships) and to give practical support in areas like catering or the provision of audio-visual equipment.

But, as we shall see, this need not leave the local church on the sidelines.

STUDENT MINISTRY AND THE LOCAL CHURCH: A PASTORAL VISION OF WELCOME AND INCLUSION

We often imagine that all that students really want from the local church is vibrant congregational worship and inspiring biblical teaching. Without doubt these things are very important, but many are not just looking for an impressive programme; they want to feel they belong. They want a spiritual home – and this, surely, is what we want to give them!

Welcoming students
Meaningful welcome can be a real challenge in larger churches, where we may confuse a 'welcome programme' with a genuine invitation to belong and to be in relationship with us. Smaller churches may be stronger at offering personal relationships but may struggle to find the resources to address the particular needs and challenges students face.

A welcome service at the start of term may be important, but it is only a beginning. Student lunches and after-church evenings with 'coffee and cake' may provide significant opportunities to introduce the church's vision and some of its leaders and allow students across the year groups to meet. However, in the end there is no substitute for personal relationships and in a larger church that will mean building a team of people committed to welcoming students at the start of the year and forming ongoing deeper relationships with at least some of them.

Integrating students and encouraging them to serve

Most students love to spend time in a real family home – they are, after all, *away* from their own family homes. Whenever possible, it is good for church pastors to set an example of hospitality to students in the use of their own homes. However, if it is limited to us, the impact will be small. Therefore, church pastors also need to be aware of some of the obstacles to church families offering hospitality to students. Some will feel intimidated by what they imagine will be the fearsome intelligence of students who visit them. Others will see students sticking together in church services (often because they are feeling somewhat insecure and uncertain themselves!) and imagine that they are not interested in 'ordinary people'. A well-timed interview with a student and their host in a Sunday service could be very significant in helping overcome such obstacles.

Some churches will feel able to integrate second and third-year students into mixed church cell or home groups. This is often an attractive option in terms of integrating students, though it may have the unintended side effect of reducing their focus on working together for evangelism among their peers. An alternative approach is to open up opportunities to serve within the church for students. Some can play a significant role in children's and youth work. Why not ask others to serve on welcome teams (this will often have the surprising effect of making them feel welcomed and integrated *themselves!*)? Others may join music teams or PA and projection teams. Or what about getting teams of students serving tea and coffee after services?

My observation is that the churches which are most effective at integrating students into their community are those which enable them to become stakeholders in their vision. Students love vision. They love to be part of something which they can see is going somewhere and having an impact, something they feel motivated to give their lives to (or at least a period of their lives). The details will vary according to the particular vision being pursued and it needs to be done in such a way as to avoid undermining their contribution to campusbased ministry, but it is an area that is important to consider carefully. Could they give a week of their summer holiday to a mission in a needy part of town? Do some have the flexibility to contribute to a social action outreach? Could some be trained to be part of a church-planting team or to pioneer a new missional community as soon as they graduate?

Pastoring Students

This is at the heart of the role of the local church in student ministry. Students need to be fed[9] with faithful, biblical teaching and preaching which handles the biblical text responsibly (and, I would argue, systematically), which stirs their hearts to love and worship God and which is well applied to the realities and challenges of their lives. Students also need to know who they can turn to for support in a crisis, for wisdom in a complex decision, for more specialist help with emotional struggles and for personal and sympathetic help when facing challenges to their faith.

However, the task of pastoring students adequately is not simply about teaching them and helping them with their problems. It is fundamentally about helping them to become

---

9   Acts 20:25-31; 1 Timothy 4:13

mature disciples of Christ who are applying the gospel to all areas of their lives. A key strategy within this will be the development of one-to-one or very small group 'discipling' relationships in which a more mature believer shares something of their life with a younger believer, enables them to discover the joy and freedom of living in the grace of Christ and helps them establish the essential disciplines of Bible study, prayer and Christian service. It seems that a particularly effective model for this is to encourage more mature students, who have had the benefit of such input themselves, to establish these 'discipling' relationships with younger believers.

Students are really very much like the rest of us: they need a spiritual home – and it is our responsibility in the local churches to give them such a home.

STUDENT MINISTRY AND THE LOCAL CHURCH: A STRATEGIC VISION OF TEACHING AND TRAINING

I began this chapter by reflecting on Philip Hacking's visit to Nottingham Christian Union to teach the Scriptures to us some twenty years ago. Such teaching within campus-based groups is invaluable and has made a great contribution over the years (though it is clearly best when it is focused on re-sourcing the group to fulfil its missional vision, rather than just replicating the teaching programme of a local church).

However, the clear and faithful teaching of Scripture is a primary responsibility of the local church and, as we have seen, a core element of its pastoral role. The fulfilling of this responsibility in relation to students is undoubtedly a particular joy. For some who are new Christians it will be their first experience of biblical truth, for some others it will be their first encounter with serious Bible teaching, for many it will be a deeply formative experience which shapes for life their understanding of the gospel and Christian living.

The material throughout this section is clearly relevant to the public teaching ministry of the church. However, that will need to be shaped by many other factors. Many churches are discovering that teaching and training of students within the church can happen in other ways also, which, rather than taking away from campus-based ministries, can actually enhance them. Our own practice has been to provide a teaching programme for second and third-year students, delivered (with a meal) in an early evening, so as to leave the rest of the evening free for study, socialising and involvement in campus-based ministry[10]. A key aim of that programme is to equip the students for their contribution to the local Christian Unions. It is in this context, alongside that of our public expository preaching ministry, that we have sought to work out some of the principles and priorities below.

A biblical grounding

The opportunity to expose keen undergraduate students to the joys of quality Bible teaching is one that is simply too good and too significant to miss! It is a first-order tragedy if, after three years in our churches, students emerge with little more than an ability to recite 'two ways to live' and a vague understanding of two or three of our theological hobby-horses! We need to plan to give them more: a foundational grasp of the 'whole counsel of God' (Acts 20:27, ESV).

A few key priorities might include:

- A basic Bible overview, which opens up the biblical narrative and enables them to begin tracing themes and connections that develop through Scripture.

- A grasp of basic Bible doctrines – working through, for example, something like the UCCF Doctrinal Basis, or our own church's confession of faith.

---

10 Our programme is called '3:16' and its development owes much to the work of my colleagues Ruth Norbury (who was our student worker) and Andrew Page (a fellow minister) as well as several student interns. Until now it has been largely run in my own home on a Thursday evening from 5:45-7:30pm.

- Developing an ability to read, interpret and apply different kinds of biblical literature (we have found it very useful to use 'Dig deeper' by Graham Beynon and Andrew Sach) developed through an in-depth look at two or three different Bible books in which they are both taught directly and given opportunities to think for themselves and have a go at teaching others.

It is probably the case that teaching of this kind will be most effectively delivered through a mixture of guided reading and interactive learning alongside talks delivered in various styles.

A practical equipping

There is always a danger in student ministry that we nuture people with a well-developed theological understanding but a rather underdeveloped view of how to actually live the Christian life.

The importance in this regard of the kind of one-to-one discipling work mentioned above is hard to overemphasise, but teaching programmes and seminars (perhaps attached to a student lunch, say) also have a role. Some of the areas that need to be covered include:

- Helping them to grow a close relationship with God through a developing practice of the spiritual disciplines of prayer, Bible reading, worship etc.

- Teaching them to be grace-filled disciples of Christ who have discovered the freedom of knowing that grace is not only the basis of our salvation but also of how we live and serve as Christians.

- Giving them the tools they need to explain the gospel clearly and persuasively to their friends, to respond to some of the common objections they will face and to challenge other world views.

- Giving practical, 'no-holds-barred' teaching from Scripture on friendship, dealing with conflict, building relationships and the many issues surrounding love, sex and marriage.

- Timely guidance on how to trust and honour God under the pressure of exams.

- Practical input on how to lead a group Bible study effectively, or how to work in a one-to-one discipling relationship, along with opportunities to have a go and receive some feedback.

- Biblical teaching on the importance of the local church, the discovery and responsible use of spiritual gifts[11], the place of baptism and Communion and the need to respect church leaders.

However, we also need to remember that all the skills we help students to develop will not remain sharp if we fail to integrate them into leadership within our churches soon after they graduate.

An integrated theology

A further danger in student ministry is that we prepare people for a lifetime of serving Christ in the church (especially those whom we see as having leadership potential) but that we fail to prepare them for a lifetime of serving Christ in the world and in wider society. We are preparing people to be godly vicars and ministers, but are we preparing them to be godly bankers, entrepreneurs, teachers, doctors, parents or social workers? Those are, after all, the kinds of contexts in which the majority of our students will be called to work out their Christian discipleship and involvement in God's mission.

We need to take very seriously the famous words of Abraham B. Kuyper that *'There is not one square inch of the entire*

---

11 The 'Network Course' published by the Willow Creek Association has been found by many to be a helpful tool for this.

creation about which Jesus Christ does not cry out, "This is mine! This belongs to me!"'. If this is true (and I believe it is) there are two major consequences:

First, that we want to produce Christians who are what Don Carson calls 'world Christians'[12]. That is, Christians who believe that Jesus must be proclaimed as Lord and Saviour in every nation and culture and whose world view reaches beyond their own national identity and cultural values so that they are able to be both as flexible and as inflexible as the gospel itself. What would be the effect on global mission if we began to pray that as many of our students would go on to serve in cross-cultural mission as currently go on to serve within the British church?

In practice this could involve:

• Encouraging students to be involved in short-term mission teams (perhaps with church mission partners?) and providing financial and prayer support for those who go, whenever possible.

• Teaching some essential principles of cross-cultural mission and encouraging them to think about how to apply those in mission situations they are facing locally.

• Training students in how to befriend international students and how to share the love of Christ with them.

• Occasional, inspirational and creative evenings of prayer for the world.

The *second* implication of Kuyper's famous words is that we need to recover a commitment to whole-life discipleship which sees no area of life as 'secular' and which seeks to honour Christ as Lord in the workplace and the public square as much as in the church and the home.

In practice this could involve:

---

12   See *The Cross and Christian Ministry: an exposition of passages from 1 Corinthians* (IVP 1993) Chapter 5 'The cross and the world Christian'.

- Beginning by encouraging students to reflect biblically on the subject they are studying – linking them (if possible) to local Christian academics in relevant fields.

- Encouraging regular prayer in church services for Christians in the workplace and in significant roles in society.

- Providing practical biblical teaching on work itself and apply some of the principles to their study so that they see the value of what they are doing[13].

- Encouraging Christian reflection on the political sphere and ensuring that Christians with an interest in this sphere are not shunned or regarded as 'suspect'!

If the Lordship of Christ extends to 'every inch' of human life and experience, our vision of discipleship must embrace the call to work for the glory of Christ in all the nations and every sphere of human activity.

STUDENT MINISTRY AND THE LOCAL CHURCH: A VISION FOR THE FUTURE

Student ministry is unquestionably hugely strategic. It is also generally great fun and deeply rewarding! On occasions others in the church may question its importance but we need to remind them that student ministry represents a key investment in the future of the church and a key contribution to God's ongoing purposes in the world.

As pastors I believe we should rejoice in the role and contribution of the various agencies who contribute so much to student ministry more widely, but we should do so not as bystanders but as participants, delighted to be involved in passing on the whole gospel that was taught to us, to those who will in turn be instrumental in passing it on to subsequent generations.

---

13   Books like *Thank God it's Monday* by Mark Greene and *Working without wilting* by Jago Wynne provide excellent material to work through.

I I

The Pastor and Gospel Partnership[1]

JOHN STEVENS

It has long been a mark of the evangelical movement to seek partnership between like-minded servants of Christ. Philip Hacking is no exception. He loved those who loved the Lord and His gospel and worked hard at generating genuine gospel partnership, the 'koinonia' spoken of by Paul in Philippians 1:4. John Stevens carefully explores the nature and shape of what such a partnership might be in today's UK scene by expounding, in broad brush strokes, the letter to the Romans.

There is no doubt that in the course of his ministry Philip was a pastor who was committed to fostering and modelling gospel partnership. His concern for the gospel extended far beyond his parish of Fulwood and the Anglican Church. His commitment to gospel partnership was evident in his chairmanship of New Word Alive and the Keswick Convention, and his support for the establishment of The Crowded House church planting network in Sheffield. Philip kindly preached for us at City Evangelical Church, Birmingham,

1   Many of the arguments developed in this essay rely on the work of Douglas J. Moo, *The Epistle to the Romans*, NICNT, N.T.Wright, *Romans*, NIBC, and Ben Witherington, *Paul's Letter to the Romans: A Socio-Rhetorical Commentary*. I have benefitted greatly from discussions as to the purpose and content of Romans with Steve Timmis and Tim Ward, and am very grateful for the comments of Jonathan Bennett on the first draft.

and was pleased to support the establishment of this FIEC (Fellowship of Independent Evangelical Churches) church in Birmingham.

The need for partnership between Bible-believing and cross-proclaiming evangelicals, irrespective of whether they are free-church or Anglican in ecclesiology, is well recognised today. Indeed it is urgent because of the dire state of the church in our country following the collapse of Christendom and advance of secularism. It has to some extent come to be institutionalised by the emergence of the regional gospel partnerships around the country, building on the heritage of the work of the Proclamation Trust and others to bring evangelicals committed to expository Bible ministry together. Such partnership grows out of relationships of confidence and trust built over time, together with a generous heart and passion for the cause of Christ and his kingdom. Philip was pioneer in devoting so much of His ministry to developing such relationships across constituencies, and succeeding generations are benefiting from the foundations that he and others laid. Investing in such relationships always takes time and energy, which might easily be thought to detract from local church ministry. However, the New Testament would suggest that the leaders of local churches are required to give time and effort to developing and preserving gospel partnership both with other churches in their immediate locality, and those more widely scattered across their region and the world. The apostle Paul in particular devotes an immense amount of his time, effort and prayer not just to planting and sustaining churches, but encouraging and exhorting them to remain in close fellowship with each other. He takes it for granted that there will be a high degree of interchange between the churches, both of people and of resources, and he writes and visits to ensure that good relationships are maintained and misunderstandings are prevented. The letters of Philippians and 2 Corinthians are obvious examples where Paul writes to foster and maintain true partnership in the gospel.

However, it is the purpose of this chapter to contend that no letter reveals more clearly Paul's commitment and investment in gospel partnership than the letter to the Romans. This letter is often wrongly regarded as if it were a theological treatise, in other words, Paul's systematic theology, or an extended evangelistic tract designed to explain the gospel. But the context clearly shows that Paul's purpose in writing was to seek to foster a true gospel partnership between himself and the church, or more likely the *churches/congregations* in Rome. It is evident from the opening and closing sections of the letter that Paul is writing in anticipation of an expected visit to Rome. The purpose of this visit is not fully disclosed in 1:8-13, where Paul simply indicates his intention at long last to come to Rome and his desire to strengthen the church and enjoy mutual encouragement with them. However, in 15:23-33 it finally emerges that Paul is coming to Rome in search of support for his next projected missionary endeavour. Paul explains that he is planning to pass through Rome on his way to Spain, where he wishes to preach the gospel because Christ is not yet known there. He does not plan to stay long in Rome, but he does want the church there to become partners with him in his mission. He is going to be asking for tangible help, specifically including financial support. His purpose in visiting is to have the church 'assist me on my journey there.' (Rom. 15:24) The term 'assistance' is something of a technical term for missionary support (cf. Acts 15:3; 20:38; 21:5; 1 Cor. 16:6, 11; 2 Cor. 1:16; Titus 3:13; 3 John 6), and means 'accompany' or 'escort'. Paul is certainly anticipating receiving financial and logistical support, and he may also be expecting that the church will provide co-workers to join his team. He also asks that the church will partner with Paul in his ministry by praying for him (Rom. 15:31), and especially for success in his forthcoming visit to Jerusalem to deliver the collection from the Gentile churches for the poor believers there. The letter to the Romans is thus, in essence, a missionary deputation letter, preparing the way for Paul's stopover visit during which he will seek practical help for his ongoing gospel ministry. Paul writes to encourage the church at Rome to partner with him just as other churches have done in the past.

A key difference, of which Paul is very aware, is that he did not plant the church in Rome, and as such he has no automatic entitlement to receive their support for his project. The whole tenor of the letter suggests that Paul is regarded as a controversial and unwelcome figure by some at Rome, and so he sets out his gospel and defends his ministry strategy, anticipating likely questions and objections, in order to prepare the way for a generous welcome.

Whatever the exact composition of the church at Rome, it seems clear from the letter that it consists of a mix of both Jewish and Gentile believers. Paul's greetings in 16:1-24 suggest at least five different household congregations at Rome,[2] and Paul is at pains to emphasise his contacts amongst both those from a Jewish and a Gentile background. Whatever factions there may be in Rome, Paul has connections with them all, whether by blood relation, cultural heritage or past ministry cooperation. It is highly likely that it is the Jewish Christians who are most suspicious of Paul and of his ministry as an apostle to the Gentiles, and his main purpose is to win them over to his visit and his mission. They may well perceive him as a traitor to his own people and culture and they are deeply critical of his 'law-free' gospel message.

The way that Paul was received by the apostles in Jerusalem shortly after this letter was written gives a good indication of the way in which Paul was viewed by many Jewish Christians at the time, much of which was the result of misinformation and negative propaganda from his opponents. In Acts 21:20-21

2   See Moo, *The Epistle to the Romans*, NICNT p. 919.

James and the Jerusalem elders greet Paul and rejoice at how God has worked among the Gentiles, but then say: 'You see, brother, how many thousands of Jews have believed, and all of them are zealous for the law. They have been informed that you teach all the Jews who live among the Gentiles to turn away from Moses, telling them not to circumcise their children or live according to our customs.' They therefore urge Paul to undertake purification rights at the temple to prove that these reports are not true. It is clear from Romans 14 and 15 that there were Jewish Christians in Rome who observed the Law, including the food laws (Rom. 14:2) and the Sabbath regulations (Rom. 14:5-6), and to such people Paul might have seemed an unwelcome visitor.

Paul writes to counter such unfounded suspicions, setting out his gospel message, stressing how it fulfils the Old Testament Scriptures and the promises that were made to Abraham. He repeatedly emphasises his concern for the salvation of his own ethnic people, and not just for the Gentiles, beginning the letter by asserting that his gospel is the power of God for the salvation of everyone who believes, first for the Jew and then for the Gentile (Rom. 1:16), and climaxing in Chapters 9-11 where he declares that his mission to the Gentiles is paradoxically the very means by which God's promises to ethnic Israel will be fulfilled.

In Chapter 15, where he makes clear his intention to seek financial and tangible support when he visits, he highlights how he is himself committed to tangible gospel partnership between Jewish and Gentile believers in the form of the collection he is delivering to the Jerusalem church for the poor believers there from the Gentile churches.[3] Paul is indicating his own credentials in cross-cultural gospel partnership,

---

3   Romans 15:25-29. It is striking what a considerable proportion of the New Testament corpus is devoted to the collection Paul organises for the poor believers in Jerusalem, indicating how vital this was as an exercise in building gospel partnership. See: Acts 19:21-22; 20:22-24; 21:17-19; 24:17; 1 Corinthians 16:1-4; 2 Corinthians 8:1-9:15.

organising the generous sharing of resources. If his Gentile churches have given generously to support poor Jewish believers in Jerusalem it is clearly not asking too much to expect the Jewish believers in Rome to give generously to support his mission to preach Christ to the Gentiles in Spain. As well as writing, Paul is probably sending Phoebe, a deacon of the church in Cenchrea where he is currently based, ahead of him to prepare the way for his visit (Rom. 16:1-2). She may well be carrying the letter to the church at Rome. He urges the church in Rome to receive her appropriately and to provide her with any material help that she might need. Their reception of Phoebe and provision of support for her is to be a precursor for the visit of Paul himself.

Romans is therefore a letter which seeks to foster and develop gospel partnership between Paul and his missionary church planting team and the various congregations that make up the church in Rome. As we read the letter to the Romans from this perspective, we are therefore taught about the fundamental basis of gospel partnership, and are challenged to develop such partnerships with others so that the gospel may be preached to the lost, who so desperately need to hear it. If the result of hearing the letter to the Romans is not to move us to work cooperatively to see the gospel preached to those who are under the condemnation of God, especially where there is little or no gospel ministry at present, then we have surely missed what the Spirit is saying to the churches through it. Broadly speaking, Paul presents three fundamental grounds for gospel partnership: (1) the truth of the gospel; (2) love for brothers and sisters in Christ; and (3) passion for the lost. In their absence true gospel partnership will be impossible

THE TRUTH OF THE GOSPEL
The first and most fundamental basis for gospel partnership is the truth of the gospel itself. In Chapters 1–11 Paul sets out for the church at Rome the content and implications of the

gospel that he preaches. He wants them to be sure that he preaches the true and authentic message of God, which is the fulfilment of His promises to Israel in and through the life, death, resurrection and ascension of Jesus the Messiah. Romans is thus essentially salvation-historical in approach. The theme of Jesus' fulfilment of the Old Testament is emphasised right at the beginning where God's gospel, which was promised beforehand through prophets in the Holy Scriptures, is said to be about Him (see Rom. 1:1-4). He is God's Son and the long-awaited descendant of David, the prototypical King of Israel and the model of the coming messianic king. The heart of the gospel is the news that this Jesus, who has been raised from the dead, has now been appointed as sovereign Lord ruling with power. In Romans 10:9 this same combination of Jesus' Lordship and resurrection form the irreducible minimum content of the faith that saves.

Having stated what the gospel is, Paul goes on to emphasise that this gospel is the saving message for all of humanity, both Jews and Gentiles alike. This gospel is the power of God for the salvation of everyone who believes, first the Jew and then the Gentile, and for this reason Paul is obligated to preach this gospel to both Greeks and non-Greeks (Rom. 1:14-16).

In Chapter 1:18-3:20 Paul sets out to demonstrate that this gospel is the universal message for all people because all people are alike under the wrath and condemnation of God. This is because they are all sinful and all fall short of His righteousness. Paul starts by stating what Jews would have regarded as obvious, namely the wickedness and slavery to sin of pagan Gentiles (Rom. 1:18-32), but then goes on to show that even Jews, who have received the law, are just as guilty before God and enslaved to sin (Rom. 2:17-29). There can be no question that the Jews need the gospel that Paul is preaching every bit as much as the Gentiles. Paul's conclusion, which is nothing other than the verdict of God spoken in the Old Testament Scriptures and supported by a catena of quotations (Rom. 3:10-18), is that there is no-one righteous, not even one, with the result that no-one will be declared righteous in God's sight by works of the law (Rom. 3:19-20) Jews and Gentiles are in the same boat of condemnation. The possession of the law makes no difference to this.

Paul then explains what God has done to make it possible for sinful men and women to be declared righteous in His sight. In 3:21-31 he explains how God presented Jesus as a sacrifice of atonement to take upon Himself the wrath that sin deserved. God punished sin by punishing Jesus, with the result that He is able to justly forgive those who have faith in Jesus and declare them to be righteous in His sight. This righteousness is given solely on the basis of faith in what Jesus has done, and not on the basis of keeping the requirements of the law, especially the requirement of circumcision. The means of salvation is thus identical for both Jews and Gentiles alike. In Chapter 4 Paul shows that it was always God's way to make people righteous by faith rather than by works of the law by looking back to the example of Abraham, who was justified by his faith in God's promise before he was circumcised. Abraham thus becomes the pattern for all believers in Jesus, who are justified by their faith even though uncircumcised (Rom. 4:11-12).

In Chapters 5–8 Paul seeks to deal with objections that Jewish Christians might have to his gospel on the grounds that his law-free message will encourage sin and will not restrain human sin and wickedness (cf. Rom. 6:1). However, Paul counters this by showing that only the gospel, rather than the law, can lead to truly transformed living. The death of Christ achieves more than just forgiveness of guilt. Jesus died as the representative head of a new humanity, thereby undoing the consequences of the sin of Adam which has affected the whole human race, and brings life in place of death (Rom. 5:12-19). Christians are united with Christ in His death and resurrection, and as such are freed from the ruling power of sin over their lives and are enabled to live a new life (Rom. 6:4). This new life is lived in the power of the Spirit not under the law (Rom. 7:6). Whereas life under the law whilst still under the power of sin could only lead to the hopeless wretchedness described so vividly in Romans 7:14-25, the indwelling Spirit enables believers who have been freed from both the law and the power of sin to put to death the misdeeds of the flesh and to meet the righteous requirements of the law (Rom. 8:4, 13). The Christian life thus remains an ongoing struggle as believers continue to live in a fallen world and await the ultimate renewal of all things, but it is not the same hopeless struggle of those who are outside of Christ.

Paul's argument in Romans 4–8 demonstrates that the law is not necessary for justification, nor for sanctification, and indeed that Christians have been released from the law because it has been fulfilled in the death of Christ (Rom. 7:1-6). This provides a fundamental basis for unity and gospel partnership between Jewish and Gentile believers since the law is relegated to the realm of a cultural preference rather than a salvific necessity.

In Romans 9–11 Paul continues his defence of his gospel by asserting that it does not imply that God has broken His promises to the ethnic people of Israel and abandoned them (Rom 9:6). Paul's theology is not a replacement theology but a fulfilment theology and he shows how the present rejection of Jesus by many Jews is part of God's unfolding sovereign plan, and that His incorporation of Gentiles into Israel by faith is a pointer to how unbelieving Jews will be re-grafted back into the nation when they turn to Christ in faith. In the course of this argument Paul makes very clear that Gentile believers have themselves been grafted into

Israel, so that they are fully included in the people of God irrespective of the fact that they are not circumcised or observing the law (Rom. 11:13-24). They share the same root of the patriarchs and the patriarchal promises. The union of Jewish and Gentile believers in Christ alike in the one nation is a further basis for gospel partnership across this otherwise insurmountable cultural divide.

This briefest of surveys of Paul's arguments in Romans 1–11 has shown how he defends his message as the authentic gospel which is identical for Jews and Gentiles alike. This is foundational for gospel partnership, as it means that there is one single message which is universally applicable to all people. There are not different messages for Jews and for Gentiles, nor different ways of salvation. Instead, one single people is produced by faith in this common message. The gospel itself demands gospel partnership between Jews and Gentiles to work together for the salvation of all people.

But if the truth of the gospel demands partnership, Paul's argument also reminds us that there can be no true partnership where the gospel is not held in common. Gospel partnership is founded on the truth of the gospel, not on mere cultural or ethnic similarity, personal preference and tastes or old boy networks. How can there be any partnership with those who would deny the key truths that Paul expounds in his letter? How can there be partnership with those who deny that Jesus is the unique, divine Son of God? With those who deny the physical and bodily resurrection of Jesus from the dead? With those who deny the wrath of God against human sin and wickedness? With those who deny that the death of Christ on the cross was a substitutionary, propitiatory sacrifice in which He bore the just judgment of God for sin? With those who deny that justification is by faith alone rather than by faith together with religious or moral good works of whatever kind, or with those who deny that faith in Jesus is the only way to be saved? In our culture today we are under incredible pressure to compromise the truth in the interests of tolerance, courtesy, public acceptability and church politics. However, gospel partnership cannot be founded on any other basis than a commonly believed exclusive and universal truth. There cannot be gospel partnership with liberals, Roman Catholics, Anglo-Catholics or Trinity-denying cults and sects, let alone other faiths.

Paul does not address the issue in Romans but we must stand apart from false teachers who would peddle such lies about the gospel and the way of salvation (cf. Gal. 1:6-9; 5:3). The gospel demands that we stand together in partnership with those who affirm and implement the truth of the gospel, but we must stand apart from those who do not. We will be regarded as bigoted, intolerant, fundamentalist and unable to come to terms with modern society if we take such a stand, but the gospel demands nothing less. If the pastor is committed to gospel partnership, he must first and foremost be committed to the gospel itself. The gospel, if properly grasped, will drive him to make every effort to work in partnership with other gospel believers and churches, but will caution him not to enter false and pragmatic alliances with those who deny the very heart of the gospel, indeed to demand the proper discipline and excommunication of unrepentant false teachers and church leaders who would advocate 'another gospel'.

LOVE FOR BROTHERS AND SISTERS IN CHRIST

If the primary foundation of gospel partnership is the truth of the gospel, a major challenge to gospel partnership in practice is the diversity of views, practices and cultures amongst those who hold to the same core gospel truths. Differences over such theological issues as baptism, orders of ministry within the local church, ecclesiology, and over cultural practices such as taste and style of music and services, can make gospel partnership difficult to implement. We all have a natural tendency to assume that 'our way' of doing things is the right and biblical one, and therefore to be judgmental and suspicious of those who do things differently. We tend to elevate our culture-bound opinions to the level of a scriptural 'regulatory principle'. Our sinfulness generates a tendency to partisanship which leads us to want to promote the success of our 'group' because we believe that it most faithfully serves the cause of Christ. In our English culture one of the major obstacles to genuine gospel partnership is often the issue of class background, as we tend to associate and identify with others from a similar background to our own and then feel either superior or inferior to those who are above or below us in the social spectrum. Many of the ways in which we express our common faith are bound up with our class and culture, including our emotional expressiveness and style of preaching, and it can be especially difficult to maintain true gospel partnership where there are those who through their class and education assume an entitlement to lead, or where others as a result of their inverted snobbery refuse to accept the leadership of gifted men who come from a higher class group. Paul tackles the problem of maintaining gospel partnership despite theological and cultural diversity in Romans 12–15, and his message is that gospel partnership founded on the truth of the gospel must be maintained and preserved by the practice of love.

Having set out his gospel in Romans 1–11, and shown that the same message is for all people irrespective of their ethnicity, in Romans 12–15 Paul goes on to explain how gospel partnership is to be maintained between people who have diametrically opposed theological views and who are culturally different to each other. The gospel does not achieve unity by creating a monoculture of absolute theological conformity. It is evident from Romans 12–15 that the church at Rome was culturally diverse. There were clearly some amongst the church who felt that they were required to continue to observe the requirements of the Jewish law, especially the food laws and the Sabbath regulations. These were most likely converts from a Jewish or God-fearing background, but may have included some Gentiles who were converted through a Judaising mission initiative. Paul characterises those who belong to this group as 'the weak'(Rom. 14:1), although they would not have chosen this epithet for themselves, because they did not have sufficient certainty of faith to grasp the fact that the law had been fulfilled and abolished in Christ so that it was no longer necessary to live in this way in order to please God. There were also others in the church who exercised freedom to live free from the obligations of the law, eating and drinking all foods and wine, and not regarding any particular day as more special than any other. These would have included Gentile converts but also Jewish converts who had come under the influence of the Pauline ministry, including those such as Priscilla and Aquila, who had been Paul's co-workers and were now leading a church in their house. They were characterised by Paul as the 'strong', (Rom. 15:1) because they have fully appropriated their freedom in the gospel (Rom. 14:14). The probability is that there were different congregations in Rome observing different practices in regard to eating and drinking and Sabbath observance. Although differences regarding eating and drinking might seem relatively trivial to us, they were hugely significant to the life and unity of the church, both because they represented deeply held convictions, and because they affected the ability of the church to enjoy fellowship. The main meeting of the early church was evidently the Lord's Supper (See Acts 2:42; 1 Cor. 11:17-34), which was a genuine meal rather than the mere symbol of a meal we have adopted in modern practice. The food that was served at the gathering of the church would determine who could attend, eat and participate. If the kosher rules were ignored then the 'weak' would be unable to fully participate. The centrality of eating together for the unity and life of the church had led Paul to oppose Peter to his face in Antioch when he had withdrawn from eating with the Gentiles in the church (Gal. 2:11-14).

Against this background it is highly likely that the law-observing Jewish Christians at Rome fear that Paul will prove a controversial and disruptive influence in the city. Most likely they suspect that he will urge and demand that they stop observing their laws and customs, and adopt his law-free lifestyle. For this reason Paul sets out his principles for how 'weak' and 'strong' gospel believers should relate to each other and, far from insisting that one group capitulate and the other dominate, he insists that they both act out of love towards each other. Romans 12–15 sets out the shape of the transformed lives that Christians should live in view of what God has done to liberate them from sin, death and the law, and the dominating ethic is that of love. The entire law is summed up in the command 'Love your neighbour as yourself,' (Rom. 13:8-10) where in the context, as in the Old Testament, 'neighbour' is clearly your fellow member of the people of God.[4] Christians are therefore to use the gifts that they have been given by God with humility to serve each other, valuing and appreciating their diversity. Christians are to share their resources with each other, caring for those who are in need and practicing hospitality. Christians are not to seek to take revenge upon those who have done them harm and are to be obedient to the governing authorities.

The need to love is most extensively spelt out in regard to the mutual interactions between the 'weak' and the 'strong' in

---

4   cf. Leviticus 19:18, where the context makes clear that the command concerns 'one of your people'. This does not mean that there is no obligation to love others. God's people are commanded to love aliens and strangers amongst them, and also to love their enemies. To regard everyone as a neighbour in the biblical sense is to collapse the categories, thereby rendering the command to love enemies as redundant, and eliminating the radical obligation to love those who are hostile. In Romans 11:28 unbelieving Jews are characterised as 'enemies', not as 'neighbours', highlighting the continued distinction.

Chapters 14–15. Whilst Paul is utterly clear that the 'strong' are theologically correct, because he is fully persuaded in the Lord Jesus that nothing is unclean in itself, (Rom. 14:14), he urges both the 'weak' and the 'strong' to put aside their respective convictions and to practice love towards each other. He urges the strong not to look down on the weak with contempt, (Rom. 14:1, 3) and to be willing to set aside their freedom to eat or drink anything for the sake of their weak brothers and sisters in Christ (Rom. 14:19-21). He urges the weak not to judge the strong because of their failure to observe the law, (Rom. 14:3-4) and to remember that they are answerable and accountable to Christ alone for their actions. Paul insists on a generosity of spirit which calls both groups to acknowledge that the other is acting in good faith 'to the Lord' and to recognise the priority maintaining peace and seeking mutual edification of the body as a whole (Rom. 14:19). Paul goes so far as to say that the different groups should exercise self-censorship and keep what they believe about these things to themselves, rather than making them a matter of public controversy and debate (Rom. 14:22). In summary, the practice of love will require the 'weak' to put aside their conviction of theological superiority which underlies their practice and stop condemning the 'strong', and the 'strong' will have to set aside the assertive exercise of their freedom in order to respect the scruples and sensitivities of the 'weak'. By setting out his principles in this way Paul demonstrates that neither group should have anything to fear from his visit to Rome. He will not be insisting that law-observing believers stop observing the law, although he will be insisting that they relativise their observance as a cultural practice rather than as a God-pleasing obligation. He will not be championing the stand of the 'strong' insisting on the exercise of their freedom, but will be urging them to set aside their rights in the greater interest of fellowship.

The principles Paul establishes in Romans 14–15 are of crucial importance if we are to foster and maintain gospel partnership. We do not face the same specific issue, but we do struggle to overcome diversity on a wide range of theological issues and practices. We are familiar with applying the principles set out in Romans 14–15 to the life of the local church, but the context of Romans suggests that we need to apply them far more widely than that. The issues at Rome were not simply ones of division and disunity within the individual congregations in the city but more likely were divisions between the different house-churches that were to be found there. Each of these churches probably had a more homogeneous practice on these issues, reflecting either a law-observing or law-free orientation, much as today different local churches reflect a common culture or a common position on secondary theological issues. The challenge is therefore not just to maintain unity within a local congregation, but between gospel-believing congregations which might have widely diverse cultural habits or theological views.

Paul's message to the church at Rome reminds us of the importance of love and the need to be willing to set aside practices and even deeply held convictions for the great sake of unity and mutual edification. Love cannot, of course, be a reason to set aside the fundamental gospel truths that Paul has highlighted in Romans 1–11, and all too often the ecumenical movement has sought to do this, demanding that love overcome doctrinal division even where that division concerns the gospel itself. However, Paul's approach to the issues of food and drink in Romans 12–15 shows that there are truths which have a second-order significance, and therefore gospel partnership cannot be founded on absolute doctrinal purity. As far as Paul is concerned, the beliefs of the 'weak' are wrong, but as long as the weak are not insisting that they are essential to salvation they are not in the same category as 'false teaching' which requires discipline and excommunication both for the sake of the false teachers themselves and for the church which would otherwise be led astray from Christ. The strong may be right to claim their freedom in Christ, but they need to both restrain the practice of their freedom and the assertion of their right to freedom in order to ensure that they do not cause their brothers and sisters to stumble from the faith. Obviously the major difficulty is determining whether particular doctrines fall into a primary or secondary category. Issues such as baptism, the cessation or continuation of some spiritual gifts and appropriate ecclesiological structures have been major causes of division. But whilst deeply held, we ought to be cautious before elevating them to a point where we refuse to maintain fellowship with those who might take a different view. To be willing to act in love does not mean that we trivialise our convictions, merely that we do not give them ultimate significance. However, where convictions in such matters are raised to the level of necessity for salvation then they are in danger of becoming false teaching which must be resisted. Thus to insist on baptism in a particular mode before admission to the Lord's Table in addition to faith in Christ is in danger of falling into the Galatian heresy. Whilst it might be possible to set aside cultural preferences in relation to the style of music, it is more difficult to maintain gospel partnership with those who insist that the Holy Spirit is only received as a result of a second Pentecostal blessing, rather than by faith on conversion, since this is tantamount to asserting that some believers have not truly been united with Christ and adding a requirement for salvation other than faith alone.

In many cases our struggle to maintain gospel partnership is not as a result of deeply held theological divisions, but as a result of our cultural preferences, which we have elevated to a level of 'rightness'. We like things to be done our way, and on our terms, and by our people. We may be willing to allow others to join with us, but only if they do so on our terms and allow us to lead and dictate how things are done. If we are to overcome this we need to have love for our brothers and sisters and to relativise our preferences and set aside our rights to have things as we want them to be in the greater interest of peace and mutual edification.

PASSION FOR THE LOST

As the letter to the Romans demonstrates, fostering and maintaining gospel partnership is time and effort-intensive, and busy pastors might be forgiven for wondering why they should make this sacrifice when they could be getting on with gospel ministry through their local church. The partnership that Paul wants to develop in Romans is not partnership for its own sake. He is not seeking to establish a 'talking shop' between churches, or to establish a purely symbolic expression of Christian unity. Paul's driving passion, which underlies his efforts to promote gospel partnership, is his desire to see the lost come to salvation in Christ. This passion is evident throughout the letter. In Chapter 1, Paul reminds his readers of his appointment as an apostle with the responsibility of calling the Gentiles to the obedience of faith in Jesus Christ (Rom. 1:5). He is keenly aware of his personal responsibility to preach the gospel both to Greeks and to non-Greeks (Rom. 1:14). He is not ashamed of the gospel, by which is meant that he preaches it to those who need to hear it, irrespective of the suffering and opposition that inevitably result, because he is passionately convinced that it is the power of God to save men and women from the wrath of God that will be poured out in fullness at the coming judgment (Rom. 1:16-17). Paul's passion is especially evident in Romans 9–11 where he speaks from the heart about his concern for the Jews who have rejected Christ and as a result stand under eternal condemnation. In Romans 9:1-4 he speaks of the deep pain this causes him, and how he would, if it were possible, exchange his own eternal salvation for damnation if this meant that his people could be saved. In chapter 10, verse 1, he tells how he prays that the Israelites might be saved, and in chapter 11, verses 13-14, his ministry to the Gentiles is motivated by a desire to rouse his own people to jealousy as they see others enjoying the blessings of the new covenant that should be theirs. As we have already seen, Paul's purpose in writing to the church at Rome is because he is planning to go to Spain, where he will preach Christ to those who have never heard of Him before (Rom. 15:28). He feels that his work in Europe and Asia has now been completed because he has established thriving churches which will be able to proclaim the gospel to their environs and regions (Rom. 15:23). Paul sees himself as following in the footsteps of the messianic servant as he preaches the gospel to the nations with the result that 'those who were not told about him will see, and those who have not heard will understand.' (Rom. 15:21, citing Isa. 52:15) Paul ends his letter by restating the goal of all his work, which is 'that all the Gentiles might come to the obedience that comes from faith.' (Rom. 16:26).

Thus Paul is motivated from beginning to end by his desire that the lost should be saved, and in order for this to be possible the gospel must be preached. His desire to foster and maintain gospel partnership is ultimately driven by a desire to see all nations come to salvation. Paul's vision is breathtaking in its scale, and is a reminder that the work of bringing salvation to all men cannot be done just by isolated local churches serving their immediate communities, but by churches working in partnership with each other to see the gospel preached everywhere. In the UK we have a long tradition of gospel partnership for the sake of world mission, with multiple agencies working to help churches cooperate to send workers around the globe. However, we too often neglect the immense missionary need in our own country and are less willing to invest in gospel partnerships to reach the communities and places in our land where the gospel is barely known. In huge swathes of the country there is little or no effective gospel ministry, especially in the North, in rural areas, amongst ethnic communities, amongst the white working-class and the benefit-dependent. The gospel will only be taken to our nation if we are able to work together in partnership, supporting and resourcing gifted church planters and evangelists who are called of God to this work. Paul is not asking the Christians in Rome to go with him en masse to Spain, but he is asking them to help foot the bill for the work that he and his missionary team will be undertaking. Paul no doubt wants the pastors and leaders of the congregations to lead their congregations in supporting him and his work, and in order to do this they will need to share his gospel vision for the lost.

CONCLUSIONS

We have seen how Paul wrote the letter to the Romans in order to foster gospel partnership between himself and the congregations in this city. He was not himself a local church pastor but rather a pioneer church-planting evangelist. Nonetheless, he wants church leaders and their congregations to support him tangibly and in prayer. Against a background of suspicion about him and his message, he sets out to build a partnership founded on the truth of the gospel that was revealed to him, expressed in love between brothers and sisters in Christ that is able to overcome their theological and cultural diversity, and motivated by a passionate concern for the lost to be saved from the coming judgment. Surely local church pastors today must see it as part of their ministry to lead their churches in developing gospel partnerships of this kind. This is not an optional extra to ministry, a time-consuming distraction from the real work. Rather, it is a vital element of the work that we are called to do.

In the course of his ministry, Philip, like Paul, was committed to such generous gospel partnership and we have much to learn from his example.

12

The Pastor as Evangelical and Anglican

GERALD BRAY

Philip Hacking has always been an Evangelical by conviction. These convictions he exercised within the context of the Church of England, a denomination he has served well for many years. Philip would be known as an 'Evangelical First' man which meant that his affiliations and friendships transcended those of his own preferred denomination, enjoying that 'unity in truth' which the gospel provides. However, he was also an Anglican and towards the end of his ordained ministry found himself occupying a high profile (often uncomfortably held) as chairman of Reform. This he took on because of his commitment to, and concerns about, the Church of England. Gerald Bray considers some of the changes within the Church of England (and indeed Anglican evangelicalism) which have taken place during Philip's lifetime and, with one eye on the future, asks what is entailed in being an Evangelical and Anglican in today's church?

When Philip Hacking entered the ministry back in 1955, he and his contemporaries knew exactly what an Evangelical was and where men like him belonged in the Church of England. As they understood it, Evangelicals were the true Anglicans, the ones who stuck to the 1662 Book of Common Prayer, the Thirty-nine Articles and the Ordinal in their original sense. In church, they wore scarf and hood when taking services and celebrated Holy Communion from the north end of the table. Relations with people of other churchmanships were often strained but they were kept to a minimum. Anglo-Catholicism was still influential in the universities and in the higher echelons of the Church, and liberalism was also strong. Evangelicals felt beleaguered and reacted accordingly, sticking pretty much to their parishes and para-church organisations and suspicious of anyone who ventured further afield or failed to toe the party line.

Two generations later the Church has changed a great deal, and Evangelicals have changed along with it, but in most fundamental respects they are still recognisably the same. They no longer insist on scarf and hood the way they used to, but they dislike being asked to wear a stole at ordination and many of them have now abandoned clerical dress almost completely. To them, even the attire of their grandparents seems 'high-church' and the liturgical sensitivities of that generation are incomprehensible. Not that they have embraced liturgical revision with any greater enthusiasm than the forebears did. But whereas opponents of the 1928 Prayer Book stuck firmly to 1662, nowadays most Evangelicals make up their own forms of worship. They sometimes use what the Church provides, but this is a matter of convenience more than conviction. The niceties of the rubrics that so excited Evangelicals in the past have been forgotten, and in some quarters the mere suggestion of using a liturgy sounds like an admission of spiritual dryness. On the other hand, Evangelicals are still as enthusiastic as ever, still as determined to get the gospel message across to others and still longing to see people turn to Christ. Grandfathers and grandsons may do things differently, but they can still pray together, and surely that is what matters most.

In the Church at large, Evangelicals remain distinctive and although they are more numerous than they once were, it cannot be said that they are any more widely accepted than they used to be. It is a matter of public record that they are seriously under-represented in the Church's hierarchy and tolerance for an Evangelical in the house of bishops is probably even less now than it was fifty or sixty years ago. Modern bishops have to be all things to all people, and that naturally works against men who hold convictions that not everyone shares. A generation ago Evangelicals were rarely asked to become bishops; today they are asked more often, but are expected to moderate their Evangelicalism so that they can minister to the whole Church – as if Evangelical faith is inadequate to do that! A generation ago, no Evangelical would have sold his birthright for such a mess of pottage, but not any more. To the dismay of the older generation, many younger Evangelicals are prepared to believe that their inheritance is only partially compatible with Anglicanism and to adjust or abandon it accordingly.

This feeling was crystallised in a book by Richard Turnbull, the Principal of Wycliffe Hall, Oxford, whose title *Anglican and Evangelical?* (London: Continuum, 2007) says it all. Needless to say, Dr Turnbull makes the two things compatible, but the fact that this could ever be doubted shows how far we have travelled in the lifetime of men like Philip Hacking. Evangelicals have often been treated with disdain by others, but in the past they always insisted that they had more right to belong in the Church of England than anyone else. Now they have begun to doubt it, and there is a real possibility that in the next generation the idea that an Evangelical can also be an Anglican will seem as strange as the suggestion that he might be a Roman Catholic. This is not because the Church of England has moved in a more Catholic direction – far from it. What has happened is that an aggressive liberalism has taken over by playing the two traditionalist parties off against each other, and in the wake of the departure of the more conservative Anglo-Catholics, Evangelicals are in serious danger of being squeezed out too.

Evangelicals now have to fight for a recognised place in the Church which they were grudgingly allowed in the past but which seems to be increasingly incompatible with centralisation, downsizing and the spread of a pseudo-ecumenical 'tolerance' where everything is allowed apart from orthodox theological conviction. Outside the establishment, the spread of house churches and 'fresh expressions' is such that the younger generation may well drift away from any commitment to the Church, challenging those who remain to leave and join them in creating a new Evangelical subculture. Already many people think that to be an Evangelical is to be 'happy-clappy', and the decay of formal worship in the name of spontaneity is far advanced. As the national church moves in an increasingly liberal direction and demands more money from its congregations, the temptation to jump ship is bound to become greater. There are now prominent Evangelical parishes that have effectively withdrawn from their diocesan structures and no longer contribute to central Church funds. Some are even talking about seeking alternative oversight from overseas bishops, apparently unaware that such a move is illegal in England, and will only lead to their formal expulsion and the loss of their property. That this outcome does not seem to occur to those who advocate taking such steps, let alone worry them, is a measure of just how far some segments of the Evangelical constituency have been alienated from the Church of England in recent years.

THE EVANGELICAL PASTOR
Given this situation, it seems timely to look again at the role of the pastor within the established church and examine afresh whether it is still possible or desirable for a man of Evangelical conviction to retain or adopt an Anglican denominational identity. In the past, many would have questioned this order – for them, being Anglican came first, and Evangelical identity was a secondary consideration. Perhaps people like that still exist somewhere, but if so, they are few and far between. Nor is that surprising,

because as John Stott famously put in his closing address to the National Evangelical Anglican Congress (NEAC) at Nottingham in 1977, Evangelicals are Bible people and they are gospel people. The Bible and the gospel have been around longer than the Church of England, and they are universal in a way that Anglicanism is not. To cling to them is more important than to be attached to the historical, geographical and political circumstances that brought Anglicanism into being, and it is with them that we must begin.

An Evangelical is a Christian who bases his faith on the teaching of the Bible. All branches of the Christian church acknowledge the Scriptures as divinely inspired and foundational for theology and practice, but they do not all give them the unique authority that Evangelicals do. At the time of the Reformation, it was the watchword *sola Scriptura* – Scripture alone – that set Protestants apart and continues to distinguish them from Roman Catholics and the Eastern Orthodox, as well as from anyone else who adds another authority to that of God's Word. It was the conviction of the first generation of Reformers that the words of the Bible were God-breathed and sharper than any two-edged sword, piercing to the division between soul and spirit, between the things of this world and the things of the next. To search the Scriptures was to find eternal life, because in them (and only in them) was the person and work of Jesus Christ to be found.

To make this a reality in the life of the church, the Reformers realised that the first need was for teaching. Great efforts were made to establish schools and spread literacy so that people would be able to read the Bible for themselves. To this day, the Church of England maintains a network of schools founded on this principle, and it is the duty of every pastor to ensure that his flock is as well-instructed in the things of God as it can be. Now that the state schools have turned away from Bible-reading and developed inter-faith religious education, the need for the Church to do this is greater than ever. It is one of the ironies of our time that although access to the Bible has never been easier, with dozens of different versions and an almost unlimited range of helps available for those who want to understand it, actual knowledge of the text is at an all-time low. Even regular churchgoers know little of the Old Testament, which is seldom read and hardly ever preached on any more. The days when it was customary to hear a series of sermons on the life of Abraham, David or Elijah are long gone, and the modern preacher is grateful if members of his congregation have any idea who those people were.

This is a situation that can only be remedied by a regular and dedicated pastoral ministry. It is not enough to give someone a Bible, tell him to read it and wait until he gets bogged down in Leviticus. A good teacher has to explain what the text is about, where it is headed, and why the 'boring' bits are important. Nothing is more harmful to the Bible's authority than the picture of someone mindlessly reading through all the 'begats' in Genesis and concluding that the text has nothing to say to him. Like everything else in the Scriptures, the 'begats' have their importance, but it takes a good pastor to teach his people what that is and to show them how something so apparently remote from their everyday concerns matters for their understanding of the God who is just as faithful to His people today as He was in generations gone by.

Teaching of this kind is especially important because without it, the deeper message of the Bible is incomprehensible. When the apostle Paul embarked on his missionary journeys, he went mainly to the synagogues of the Greek world to preach his message, because he knew that there he would find people who would understand what he was talking about. Not everyone agreed with him, to be sure, but those who did had their eyes opened to appreciate more deeply what they already knew. Paul was building on a foundation of teaching which bore fruit in the establishment of new congregations of committed believers in Christ. Where no such foundation existed, as was the case at Athens, his message went unheard, and although one or two people were converted, there were not enough to start a church.

Closely related to teaching and built directly upon it is preaching. Some people see these things as essentially the same, and the overlap between them is so great that often they are. Even so, a distinction must be made between instruction (teaching) and exhortation (preaching). In the former, the emphasis is on conveying the facts, so that people know what it being talked about. In the latter, the emphasis is on persuading people to submit to the authority of those facts and apply them to their lives. The most appreciated sermons are often those that expound well-known passages of Scripture because the hearers are being asked to meditate more deeply on what they know already. In earlier times it might have been enough to translate the Bible and give it to people to read because it would have been the only book they possessed. Today however, we compete with an information universe that bombards us with facts. The sheer volume is too great to absorb at any depth, so even if we agree that they are both true and important, they do not change our lives.

This is the danger that the preacher is called to counter. He has to lift the words off the page of a book and put them in the hearts of his hearers. Of course, it should go without saying that all true preaching must be exposition of Scripture. It is not difficult to amuse a congregation with funny stories or give them good advice, but that is not what the pulpit is for. The preacher is there to open up the Word of God and to apply it to the lives of those who have come to hear him. To do this effectively, he must immerse himself in the text and meditate deeply on its true meaning. Sadly, it has to be said that the majority of modern commentaries on the text are more of a hindrance than a help in this. Commentaries nowadays tend to go into great detail about the meaning of the original words and may tell us a great deal about the background of the author and his readership, about the controversies that have arisen over the interpretation of particular phrases and about the views held by different scholars. But none of these things is likely to get the ordinary Christian closer to God, and it is this that must be the chief aim of the preacher.

The preacher is the man who makes the link between the Bible and the gospel. The Jews had the Bible, but how were they to hear the gospel without a preacher? The gospel is the message of Scripture, the truth that lies behind it and that is found in it. The gospel is the story of man's rebellion against the God who created him, and of God's response to that rebellion. Instead of wiping us out as we deserve, God the Father chose to send His Son into the world to save us from destruction by becoming sin for us and paying the price of our redemption. By the blood which He shed on the cross He has obtained forgiveness for us and opened the way for us to live with Him for ever.

Throughout its history, the church has been constantly assailed by attacks made on the gospel message. Some say that Jesus was just a man and not the Son of God. Others claim that we are not so sinful that we cannot save ourselves by our own efforts. Many find the language of condemnation and death repulsive and tell us that a God of love would never be so unkind. The precise nature of the attacks changes over time, but Satan never ceases trying to suppress the Word of truth by any means he can. This is where the preacher has to be a good pastor, and not merely an accomplished orator. He has to understand where his people are itching and scratch there, not somewhere else where the effects will be blunted.

This needs to be said because one of the failings of the church is its tendency to go on fighting old battles long after the action has moved elsewhere. The sixteenth-century Reformers lived in a church that had appropriated the sacrifice of Christ and used it as a means of manipulating people by subjecting them to the authority of its priesthood. The Reformers therefore had to emphasise that Christ died once for all time, that His sacrifice could not be repeated, either by the priest or by anyone else, and that 'the benefits of His saving passion', to use the words of the Prayer Book, are freely available to all who believe in Him.

That is still true today, but the ground has shifted somewhat and the attacks we now face are different. Very few people are in thrall to the priesthood as they once were. We are dealing with a world that is more concerned with suffering than with punishment, with feelings than with facts. That we have sinned and deserve the death that Jesus died on our behalf may be vaguely acknowledged, but modern people are more bothered by what they see as the pointlessness of suffering. Did God have to send His Son to die? What normal, loving father would do a thing like that? Surely he could have forgiven us without putting His own child through such pain! More often than not, this is the issue that the modern preacher has to address and he can only do so if he has a clear and compassionate understanding of the people to whom he is called to minister. The pastor who has comforted the grieving, who has challenged the wayward and who understands the secret suffering of those who do not (or cannot) speak up for themselves – this is the pastor who can preach the Word of God with the sensitivity and the effectiveness that the message demands.

It is the man who understands people who will know how to apply the Word to their lives. A doctor who has been to medical school may be able to conduct operations on an anaesthetised patient and develop great skills as a consultant. But the general practitioner who has to talk to his patients and walk them through the operation needs to understand where they are coming from and how best to get what is needed across to them. Reading the textbook will only confuse and probably frighten the untrained; it has to be interpreted and expressed in ways that they can absorb and accept. This is what the preacher is called to do and, like the general practitioner in medicine, his skill as a pastor is at least as important as his mastery of the message he is trying to get across.

Today we live in a church where good preaching is rare. For many clergymen it is a chore that interrupts other activities. Often they do not believe that it is central to their ministry and do not give it the care and attention that it needs and deserves. Small wonder that congregations are unimpressed and want the agony to be as short as possible. Ten minutes is a long time to listen to someone who has nothing to say and too often that is what we get. Even when the minister does have a message, it is often something that has come off the top of his head and not from his study of the Scriptures, so its relevance is open to question. Whether it is true or not is beside the point – it has nothing to do with me because it does not speak to my spiritual condition. This is why the preacher must stick to the Bible and find in it the message of the gospel. Every true sermon is fundamentally evangelistic, because every good preacher knows how to touch his hearers with the claim of Christ on their lives. Some will be hearing it for the first time; others will be applying it to parts of their lives that may have been relatively impervious to the message up to now. Congregations are full of all sorts and conditions of people, but the gospel speaks to them all and gives them new life in Christ. It is the preacher's privilege to be the midwife of that new birth and it is his pastor's skill that produces the safe delivery we so earnestly hope and pray for.

THE ANGLICAN PASTOR

So why be an Anglican? The call of the pastor to preach and teach the Word of God as an Evangelical is universal, and nobody would suggest that ordination in the Church of England is the only way to do it. Some of the greatest preachers in England have ministered outside the national church, and it would be churlish in the extreme to belittle their ministry because of that. It was the glory of Anglicanism at the time of the Reformation that it was open to receiving truth from whatever quarter it came. Anglicans did not buy into one particular theology or model of the church to the exclusion of all others, but sought to achieve a *via media* between different positions that would preserve the best of each. The resulting synthesis has not been to everyone's taste and there are things about it that Anglicans of all kinds find difficult to accept. This should remind us that not only are we a 'middle way' between extremes, but also that we are 'on the way', pilgrims on a journey to the celestial city which we have not yet reached. If we are joined by other pilgrims, where they have come from matters less than where they think they are going. If we are headed in the same direction then we are one with them, and the route by which they have come to us should not disturb us unduly.

Evangelical Anglicans have never been so tied to the structures of the institutional church that they have been unable to see beyond them. In the days before the rise of modern ecumenism, when it was rare for ministers of other denominations to be welcomed into Anglican churches and even laypeople were barred from Communion if they belonged to another church, Evangelicals generally ignored the rules and welcomed everyone who loved the Lord Jesus in sincerity and truth into fellowship.

This is still the case today, but the context has changed dramatically. Today, the Church officially welcomes people from other denominations and sponsors joint ecumenical projects in which ministers of other churches function in almost exactly the same way as Anglicans. The challenge no longer comes from the exclusivity of the institutional church but from the virtual disappearance of denominational boundaries in a host of different para-church organisations. Today laypeople of all ages are engaged in camps, societies and missionary endeavours that have little or nothing to do with official church structures. Many of them attend the church they do because it is the best one in the neighbourhood, and if they were to move elsewhere they would look for something similar, whether it is Anglican or not. Perhaps even more significantly, many younger people have left the established denominations to join (or to start) new churches that meet in a variety of venues and have little of the formality associated with traditional structures.

Another problem is that young men of Evangelical conviction who might offer themselves for the Anglican ministry are faced with some hard choices. It was not easy for Evangelicals in Philip Hacking's day, but at least there was a recognised network of colleges and parishes in which he and his peers could train and there was little interference from the hierarchy. Nobody asked about their views on women's ministry, and homosexuality was not mentioned. Today, while it is still possible to be accepted for training without being either in favour of women's ordination or pro-gay, those who resist the modern trends are liable to find that their options are significantly (if unofficially) narrowed. Furthermore, the prospect is that this situation will get worse in the future, which is a significant consideration for someone who expects to spend the next forty years or so in parish ministry.

This is particularly galling when we realise that, on the whole, the more conservative ordination candidates are now getting the best theological education. It is the Evangelicals who insist on keeping their colleges open and who invest in them, raising the standard of the courses being offered at a time when the rest of the Church is cutting back, preferring to ordain people who have done nothing but a part-time course with very little emphasis on the Bible or on Christian doctrine. The truth is that an increasingly large number of ordinands are simply not qualified for the task ahead of them and as they become the majority in some dioceses, the prospects for the Church's ministry look dire. But in spite of the increasingly obvious fact that Evangelical candidates are better prepared and more dedicated than most of the others, they are effectively discriminated against because their views are unpalatable to those in charge. As it becomes increasingly clear that an undertrained woman is more likely to become an archdeacon, dean or even bishop than a well-trained but too conservative man, the demoralising effect of this is bound to have serious consequences. Of course, nobody should go into parish ministry with an ambition to rise in the hierarchy, but the parish clergy are entitled to expect that those who are put in authority over them will be people whom they can respect and trust. There have already been difficulties with Evangelical clergy who have rejected the liberal views of their diocesan bishops, and their numbers are almost bound to increase in the years ahead.

Worse still, ordinary laypeople do not understand what is going on in the Church and often take it out on the local clergyman, who is presumed to be supportive of whatever the hierarchy does. When I was a curate in east London, the then Bishop of Southwark (Mervyn Stockwood) announced to the world that he was in favour of 'free love', and I was immediately accosted in the local newsagent's, as if that had been my personal decision. The price of such irresponsible behaviour is often paid by the troops on the ground who are far away and out of sight – and many of those troops will be young and perhaps idealistic Evangelicals who will be easily discouraged by such shenanigans. Unfortunately, what was irresponsible a generation ago now seems increasingly likely to become official policy. At the very least, there seems to be little prospect of disciplining a bishop now in the way that the late John A. T. Robinson was sent in 1963 from the suffragan see of Woolwich to Trinity College, Cambridge, because of adverse public reaction to his (then) scandalous book *Honest to God*. If the drift of the Church of England is away from the Bible and the gospel, what place can there be in it for Evangelicals?

Perhaps the best way to tackle this thorny question is to look behind the abuses to the foundations on which the Church is based. For all its indiscipline, the Church of England remains firmly rooted in the principles of the Reformation. There is nothing in its official doctrine or formularies (the Book of Common Prayer, the Thirty-Nine Articles and the Ordinal) that contradicts the teaching of the Bible, and a great deal that promotes the preaching of the gospel. Those Evangelicals who, a century ago, took their stand on these documents were not mistaken, and although they are less well-known and much less used than they were then, they remain the standard by which the teaching of the Church must be judged. Evangelicals have a responsibility to maintain that teaching and promote it as much as they can. Recent developments in the Anglican Communion have raised the issue of our corporate identity. This has brought the formularies into prominence once more, and it is entirely possible that they will play a greater role in the next century than they have in the last one. Certainly, this is no time for Evangelicals to give up hope and abandon a leaky but still seaworthy ship. It does, however, put a special responsibility on their shoulders. If those who defend the formularies do not know or use them, who will? It is no good saying one thing and doing another, and Evangelical colleges (in particular) have a duty to inculcate these principles into their students. They will not get them anywhere else, and if they do not get them, then the positions they claim to be defending will be abandoned by default.

Evangelicals are still free to preach the gospel from their pulpits and to call men and women to Christ. Equality-minded secular governments may seek to curtail this freedom in the future, arguing that the Christian message is offensive to racial, religious and sexual minorities, but if they do so it will affect all denominations and some of the smaller or independent churches may find it even harder to maintain their distinctive witness. There is a very real danger that the

Church of England will be pressured into supporting this secular drift by permitting same-sex marriages on church premises (and between clergy), and Evangelicals are needed who will speak out plainly and risk the consequences if necessary. Other churches will undoubtedly support them in this, not least because they know that if the Anglicans give way their own chances of being able to resist the tide will be greatly diminished. No-one should pretend that the battle will be easy, but being an Evangelical has never been comfortable. It took our eighteenth-century forebears two generations to turn England around and create the Victorian ethic that lifted the nation to greatness, and there were downs as well as ups along the way. We should not expect to have an easier time of it than they did, but we must remember that we serve an Almighty God, who is able to move whatever mountains the forces of secular materialism can range against us.

The Anglican clergy also have an entrée into the homes of the nation that few others can claim. Admittedly, they are not welcome everywhere or by everyone, but there is still a residue of respect and goodwill that can be tapped for the preaching of the gospel. In the parish where I live, which is not Evangelical and which contains a high proportion of academics and other independent-minded folk, the local vicar sends a yearly letter to the entire parish, asking non-churchgoers to support the work of the church as being of benefit to the whole community. The results are astonishing – every year the church receives thousands of pounds in donations from people who never set foot inside the door but who nevertheless think that it is doing good work and want to support it. Evangelicals may recoil from making a blatant pitch at the uncommitted in that way, but at least it shows that the institution is more highly thought of than the media might suggest. Baptisms, weddings and especially funerals continue to provide opportunities for sharing the Word of God with people who would not otherwise hear it, and these should not be lightly dismissed. For every person who has a Damascus-road experience and turns to Christ there are a hundred more who come in only gradually, often through making contact in this kind of way.

The Church of England has suffered from financial mishaps and declining congregations, but it alone maintains the aim of providing pastoral care to the entire nation. It stays in the inner city when other groups have left and its clergy are there at night after the social workers and professional caregivers have gone home to the suburbs. It makes its presence felt in the workplace, in hospitals, in schools and in prisons. It has opportunities in the media that it tends not to use to good effect, but whose fault is that? Above all, it is forced out of itself and into wider society. Evangelicals are very good at building walls around themselves and steering clear of the wicked world outside, so anything that combats this tendency is to be welcomed. A house church may appeal to its members, but after the initial enthusiasm dies down, new people stop coming, a clique is formed, and as differences of opinion start to emerge, it often falls apart. It is seldom a credible witness to anyone and may be easily swayed by a false teacher whose personal charisma is more attractive than his message.

Anglicans are in for the long haul. Most of our churches have been around for a very long time and they are not going away in the foreseeable future. Many of them are repositories of the local community's history and all of them represent the face of Christianity in this country, whether they want to or not. If they disappear then so will the public expression of our faith and the church will retreat to the catacombs from which it emerged seventeen centuries ago.

It is pointless trying to pretend that the calling of an Evangelical Anglican pastor is an easy one. It never has been and it never will be. To carry the cross of Christ is always difficult and demanding, and we are no strangers to martyrdom. There may be suffering ahead of which we have little inkling and troubles of a kind we have never before seen. But the fields are still white for harvest, and the labourers are few. The God of grace who raised His Son Jesus Christ from the dead is the same God who will raise His church from its slumber, and the pastor who is faithful and committed to that task will have the joy of knowing that he has been a good and faithful servant of the One who invites him in to share in His eternal life.

Gerald Bray is Director of Research for the Latimer Trust, London.

Christian Focus Publications
publishes books for all ages

Our mission statement –

STAYING FAITHFUL

In dependence upon God we seek to impact the world through literature faithful to His infallible Word, the Bible. Our aim is to ensure that the Lord Jesus Christ is presented as the only hope to obtain forgiveness of sin, live a useful life and look forward to heaven with Him.

REACHING OUT

Christ's last command requires us to reach out to our world with His gospel. We seek to help fulfil that by publishing books that point people towards Jesus and help them develop a Christ-like maturity. We aim to equip all levels of readers for life, work, ministry and mission.

Books in our adult range are published in three imprints:

Christian Focus contains popular works including biographies, commentaries, basic doctrine and Christian living. Our children's books are also published in this imprint.

Mentor focuses on books written at a level suitable for Bible College and seminary students, pastors, and other serious readers. The imprint includes commentaries, doctrinal studies, examination of current issues and church history.

Christian Heritage contains classic writings from the past.

Christian Focus Publications Ltd,
Geanies House, Fearn, Ross-shire,
IV20 1TW, Scotland, United Kingdom.
www.christianfocus.com